The Natural Heritage of Jammu-Kashmir-Ladakh

Wildlife-Forests-Flora-Rivers-Lakes

Attention Authors

'We Convert Fighters into Writers'. That's the motto of Manas Publications since more than four decades. Our message to the world is that India can win the battle not only by the bullet but also by the pen. There is no dearth of intellectuals in our country, but their knowledge is confined to them only. No sincere effort has been made by any other publisher to channelise their knowledge in national interest. That is why the talent of a large number of intellectuals remains latent. An author transforms his knowledge into a manuscript, and it is our job to spread his/her knowledge by converting it into a beautiful book. For over four decades, Manas has been motivating the intellectuals by publishing their manuscripts and would like to publish your manuscript too. So if you or your colleagues have any manuscript ready for publication or are working on it, kindly contact us with detailed synopsis and list of contents. We will transform your work into a valuable publication. If you wish, we can also suggest you the suitable subjects for writing the books related to your area of expertise. Manas is known for its publishing quality and commitments. We take utmost care in production and give wide publicity to the book as well as its author through our national and international distribution network.

For the Rai family
Rajendra, Rani, Animesh and Mridu

Some of the important books written by Parvéz Dewan, are:

- The Other Kashmîr: Almost Everything About
  Aksai Chin, Baltistan, Gilgit, Hunza, Mirpur, Muzaffarabad (Manas)
- People and Culture of Jammû–Kashmîr–Ladâkh (Manas)
- Amazing Ladakh (Manas)
- Religion in Jammû–Kashmîr–Ladâkh (Manas)
- A History of Jammû (Manas)
- A History of Kashmîr (Manas)
- A History of Ladâkh–Gilgit–Baltistân (Manas)
- Parvez Dewan's Jammû–Kashmîr–Ladâkh: **Jammû** (Manas)
- Parvez Dewan's Jammû–Kashmîr–Ladâkh: **Kashmîr** (Manas)
- Parvez Dewan's Jammû–Kashmîr–Ladâkh: **Ladâkh** (Manas)

- Hiñdi-Urdû: A Language Survival Kit (Lonely Planet, Australia)
- The Civil Services (20/ 20 Publications, Delhi)
- India's Western Himâlayas (co-authored; APA, Singapore)
- Hanûmân Chalîsâ (Viking-Penguin)
- The Names of Allâh (Viking-Penguin)
- The Book of Hanûmân (Viking-Penguin)
- Tibet: Fifty years after (Shubhi)

Contents

Jammu, Kashmir, Ladakh: The State as a whole

The Natural Heritage of Jammu-Kashmir-Ladakh

Wildlife-Forests-Flora-Rivers-Lakes

Parvéz Dewân, IAS

Manas Publications
(We Convert Fighters into Writers)
New Delhi-110 002 (INDIA)

MANAS PUBLICATIONS
(We Convert Fighters into Writers)
(Publishers, Library Suppliers, Importers & Exporters)
4402/5-A, Ansari Road (Opp. HDFC Bank)
Darya Ganj, New Delhi-110 002 (India)
Off. (23260783, 23265523, Fax: 011-23272766
E-mail: manaspublications@vsnl.com
manaspublications@gmail.com

ISBN 978-81-7049-425-6
₹ 995/-

Designed at
Manas Publications

Printed in India at
RK Offsets, Delhi
and published by Mrs Suman Lata for
Manas Publications, 4402/5-A,
Ansari Road, (Opp. HDFC Bank),
Darya Ganj, New Delhi-110 002 (INDIA)

The Baghliar Power project on the banks of River Chenab

River Jehlum

The Sind River, Sonamarg

Rafting on River Zanskar, Ladakh

The Confluence of the Indus and Zanskar rivers

Waterfall, Pattika, 'Azad' Jammu Kashmir (POK)

Pangong Lake

Viola odorata L. (Gul-e-Banafshan), Ladakh

Xanthium strumarium L. (Gul-e Cheero), Gilgit

Badam Vaari (Almond garden) in Srinagar

A grove in Kokernaag near

Snow Leopard

Ursus Bears

Markhor

Black Panther (Seh)

Blue Sheep

Ibex

Yellow bellied Marmot

Pashmina Goat

Langur

Kiang

Yak

Snow Cock

Hoopoe

Brahminy Duck

Hangul

Pronunciation

This book has used diacritical marks to double the value of three vowels: a, i and u. Therefore

'a' is as in 'c*a*thedral'

'â' is as in 'f*â*ther'

'e' is as in 'g*e*t'

'é' is as in 'caf*é*'

'i' is as in '*i*t'

'î' is as in '*e*at'

'ñ' is a brief, almost silent 'n,' much as in 'mo*n*k.'

'o' is always as in 'g*o*'

'u' is as in 'p*u*t'

'û' is as in 'f*oo*d'

'ts' is much like the 'z' in 'Mo*z*art'. Most Hindi, Urdu and English-speaking people settle for the 'ch' sound. They thus turn 'Tséwâñg' into 'Chéwâñg,' which the people of Ladâkh find quite acceptable.

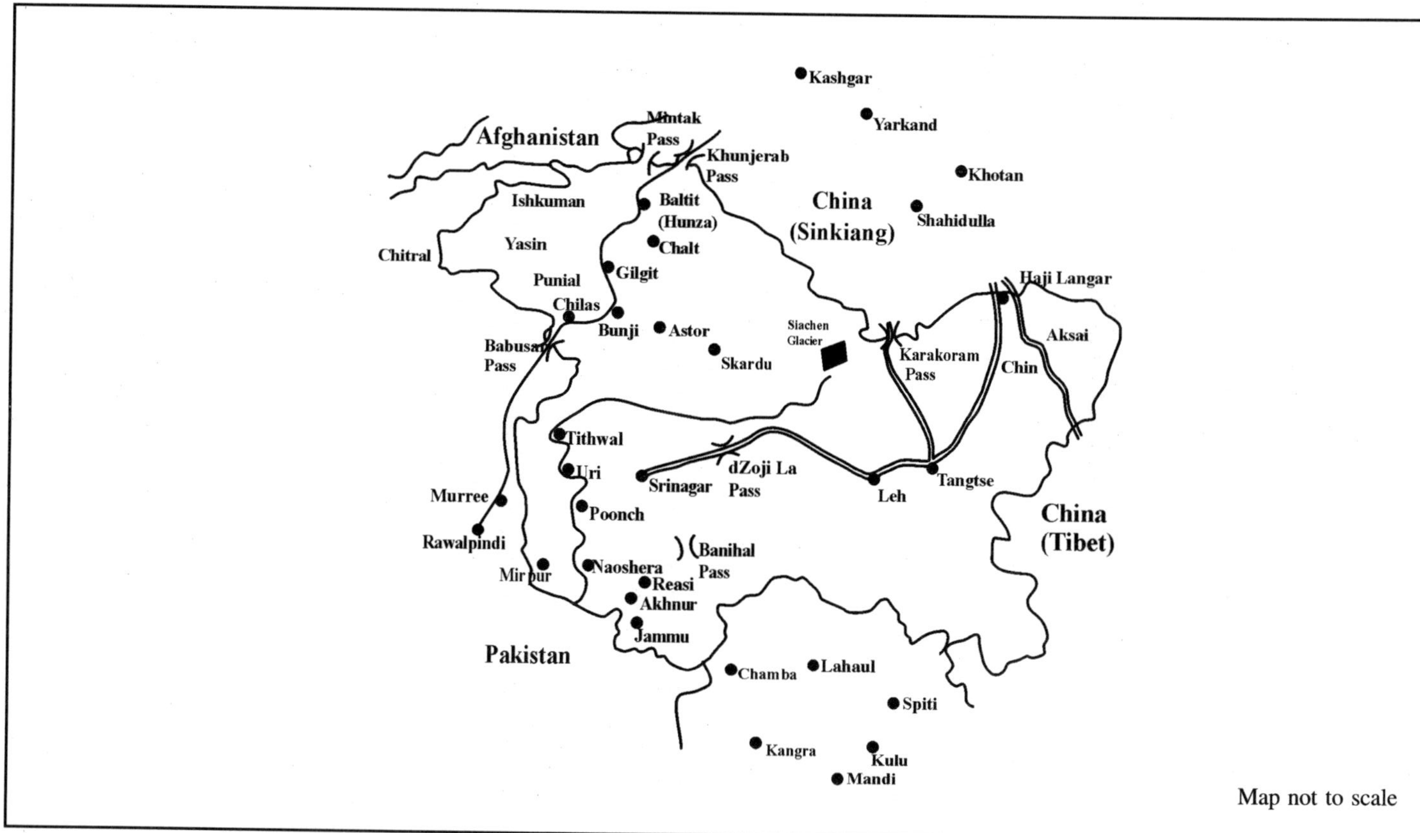

Jammu and Kashmir (including Ladakh)

Preface

The joys of living amidst nature

Despite all the urbanisation of my state you still have to make an effort to keep nature out of your house, because by default it is likely to press itself in (sometimes in ways that are not wholly welcome).

They say that in 'Gilgit-Baltistan' (in the occupied part of Kashmir) there is a seismic tremor every three minutes, on average. In Srinagar when I would sit typing this series of books in my glass-walled cottage perched above the Dal Lake, during what was the rainy season in the rest of India the sky above the Hari Parbat/Koh i Maran would flash with noiseless, rainless lightning once in every few minutes.

That one can't keep nature out is something I learnt the nice way while constructing a wooden cottage in my official residence within the Raj Bhavan (gubernatorial palace) complex, which is inside a several miles-long city forest in Srinagar. Two of the walls of the cottage were all-glass, except for their raw wooden frames, which had the fragrance of the deodar trees that they came from. While the hut was being constructed the forest outside and the space inside merged into one. You could not tell where the room ended and where the forest began. I assumed that even after curtains were fitted things would remain the same whenever the curtains were opened.

It did not work that way. Even when the curtains were bunched together tightly and covered only the vertical wooden frames, they came in the way. Not having travelled enough then I did not know that in some very upmarket forest lodges across the world they did not have curtains at all—or the curtains would be bunched above, and not between, the windows.

Even more exciting was the almost-invisible chain link fence that separated the lawns of my house in the Raj Bhavan from the forest beyond. Punctually, for three weeks every June, a creeper that went up the fence and was hardly noticeable the other eleven months would come alive with red flowers. Because the fence could barely be seen, it seemed as if red flowers were climbing towards the sky on their own, against the green and yellow leaves and brown wood of the thick grove behind.

There was a family of exactly four leopards, two adults and two cubs, in that forest. I lived in that area for almost nine years and, on an average, got to see one member of the family once a year—not more. The first of these sightings was in late winter when much of the snow had melted and I saw this baby leopard amble down a slope near my office, lost in some pleasant thought, because he had the most beatific baby-smile in the world.

It was in Padam (Zanskar) that I realised how rare these sightings could be. My office had glass walls including on the side that faced the mountain where snow leopards and ibexes were most likely to come. This was the wall behind the back of my swivel chair. Therefore, I would face the mountain only during breaks. Two young wildlife experts, from Austria and Germany, decided to spend the winter in Zanskar in order to photograph these elusive animals. Through them I understood how my office was the only covered place in town to spot leopards and ibexes from—because it was the only building perched above the river that divided the mountain from the town. The mountain was covered with smooth, white snow, because of which it was easy to spot any coloured object of the size of a dog or bigger. Moving animals would be easier still. Despite all these advantages—and despite my European friends' sharp eyes and fancy lenses—I was able to spot ibexes only a few times and the snow leopard perhaps only once, fleetingly.

The human behaviour of animals Even though my father made sure that we spent at least one month in the mountains during our vacations every year, I got down to studying animal behaviour only when I was twenty-two and had joined the civil service. (A major influence had been Dutch filmmaker Bert Haanstra's classic documentary *Ape and Super-Ape).*

There was hardly any traffic on the rough Basohli-Banni track in those days—maybe a few trucks a day, and those only during the daylight hours. Hill animals, like the simple people living in remote mountain villages, unconnected by roads, had hardly seen any vehicles and, therefore, did not know how to respond.

We were touring the hills of Banni. It was late in the night when my work got over and we started driving back to the headquarters. A rabbit got caught in the beam of the front lights of my jeep. That's right, once the beam hit him he could not get out of it, like in space-travel films in which they trap good and bad people in laser beams. He ran at exactly the same speed as the jeep so that he remained within the beam all the time. This went on for almost a kilometre. To spare the poor creature its agony I requested my driver to switch off the lights without stopping the jeep. The rabbit seized the opportunity and ran away from the mud road.

Urban animals, like urban humans, on the other hand, know how to react to urban situations.

Jammu city has for decades had the second highest vehicles-per-kilometre-of-blacktopped-roads ratio in Asia after Tokyo (or so they say). Billu Saand, a bull as long as a luxury car—and as tall—had gone rogue and had earmarked for himself a spot outside the police headquarters. Any car that dared encroach on his turf would have its bonnet ripped out, as I saw for myself.

Though Kargil is very sparsely populated, there is enough traffic on the highway to keep its wildlife trained. On a good summer's night, an hour or two after sunset, you are more or less guaranteed a couple of fox sightings, with their enormous mink-like tails—if not other animal sightings as well.

Bird sanctuary on the highway Kargil district is like one huge wildlife-and-aromatic-plants sanctuary.

One morning I had to get up and leave Kargil town at four, in order to reach the dZoji La pass by seven, after which they would stop vehicular traffic. That three-hour drive was like going through a busy bird sanctuary—one that is very popular with our winged friends. There were a few score birds just above my car (and a few on or just above the road) at any given time. I am no expert but I think I saw at least half a dozen different species that morning. It wasn't migration time. Maybe that was why they were flying very low, in small groups and not in formation.[1]

Back in Srinagar—by now I was on the wooded, hilly Gupkar Road—every evening around dusk during the migration months (see below) a few thousand birds—normally of one species at a time and all in formation—would glide over my house, to rest after a day of activity.

Birds migrate to Kashmir in summer from the boiling south and in winter from the freezing north. The Bee-eater from Cape Colony, the Golden Oriole from Transvaal, South Africa, and the Paradise Flycatcher from Java come in the summer. Mallards (neluj and thuj), Pintail ducks (sokha pachhin) and Wigeon ducks arrive in winter from Kashgar, Tomsk and Tobolisk (Siberia).[i]

Prof. B.L. Kaul adds that in the 1970s and '80s it was noticed that 'some of [Kashmir's] winter migrants also come from [the] wet lands of Bharatpur in Rajasthan and Harike in the Punjab.'[ii] Having run a lodge inside the Bharatpur sanctuary for four years I find this counter-intuitive, but Prof. Kaul is an expert. My guess is that this must be during the years when Lake Bharatpur dries up, which has been happening frequently since the 1970s.

And then in early November Mânsar Lake, in somewhat warmer Jammu, has thousands of birds flying over it.

---

1. The numbers and varieties were unique to Kargil, but much of it had to do with the time of the day. Once while returning from a party around 4 a.m. in Delhi I found dozens of birds flying equally low above the always-uncongested road next to Nehru Park.

262 species of birds have been spotted in the Valley of Kashmir, 225 in Ladakh and 183 in Jammu province.[iii] Many of these must be common to all three regions, because in all the state sustains a little more 300 species.

The valley bathed in herbal perfume In August and September the serene, Central Asian Suru valley of Kargil acquires a haunting new attraction. The *sarsing* tree (elagnus hortensis) suddenly starts exuding a sweet scent. This is also the time when the cherry-sized fruit of the same name ripens. These trees line the road that runs through the valley. One tree is enough to cover an entire village with fragrance. The stretches that pass through Sankoo, Khachen, and Grong-Minji in Suru valley, and Poyen and Shalikchay near Kargil town, are particularly fragrant. The perfume starts floating in the air well after sunset, say around seven or eight at night. The scent is much like that which emerges from central Indian temples in the evenings. It is as if God has spilt water-reservoir sized bottles of herbal perfume on each of those villages.[2]

In short, to be in Jammu & Kashmir is to be close to nature all the while. And because my career in the state has almost entirely been in field assignments and my official residences have mostly been on the outskirts I have been closer still.

The flip side But, as I hinted above, this has its flip side.

The water table below my official house in Jawahar Nagar, Srinagar, was so high that the ground-floor flush toilet was useless, because—how do I put this delicately?—what went down always came up, and within minutes.

Once when I had to go to my office in the Raj Bhavan, Srinagar, at night, I found the guard poking a medium sized insect. I assumed it was some kind of a centipede, and then saw half a dozen more nearby. They were scorpions, the guard informed me. I am glad he did because I had seen identical creatures on the steps leading into my house and also inside my office and had taken them lightly. (I had thought that scorpions were at least as big as a fist.)

A snake found my wood-and-glass cottage in the Zaberwan mountains (Cheshma Shahi) as inviting as my outstation guests and I did. So, it decided to make a nest under the wooden planks of the living room. No, not in some remote corner but in the passage as soon as you entered the house. During the day, when I was in my office in the city, I am told that he would dangle from the ceiling. Fortunately, he never ruined my weekend mornings. The snakes of Kashmir are mostly non-poisonous, but still...

Then there was this huge bear that would, on balmy nights, hug one of the wooden stilts that my cottage rested on, scratch it throughout the night, and

2. For a few days every year—in late September/ October—the entire air around Lutyen's leafy central Delhi is similarly displaced by the perfume of what journalist Vichitra Sharma informs me are the flowers of alstonia trees.

sometimes shake it. Compared to the snake, during these bear visits I felt almost as safe as I would be in Singapore.

(This has a nice side, too. During late spring and summer you are guaranteed bear 'hearings' on the stretch of road that leads uphill from the Cheshma Shahi to the Pari Mahal. You can hear them move in the bush—and, maybe, catch a glimpse of dark fur between the thick foliage. Just as the length of the day varies every day, these bears come a few minutes late every day when days lengthen and a minute or so sooner as days grow short—but all around 9.30p.m. The bears are 'safely' tucked behind a chain-link fence, which they periodically rip open.)

You don't have to believe any of this No, seriously, there have been so many amazing things to learn about nature in this mountainous state. For instance, Lake Pangong always freezes, punctually, on November 14. Some lakes (e.g. Chang Chenmo and Tsomo Riri) in Ladakh have water coming in (mainly snow melting on the mountains above) but, because the lakes are surrounded by mountains all around, the water does not flow out at all. Then how do these lakes maintain the same level? Through the evaporation of the water in the warm months. This is a form of distillation, which means that the salts inside these lakes are so thick that no animal or vegetable life can survive inside.

I used to go to a celebrated spring near Basohli the water of which was 'warm in winter and cool in summer.' (My theory is that—like the water of most springs—it remained at the same temperature throughout the year but seemed to be warmer or colder than the air outside).

'Battery Chashma' above Patni Top is another phenomenon. The water of this tiny spring is so pure that truck drivers would use it instead of distilled water in their old-style lead-acid batteries. I, being me, immediately ordered that these waters be bottled and served to premium guests at the holiday cottages run by the Tourism department (of which I was the Commissioner) at Patni Top. (There isn't enough water for wider sales) I dreamt of creating a niche brand to rival Evian and Perrier. The problem was that a local laboratory gave us a report saying that the water was unfit for human consumption.[3]

And then there is a tiny water channel on the trekking route from Padum to Zangla (Zanskar). It seems that it flows upwards. Obviously, reservoir-action is at work.

Our mediæval ancestors had found ways of pushing water up to the higher floors of the Basohli palace and about ten or fifteen feet uphill in Banni.

3. Around that time *India Today* carried a report according to which half the bottling plants of India's leading bottlers of drinking water were supplying water that was unfit for human consumption.

There was no reservoir, natural or artificial, in Basohli. Hence the royals used a thin, spiral clay pipe which rose upwards and can still be seen here and there in the ruins of that palace. At Banni, too, they used a spiralling pipe to send water up to the stream's bank, which was well above the stream. In this case the fact that the stream had for scores of miles been coming down a hill was probably used to send it a few feet uphill to the bank.

The Romans created great aqueducts. The kings of Jammu & Kashmir fashioned exquisitely beautiful ones, made of wood. Dogra-era aqueducts can still be seen along the Uri road in Kashmir and on the mountain slope leading down to Bhaderwah town. (There is one on the Akhnoor road, too, but that one is made of more prosaic materials.)

Studying the food chain of the bigger animals has been even more fascinating. (See Kashmir> Wildlife, Sanctuaries, Fishing> in particular the last paragraph titled 'Predators.') But nothing ceases to amaze me as much as the breeding habits of black necked cranes. How do cranes sitting 3000 miles away in, say, Yunan or Vietnam know exactly which lake in distant Ladakh has been allotted for their mating and breeding? I don't think two BNC couples have ever landed up at the same lake to breed. The choice of marshlands is even more interesting. (See Ladakh> The birds (avifauna) of Ladâkh> Crane, black-necked).

Water snakes' with glowing hoods The most remarkable experience of them all has been a night halt at stunning Shesh Nâg (3,574m.), where there is a huge fresh-water lake made of icy, whitish-green water. My senior colleague G.J. Nahvi had taken me there to supervise arrangements for pilgrims.

Two days before the auspicious Sâwan Purn-mashi (in August), under an almost full moon, we saw an incredible sight around ten in the night. A few thousand glowing water animals swam from the distant end of Lake Shesh Nâg towards the end closest to the pilgrims' camp. They swam in formation, swaying (they seemed to be dancing) as they moved. They took at least twenty minutes to reach our end of the lake and almost equally long to return.

The officers stationed at Shesh Nâg, all of them Muslim, informed us that these animals were water snakes and the glow we saw was that of the *manîs* on their heads. Now, Shesh Nâg also happens to be the name of the famous water-cobra of Hindu mythology. The Hindus believe that after a cobra has lived long enough (a hundred years), it grows a natural, light-emitting *manî* (jewel) on its hood.

I don't know what the scientific explanation is. I am just telling you what we saw.

Does this happen throughout the year? Perhaps not. One scientific theory is that these snakes hibernate for the rest of the year. Perhaps they come out only during this, the warmest, time of the year. In any case, who knows? Officials go there only for the 40 days of the Amarnâth Yâtrâ. In 1998 these sightings were reported during the five nights before the *Pûrnmâshî* (full-moon night). As I said, you don't have to believe any of this. It's just that we wildlifers and explorers tend to have a lower to threshold of credulity.

References

i Kaul, Prof. B.L., Feathers Are Ruffled by Winds of Change in Kashmir, Greater Kashmir, 31 October 2010.

ii Kaul, Prof. B.L., Feathers Are Ruffled by Winds of Change in Kashmir, Greater Kashmir, 31 October 2010.

iii. Kaul, Prof. B.L., Feathers Are Ruffled by Winds of Change in Kashmir, Greater Kashmir, 31 October 2010.

Glossary

'AJK': 'Âzâd' Jammû and Kashmîr. Pâkistân has illegally occupied a large part of the state of Jammû and Kashmîr. It has divided POK (Pâkistân Occupied Kashmîr) into three broad entities: i) the so-called 'AJK' (which is mainly occupied Jammû plus the Muzaffarâbâd area/ Kishen Gañgâ valley of occupied Kashmîr); ii) the so-called 'Gilgit-Baltistan' (which consist of occupied Ladâkh-Gilgit), and iii) Shaksgam (which Pâkistân has ceded to China). People wrongly assume that 'AJK' and POK are synonyms. 'AJK' is only one part—and a very small part, at that—of POK. The quotation marks around the word Âzâd (meaning 'free' or 'independent') and around the acronym AJK draw attention to the fact that 'AJK' is not an independent political entity but is an occupied territory.

galî, gallâ, lâ: These are, respectively, the Urdû, Dogri and Ladâkhi words for 'mountain pass'.

gurudwârâ: Sikh temple.

HP: Himâchal Pradésh, the state on the eastern boundaries of the Jammû and Ladâkh regions of J&K.

J&K: Jammû and Kashmîr, the name of the state that Jammû is a part of.

jâgîrdâr: A *jâgîrdâr* was a person whom the king (all right, the state) had given a *jâgîr*. In turn, a *jâgîr* was a large tract of land, normally consisting of one or more villages. The *jâgîrdâr* was much more than a headman. He collected land revenue (and, sometimes, other taxes) on behalf of the state, was responsible for law and order and maintained a number of soldiers—cavalrymen as well as foot soldiers—for the army of his state.

jeepable road: A track on which only rugged sports-utility vehicles can ply.

kol, kuhl: Water channel.

LoC: Pâkistân has illegally occupied 35.15 per cent of the state of Jammû and Kashmîr. India actually administers 45.62 per cent of the state.

(China is in the illegal occupation of the rest.) A 'Line of Control' separates the portion where the Indian tri-colour flies from the portion illegally occupied by Pâkistân. It is not an 'international border' (IB) because neither side accepts it as that. It serves the same purpose as a border but lacks the legal status of one.

mañdir: Hiñdû temple.

masjid: Mosque.

motorable road: 'Motorable' means that in theory a car (or bus) can drive on that road. In practice most 'motorable' roads are only 'jeepable'. A 'motorable stretch' (or motorable distance) is one on which you can travel in a vehicle. You don't have to walk on that stretch, except for exercise.

nâllâh: Stream.

pass(es)/ mountain passes: What is a pass? A pass, more precisely a mountain pass, is a gap between two mountain peaks. It is the highest point on a segment of a mountain road. There might be more than one pass on a road, and the next pass might be higher still. There always are mountains on the right and left of a pass. These mountains are much higher than the pass. The job of a pass is to help you cross from the place behind you to the place in front, without having to climb all the way to the top of the mountain. A pass is called a *gallî* in Urdu/ Kashmîrî, a *gallâ* in Dogri and *lâ* in Ladâkhî.

POK (Pâkistân Occupied Kashmîr): These are areas of Jammû & Kashmîr that are under Pâkistân's illegal occupation.

roadhead: This is the place to which one can travel in an automobile. In Indian English, it is the point till which there is a 'motorable' road. After this place one has to walk (or ride a pony) to get to the final destination. Conversely, on the return journey, this is the point where the trek ends and the 'motorable' road begins.

sâdhu: A Hindû ascetic, who normally lives a very frugal life.

-sar: The Hindi-Sanskrit-Dogri word for 'lake'.

sarai/ serai: A rest house, as in caravanserai.

TRC is an important abbreviation to remember. It stands for 'Tourist Reception Centre.' Jammû has a fairly elaborate TRC and is supposed to offer every facility needed by a tourist, including reasonably priced accommodation. Katrâ, too, has a TRC though not as elaborate.

trekker: Indian English. A trekker is someone who treks.

yâtrâ: a Hindu pilgrimage; a journey towards a sacred shrine. '*Yâtrâ*' literally means 'trip' or 'journey'. There are several important Hindu shrines in the Himalayas, especially in J&K, HP and the UP hills. Devotees normally trek up to the shrine once a year on a designated day (or set of days).

These *yâtrâs* normally take place in summer, because in winter it would be difficult to reach the concerned shrine because of the snow. In a religious context, *yâtrâ* means 'pilgrimage'.

These *yâtrâs* have a fixed starting point, normally a temple at the bottom of that hill. Devotees gather there and then trek up to the shrine in a long procession. Most *yâtrâs* terminate at the hilltop shrine where, often, a colourful fair is held. *Yatris* (pilgrims) return to their homes in the plains or foothills not in a procession but when they please.

Pilgrimages in the hills are normally connected with Lord Shiv or the Mother Goddess Durgâ (in one of her several manifestations). Lord Shiv's wife, the goddess Pârvati, is one of Durgâ Mâtâ's best-known incarnations. Yet, some of the Mâtâ's major forms (especially that of Srî Mâtâ Vaishno Dévî jî and Ragnya Dévî) are connected with the story of Srî Râm.

yâtrî: Hiñdî for 'pilgrim'; the Dogri word for 'pilgrim' is *yâtrû*.

Jammu

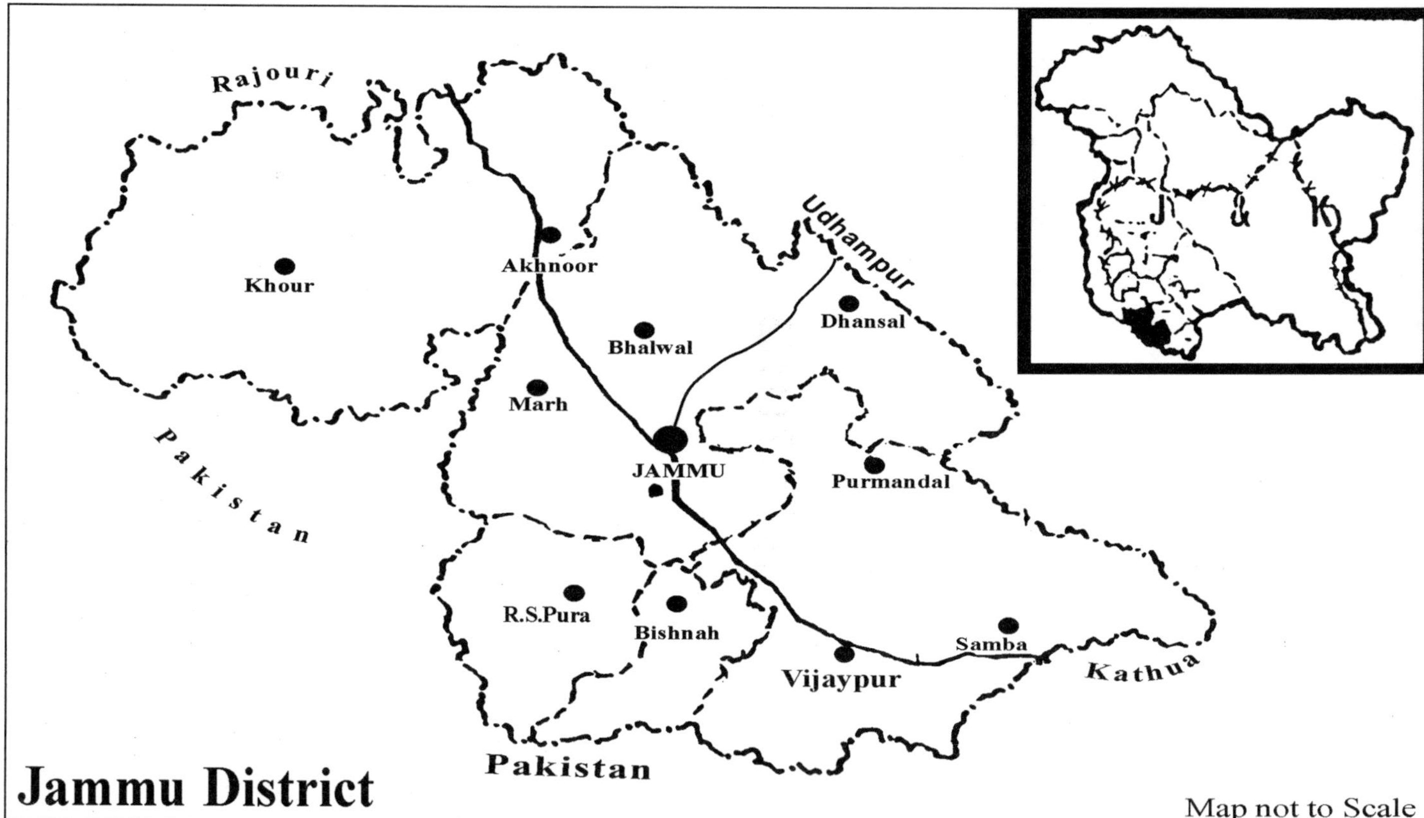
Jammu District
Map not to Scale
Rajouri
Udhampur
Kathua
Pakistan
Pakistan
Khour
Akhnoor
Bhalwal
Marh
Dhansal
JAMMU
Purmandal
R.S.Pura
Bishnah
Vijaypur
Samba
J
&
K

Chapter-1

Wildlife

Snakes: Several species of snakes that infest the *kandi* (semi-arid) belt of Jammû-Kathuâ are poisonous. The Sâmbâ krait is, arguably, the most poisonous snake in India. Snakes are worshipped in this belt to a much greater degree than in other Hindu areas. Surely there is a connection.

Parks and Sanctuaries

It is advisable to wear khaki, green or camouflage in all sanctuaries and national parks. Please do not disturb the animals with loud noises, radios/ music systems, motorboats, diesel generators and the like. (I am thought of as a Luddite, an enemy of progress, because of my refusal to allow motorboats at many tourist destinations). Please don't leave behind non-biodegradable garbage. Flash photography can irritate some animals into violence, and scare others needlessly.

National parks are a 'higher' category than sanctuaries.

National Park

Snow wolf in the Kishtwar National Park

The Kishtwâr High Altitude National Park 33°20'-34°00'N, 75°40'-76°10'E. Area: 400 sq. km./42,500 ha. (According to a conservative estimate, the area of the park is only 310 sq. km).

Bacha (1986)[i] called Kishtwâr 'arguably the most important cis-Himalayan area in [Jammû and Kashmîr] on account of its fairly large size and diverse mammalian fauna, including a number of rare and endangered species'. Till 1948, forest contractors would mow down the trees for logs. The government brought in some checks after that. The area was declared a national park in February 1981, and deforestation more or less came to an end.

The Government of India has included Kishtwâr among the seven national snow leopard reserves of the country.

Location: The park is 40km north-east of Kishtwâr town, district Dodâ. The Rinnay River is in the north, the Kibar Nâllâh (stream) catchment is in the south, the Mârwâ River in the west, and the main divide of the Great Himâlayas in the east.

What is good about this park is its topography which varies widely between medium and high altitudes (i.e., from 1,700m above the sea to 4,800m)., as well as the vegetation which, too, varies accordingly.

Climate: The monsoon hardly ever reaches Kishtwâr. There is some precipitation in March-April and July-August—when a raincoat would be needed. The park receives an average of around 760mm. of rainfall in a year. Snow mainly falls in December and January. In those months, it is very difficult to travel to the park because of the snow. Mean maximum and minimum temperatures recorded at Sirshi by Kurt (1976)[ii] and Bacha (1986) were 13°C and – 7°C in January and 35°C and 11°C in July. Therefore, please dress accordingly. Except for July, there is a nip in the air even in summer.

Flora: Bacha mentions thirteen types of vegetation.

In the region between 1,700 and 2,400m we can expect to find pristine groves of cedar and blue pine, and moist temperate deciduous forests, especially horse chestnut (Aesculus indica), walnut (Juglans regia), maple (Acer spp)., poplar (Populus ciliata), hazel (Corylus cornuta), bird cherry (Padus cornuta), ash (Fraxinus cornuta) and yew (Taxus wallichiana).

Between 2,400m and 3,000m we will find silver fir (Abies pindrow) and spruce (Picea wallichiana), interspersed with cedar (Cedrus déodâra) and blue pine (Pinus griffithii). The expensive chilgozâ nut (Pinus P. gerardiana) grows in a few patches in the Dachan Range.

The sub-alpine zone lies between 3,000m and 3,700m, which is the tree line. Here we find silver fir and birch (Betula utilis) forests together with birch-rhododendron (Rhododendron campanulatum) scrub.

There are some alpine pastures above the tree line.

Other trees that grow in the area are Pinus wallichiana, Quercus spp., and Ulmus spp. The main shrubs are Parrotiopsis jacquemontiana, Viburnum spp., Desmodium tiliaefolium and Rosa spp. The major herbs include Primula spp., Brachypodium spp., Anemone spp., Dipsacus mitis and Artemisia vulgaris.

Fauna: The fourteen or fifteen species of large *mammals* that live in this park include the musk deer and Himalayan bears, black as well as brown. Kishtwâr has more brown bears than elsewhere in the Himâlayas. The more populous species are: brown bear (Ursus arctos), bharal (Pseudois nayaur), wild boar (Sus scrofa), Himalayan musk deer (Moschus chrysogaster), goral, a few hanguls (Cervus elaphus hanglu), ibex (Capra ibex sibirica), langur, leopard (Panthera pardus), snow leopard (P. uncia), perhaps the markhor (Capra falconeriare), Indian muntjac (Muntiacus muntjac), serow (Capricornis sumatraensis) and the Himalayan tahr (Hemitragus jemlahicus).

The Himâlayan Tahr: Phylum: Chordata; Order: Artiodactyla; Family: Bovidae; Genus: Hemitragus; Size: Length: 90-140 cm., Weight: Male 73 kg., female: 36 kg.

In addition, there are fifty species of birds.

Bacha listed twenty-eight species of *birds* including the koklass

(Pucrasia macrolopha), the Himalayan monal (Lophophorus impejanus) and pheasants. The Himalayan jungle crow, griffon vulture, bearded vulture, golden oriole, paradise flycatcher, white-cheeked bulbul and Indian mynah have also been reported, though not as frequently. The Himalayan snowcock (Tetraogallus himalayensis) and western tragopan (Tragopan melanocephalus) probably also come visiting.

Best viewing season: Mammals: September to March; Birds: March to May.

Where to stay: There is a two-bedroom hut in the sanctuary in which people camp for the night. There are rest houses in nearby Ikhala and the Sirshi Forest.

How to get there: Kishtwâr is around 250km. from Jammû town. For visitors to the Park, there is a road up to Ikhala. However, buses ply only so far as Plamer (20 km. north of Kishtwâr).

Biosphere Reserves

(This is the category that ranks after 'National Parks'). There are no biosphere reserves in Jammû province.

Wildlife Sanctuaries

The Jasrotâ Wildlife Sanctuary: (63km. from the Jammû Railway station). Area: 10.04sq. km. Location: district Kathuâ. This sanctuary is located, between 336 and 520 metres above the sea, on the right bank of River Ujh, north of village Jasrotâ. The then Mahârâjâ of Jammû & Kashmîr declared it a Game Reserve under the provisions of the Old Game Act of 1942.

Flora: The area is famous for its bamboo plantations. Broad leaved species that grow here include Acacia Catechu A. Arabica, Dalbergia Sissoo and Lannea Grandis. The main shrubs are Lantana camara, Carisa spinarum and Dodonea Visacosa.

Fauna: Among the *mammals* found here are the cheetal (axis deer), the barking deer, jackal, wild boar and rhesus monkey. The cheetal is the main animal of the sanctuary. Snakes are common. Sometimes leopards have been sighted.

Porcupines are also encountered.

Avifauna: The migratory and resident birds that visit or live in Jasrotâ include the pheasant, peafowl, red jungle fowl and jungle bush quail. Species found less frequently include the green pigeon, blue rock pigeon, black partridge, woodpecker, waterfowl and babbler. During the monsoons, the Ujh barrage attracts a number of water birds including the mallard, pintail, gadwall, common teal, widgeon and common pochard.

The viewing season: Mammals: September to March. Birds: March to May.

Climate: Jasrotâ, like, say, Delhi, is very hot in summer and fairly cold in winter. The average annual rainfall is 1000 mm.

Contact person: The Wildlife Warden, Kathuâ.

How to get there: If you are driving up from Punjâb, Haryana, Delhi or beyond, you can turn right from the highway almost sixty kilometres before Jammû. If you are coming up by train, you can get off at the Kathuâ (Gobind Sar) railway station and then take a taxi or bus to the sanctuary, which is 65km. from the Jammû airport.

The Nandni Wildlife Sanctuary: Area: 33.72sq. km. Location: 26 km. from Jammû town, in the direction of Katrâ/Srînagar. This is a pine forest right on the National Highway. Established: 1981.

Fauna: There are some eight mammal species in the area, including the leopard, wild boar, rhesus monkey, goral and grey lañgûr.

Avifauna: The birds found here are the Indian mynah, blue rock pigeon, peafowl, red jungle fowl, chîr pheasant and chakor. Pheasants are the predominant bird variety.

Best viewing: Mammals: September to March. Birds: March to May.

*Climate:*At any given time of the year Nandni is three or four degrees colder than Jammû or Delhi. That's because it is at a higher altitude, has a decent forest cover and, above all, is not very sunny.

How to get there: Everyone who has ever driven up to Katrâ or Srînagar has passed through Nandni. It is 26 km from the Jammû airport, 28 km. from the Jammû railway station and, from the opposite direction, 274 km from Srînagar.

For reservations contact the Regional Wildlife Warden (Jammû Region), near Hotel Jammû Ashok, Mâñdâ (Râmnagar).

The Râmnagar Wildlife Sanctuary: This sprawling sanctuary is better known in Jammû town as the Râmnagar Rakh (pron: ruckh). A *rakh* is a grass-reserve, which is what this place used to be. It has been upgraded since. It is located in the catchment area of the Kar Nâllâh (rivulet) of River Tawi. Established: 1981.

Area: 31.5sq. km. (or 12.9sq. km., depending on how much of the Jammû city forest one counts as part of the sanctuary). Altitude: Between 430 and 611 metres above m.s.l. Temperatures inside the sanctuary are always two or three degrees lower than in the rest of the town.

Location: Theoretically, the sanctuary is 6km. from Jammu town. In fact it is just beyond the Raj Bhawan, Jammû, on the National Highway itself. Its main entrance is from behind the Janipura neighbourhood in the western part of the town.

Zoo: There is a small zoo to get to which you should take the BC Road (part of the National Highway) in the direction of Hotel Ashok, Jammû (i.e., in the direction of Katrâ). Just before the hotel is a lane on the left, which leads to the zoo.

The wildlife: There are eight *mammal* species in this sanctuary, including nilgai, fox, wild boar, monkey, jackal, rhesus monkey and the barking deer.

There are also 15 species of bird, including the pheasant and jungle fowl. Hobby hunters used to kill wild boar on Sunday mornings. Not much is left of that species now.

There normally are two male and two female leopards in the zoo. Theirs is the most popular enclosure. One of these pairs was brought from Rajourî and the other from Râmnagar (Udhampur).

Five nilgais were brought to the sanctuary on its creation. By 1997 their population had swelled to eight.

In 1983, a Deer Park was created here. Barking deer, nilgais, Sâmbârs and pea-owls have been successfully bred in the park. In 1997, the park had eight barking deer. In 1984, eight spotted deer had been brought here from Mysore. By 1997, there were 32 spotted deer in the sanctuary.

The bears in the sanctuary have been brought from Dodâ and Mânsar.

Yousuf Ganaie, Natrang, the Srînagar Correspondent of All India Radio wrote around the year 2003, "Sometime back a tiger appeared in this forest and killed a few deer and a neelgai. The deer killed by the tiger were from the small zoo maintained by the Wildlife department at one end of the sanctuary. It was last year that the department fenced almost half the length of this sanctuary, making its interior safer and relatively less accessible to the trespassers. The Gujjars and Bakerwâls who accompany the sheep, ruthlessly cut the branches of the trees for feeding their herds. I saw a few Bakerwâls trying to damage the fence in their attempt to cross".

Avifauna: Every September several migratory birds including mallards come over from the colder parts of Europe for the four-month winter. Peacocks have been brought here from Miran Sâheb. Not all birds from outside have done as well at Râmnagar, though. Few migratory birds brought over from Srînagar have survived. The sanctuary also plays host to the Indian mynah, blue rock pigeon, peafowl, red jungle fowl, jungle crow, golden oriole and white cheeked bulbul.

The sanctuary has a small pond in which ducks swim. Sometimes the resident mongoose eats the ducks up.

Animals given to the army: The Indian Army runs little sanctuaries at nearby Miran Sâheb and Ratnu Chak. The Râmnagar authorities have donated animals to these sanctuaries. In turn, in 1994, the 12 Engineers Regiment of the Army gave some chinkaras (gazelles) to Râmnagar.

Accommodation: It is possible to stay inside the sanctuary in a cottage that has two bedrooms. For reservations: Regional Wildlife Warden, near Hotel Jammû Ashok, Jammû. The said hotel is somewhat pricey, but is very close to the sanctuary.

Best viewing season: Birds: March to May. Mammals: September to March.

The Surinsar-Mânsar Wildlife Sanctuary: Around 60km from Jammû town. (The two lakes are several miles apart. However, they are part of the same forest continuum). Area: 97.82 sq. km. (Conservative estimate: 39.58sq. km) Established: 1981.

Eight species of mammals and fifteen of birds live in this sanctuary for at least a part of the year.

Flora: The mixed-scrub forest consists mainly of broad-leaved species interspersed with stands of Pinus gerardiana. Common broad-leaved species are Acacia spp., Mallotus phillipensis, dalbergia sissii, ficus religiosa and bahunia variegata.

Fauna: The eight species mentioned include goral, wild boar, barking deer and leopard.

Avifauna: Species found here include the black partridge, red jungle fowl, peafowl, grey partridge, green pigeon, blue rock pigeon and rufus turtle dove.

Best viewing: The Wildlife Department recommends: Mammal viewing: September to March. Bird viewing: March to May.

However, my personal experience is that migratory birds, by the thousand, visit between late October and early April. Some species of duck stay on even in April. Tortoises and several kinds of fish dwell in the Mânsar Lake. Fishing is a taboo for religious reasons. In 1983 the government created a Deer Park here.

Climate: Somewhat colder than Delhi or Jammû at any given time.

How to get there: The sanctuary is 58km from Jammû airport and 56km. from the Jammû railway station. If you are coming up from Delhi by train, you could possibly get off at the Sâmbâ railway station (if your train halts there) and then take a taxi or bus up to the sanctuary.

Wildlife in Kathuâ District

The Kathuâ wildlife division has an area of 467.27sq.km. The forests of Kathuâ are home to 178 species of plants, 10 species of wild animals, 71 bird species and several species of snakes and lizards. The trees that grow most commonly in Kathuâ are bamboo, *chîr* (pine), *khair* and some broad leaved species. Khair grows in the semi-arid hills—especially in Basohli and Billâwar—and yields *kat-thâ*, an edible wood used in *pân*, a Central Indian 'dessert'.

The Billâwar Forest Division has an area of 642.47sq.km. The majestic déodâr grows in Lohâî Malhâr and Bannî. Elsewhere, the most common trees are *chîr*, *oak*, *kail*, *khair* and some broad leaved species.

Kathuâ plays host to the sarus as well. This migratory bird—which is a crane—spends some time in the district. Twenty-four such birds were counted in the district in 1999.

Wildlife in Poonch District

Almost 30 per cent of the district consists of forests—83,914 acres, to be precise. Its wildlife is supposed to be unique because both oriental and 'palearctic' species are found in Poonch. Urbanisation and 'development' have played havoc with the wildlife of Poonch by encroaching on the forests where this wildlife used to roam about.

Before independence (1947) there were nine markhor game reserves in the Poonch-Haveli tehsil alone. In addition there were 41 shikargahs (hunting reserves). Many of them have survived.

Mammals found in Poonch: The ghoral, leopard, brown bear, musk deer and markhor live in the district, some of these species being rare.

Birds ('avifauna'): Again, some of the species are rare and include the moral, rock partridge, kohlas, snow cock, chakor, black partridge and pheasant.

Fishing in Jammu District

The Tawi flows past Jammu city. Among the fish found in the river are mahaseer, seeng and mali. The other places in the district that are good for fishing are Akhnoor and RS (Ranbir Singh) Pura. You can get fishing permits from the Fisheries Department, Old Secretariat (Mubarak Mandi), Jammu Tawi.

Wildlife in Rajouri District

Animals that live in the district include the black bear, the brown bear, the wild bear, the *jungli* (wild) cat, the cheetah, the log deer, the musk deer, the Indian fox, the goral, the hare, the jackal, the langur, the snow leopard, the monkey, the porcupine, the grey musk shrew and squirrels.

Birds: Birds found in the district include the bulbul, chakor, Ram chakor, house crow, jungle crow, dove, egret, falcon (shikar), common pea fowl, red jungle fowl, kingfisher, common pariah kite, koel, Indian mynah, nutcracker, green partridge, monal pheasant, koklar pheasant, Himalayan tree pie, black rock pigeon, grey quail, swallow, tailor bird, white backed vulture and wagtail.

Silk Worm: Eight thousand families in Rajouri are involved in the making of silk, mainly rearing silkworms.

Fish: The government has established a trout hatchery at Phaini (Budhal). In addition there are fish farms at Muradpur, which is seven kilometres from Rajouri town. Fish to be found there include the common carp, gross carp, silver carp, rehu and rigal. There are fish-ponds at Behrote, Chhani-parat, Dharamsal, Panjah, Rajpora-Kampla and Saranoo as well.

References

i Bacha, M.S. (1986). Snow leopard recovery plan for Kishtwâr High Altitude National Park, Jammû and Kashmîr State, 1986-87 to 1989-90. Department of Wildlife Protection, Srînagar. 51 pp.

ii Kurt, F. (1976). Study plan for IUCN/WWF Project No. 1103 (22-4): Hangul, India—Ecological study to identify conservation needs. Unpublished report. 20 pp.

Chapter- 2

Flora, Fauna and Sacred Groves

Some Sacred Groves of Jammû

From Jammû to Kerala there is a tradition of planting groves around temples. In Jammû and some neighbouring areas, especially Puñjâb (Indian as well as Pâkistâni), rural Muslim shrines normally consist of raised graves without roofs or walls. Groves are grown around them as well.

Like Kashmîr's Tsrâr (Chrâr) é Sharief, these groves promote ecological awareness. Religious taboos make sure that no one injures green trees.

Bhallo Bâbâ went into a *samâdhi*, together with his mother. Before doing so he decreed that the mangoes of that grove should not be sold but used only in religious ceremonies. At the Shiv ji temple (Purmandal), too, trees are felled only for religious ceremonies such as weddings and cremations.

Scary legends ensure that these taboos are enforced.

Apparently, a Gujjar once lopped the leaves of the sacred tree at Peer Bâbâ (Keuli, Billâwar), and fed them to his camels. It is said that all the camels that ate the leaves died. As a result, no one dares pluck leaves from that holy tree anymore.

A huge branch of the main tree at Peer Bâbâ (Bañdrâl Khurd) broke off during a storm and was sold. The vehicle in which the branch was being carted away got jammed. Devotees got the message. They carried the branch back to the spot where it had fallen.

The entry about 'Nâgbani' in the chapter about 'Jammû district' records a similar incident, which, too, had contained a divine warning.

At Buâ Dév (Changran), Râjâ Mandleek (Mandâl), Gargal Peer Bâbâ (Billâwar), Kâlkâ Mâtâ (Meen), Raal Dévatâ (Godan), Nâg-Dévatâ (Surinsar), Buâ Dâti (Palourâ), the Kalyânpur Temple and the Uttarbehni Shiv Temple people make sure that no living tree is hurt. They use only dead or decaying wood. Even the lopping of leaves and branches is a taboo.

Jammû and Samba Districts

Bhallo Bâbâ (Akhnoor-Mathwâr road) (five bîghâs) *Flora:* Mango, jâmun, banyan, Lannea, karañgal, berry, toonâ, Dodonea, Carissa and Justicia adhatoda. *Fauna:* Squirrel, pigeon, monkey, mongoose, treepie, drongo, bush cat, snakes and insects.

A dispute once arose between some Râjput and Karkyâl youths about the ownership of a mango tree. Bhallo Bâbâ asked his friend Bagra to mediate. Bagra requested Bâbâ to guard the tree, which was laden with fruit, while he was away. When the Bâbâ returned from his bath he caught some Karkyals stealing mangoes from the tree. The Bâbâ told them to fix each mango back on the very branch that it had been plucked from. The youths said that this was not possible. So, the Bâbâ went into prayer and miraculously restored all the mangoes to where they had come from.

Bhallo Bâbâ was probably a cowherd.

Every year a fair and a grand prayer are organised at this shrine on *Basañt Pañchami*, the spring festival.

Nâg Dévatâ (Nâgbani, on the Jammu-Marh Road**)** (10-12 acres) *Flora:* Mangifera, Albizia, Eriobotrya, Nerium, Ficus, Bauhinia, Cassie, Melia, Murraya, Carissa, Butea and Woodfordia.

Fauna: Squirrels, snakes, mongoose, birds and insects.

A great Nâg Mañthan (churning of snakes) took place in the universe a while after its creation. It is said that one snake was left for Srî Krishna, the deity, at this grove.

Nâg-Dévatâ (Surinsar) (0.5 acres) *Flora:* Phoenix sylvestris, Dalbergia sisso, Grewia, optiva, Carissa opaca, Lantana, Ficus racemosa, Caryopteris odorata, Barleria cristata and hydrophytes.

Fauna: Duck, grebe, kingfisher, treepie, drongo, mynah and starling.

There is a Narsingh Dev ji (Narsimh) temple nearby.

Bhairh Dévatâ (15-km from **Nagrotâ**) (two acres of village common land) *Flora:* Acacia modesta, Mallotus phillipensis, Acacia catechu, Butea monosperma, Justicia adhatoda, Carissa opaca and Murraya koenigii. *Fauna:* Macaca mulatta, Gallus gallus, Streptopelia orientalis, Dendrocitta vagabunda, Herpestes edwardsii, Tor putitora and other water animals.

There is a mediæval temple in the grove. Hindus and some Muslim communities hold it in equal reverence.

Shivji temple (Purmandal) 20 km from Kâlu Chak on the Jammu–Pathankot Highway) (2,750 acres. Exactly one-half of this land belongs to the Forest Department). *Flora:* Aegle marmelos, Bombax ceiba, Albizia lebbeck, Syzygium cuminii, Ficus religiosa, F. bengalensis, Ficus palmata, Woodfordia fruticosa, Murraya koenigii, Capparis sepiaria, Datura saaveolens, Lannea coromandelica and Acacia nilotica. *Fauna:* Birds, insects and small mammals.

Véni (or Bâni) Dutt built this temple in the late 18th or early 19th century—if not several thousand years before, as the legend claims.

Shivji temple, Purmandal

Kathuâ District

Uttarbehni Shiv Temple (Billâwar) (two acres) *Flora:* Shîsham (sissoo), Banyan, Bill, Berry, Ḳhair, Phulai, Siris, Barenkar, Ganeera, Ohi, Kakoa and Simbal. *Fauna:* Birds, insects and small mammals.

Peer Bâbâ (Mandâl, Billâwar) Muslims as well as Hiñdus revere Peer Bâbâ. *Flora:* The late 18th/ early 19th century Ficus bengalensis (banyan) tree here is considered particularly sacred. *Fauna:* Birds and insects.

Peer Bâbâ (Kéuli, Billâwar) *Flora:* There is a banyan tree in this grove that is said to have been planted around AD 1500. *Fauna:* Barbets, starlings, rosy pastors and green pigeons come to this tree.

Râjâ Mandleek (Mandal, Billâwar) *Flora:* There are around three hundred berry, Aamla and Kaam trees. *Fauna:* Birds, insects and small animals.

Bâbâ Suryâl (Katwalat, Shama Tâlâb, Billâwar) *Flora:* A Ficus racemosa (Rumbal) tree planted in the late 19th century grows here. *Fauna:* Birds and insects.

The shrine is said to miraculously cure people with snakebites.

Kâlkâ Mâtâ (Meen, Billâwar) *Flora:* Mango and Phulai trees planted in the late 19th century grow here. *Fauna:* Birds and insects.

Peer Bâbâ (Bañdrâl Khurd, Billâwar) *Flora:* A jâmun tree planted in the 1850s grows here. *Fauna:* Birds and insects visit the tree.

Gargal Peer Bâbâ (Billâwar) *Flora:* Many of these berry and Kakoa trees were planted in the 1940s. *Fauna:* Birds and insects.

Raal Dévatâ (Godan, Billâwar) *Flora:* There are around a hundred Dodonea viscosa, Ziziphus nummularia, Adhatoda vasica and Capparis sepiaria trees and bushes. *Fauna:* Dove, parrot, drongo, mongoose, snakes and insects.

Buâ Dâti (Palourâ, Billâwar) (4 acres) *Flora:* Toon, Kakoa, Dhraink, Kikkar, Rajain, Rehaar, Phulai, banyan, Bala, Barankar, Hedma, berry, Siris, mango, Kaseer, Dhamman, Tut, Sarpenkh and Kali Barenkar.

Bâbâ Kailâkh Nâth Temple (Thathar, Ban Tâlâb, Billâwar) (18.6 acres) *Flora:* Banyan, Mitragyna, Kakoa, Kikkar, Tahli Lannea, Mimosa, karañgal, Dhamman, Khair, Garna, berry and Rehaar. *Fauna:* Birds: Batér (quail), partridge, Grey Hornbill, tilyar, oriole, barbet and parakeet. Land animals: Mongoose, squirrels and snakes.

This is the shrine of the guardian deity of the Seth Brahmins. Women bathe under Kaam trees (Mitragynacparvic folia) here. A large banyan tree once toppled over and fell on a wall, where it now rests. However, it is still green, which miracle is attributed to the Bâbâ.

Bâbâ Kailâkh Nâth is one of Vâsuki Nâg's sons and a brother of Bhairh Dévatâ.

Buâ Dév, Changran (Kathua–Nagri Road) (2.5 acres) *Flora:* Date palm, banyan, Kamilla, Rumbal, Garna, Azeratum (Neela Phulnu), ferns, Barenkar, Simbal, Tahli, Tunu, jâmun and Aamla. *Fauna:* Marsh birds and insects.

Râjputs, Brahmins and some Muslim groups revere the deity.

Kalyânpur Temple (Tarna) (3 acres) *Flora:* There are around 250 mango trees and a hundred phagwara, kamilla, Tooni, Aamla and Amrood (guava) trees. *Fauna:* Insects and birds.

Shiv ji Temple (Airwan, Kathua–Panduri Road) (30 acres) *Flora:* Nerium, Mallotus, Ficus, peach, Dhraink, Siris, Kaimbal, karañgal, Bauhinia, Daronkal, Vasuti, Dhud Bana, Garna, Bans, Saru, Safeda and Subabool. *Fauna:* Mongoose, snakes and almost thirty species of birds. The jungle cat, fox and jackal have also been reported.

Mâtâ Bâlâ Sundari (Nagri Parole) (12 acres) *Flora:* There are some three hundred mango, banyan, jâmun, Rumbal, Safeda, Tahli, Sirin, Panjfulli, Garna, Barenkar and berry trees. *Fauna:* Barbet, Rosy Pastor, starling, cuckoo, treepie, drongo and insects.

This is said to be a 10th century AD shrine.

Râdhâ-Krishna temple (Kishanpur, 3 km. from Billâwar) (1 acre) *Flora:* There are around fifty mango, guava, mulberry, banana, peach, Garna, Daronkal, Dhaii, Dhraink, jâmun, Flacaurtia and Ficus racemosa trees. The grove also has some very old banyan and berry trees. *Fauna:* Birds and insects. A rivulet flows through the area, which kingfishers, wagtails and lapwings often visit.

Shiv Temple (Tilla, 2 km. from Billâwar) (3 acres) *Flora:* There are around two hundred and fifty mango, date palm, Kakoa, berry, Kainth, Aamla, Tunu, karañgal, Simbal, Champ, Palaah, Darounkal, Basuti, Raal, Kareer, Bedda, Rumbal, Dhraink and Khair trees. The Panj phulli weed is a major menace. *Fauna:* Birds: The treepie, drongo, barbet, green pigeon and cuckoo can often be seen in the early morning.

Udhampur District

Nâg Dévatâ (Mânsar) (1 acre) *Flora:* Nelumbo nucifera, Phragmites, Typha, Ipomoea, mango, Polygonum glabrum, toonâ ciliata, Buddleja, Terminalia and Salix.

Fauna: Turtle, terrapin, moorhen, kingfisher, grebe, mallard and cormorant.

In the 1970s a strange, saucer-shaped coelenterate, later named Mansariella lecustris, was discovered in the lake near the temple.

The legend of the lake, and its twin, Surinsar, has been recorded in detail in chapter 12, under 'Udhampur Reasi' district.

Dodâ District

Kâli Nâg (Sungli, Bhaderwah) *Flora:* The Vâsuki (or Bâsuki or Bâsak) Nâg is said to have rested under the Fraxinus hookeriana (Sinnu) tree that still grows here, after Garud, the gigantic eagle, chased him out of Kashmîr. The great Nâg is said to have left a tuft of hair under a rock here. (The snake king finally settled at Vâskund).

Rajouri District

Flora

The climate of Rajouri varies from place to place, depending on the altitude. So does the vegetation. Chir (pine) trees are found in most parts of the district, except in the alpine zone. As a result, resin is an important product of Rajouri.

(i) The vegetation of the semi tropical zone includes the kamila, khair phulai, amaltas, amla, shisham, jamun, anardana, kau and bargad trees. Shrubs that grow by the rivers and rivulets include garund, rausont, snathe and nerium indicum.

(ii) The temperate zone: Here we find the rare chikri tree, fir, oak and quercus senioarpifolia (kharsu). The endangered chikri tree grows mainly around Thanna Mandi, where they sell you kitschy handicrafts (including toothpicks) made of its wood. What a fine use of the wood of a dwindling species.

(iii) The 'alpine' zone: Fir, rhododendron, willow and juniper grow here.

Shâhdrâ Sharief (2.5 acres) *Flora:* A citrus tree, some oaks and an Oriental plane tree grow here. *Fauna:* Birds and insects.

Algae

Algae found in Jammû province include:

1. *Chara braunii:* Mânsar-Surinsar Lakes
2. *Chara benthamii:* Mânsar-Suninsar Lakes
3. *Chara contraria:* Kuñjwâni,Tikri Stream
4. *Chara corallina:* Mânsar-Surinsar
5. *Chara brachypus:* Kahnâ Chak Pond
6. *Chara fragilis:* Mânsar-Surinsar
7. *Chara vulgaris:* Tawi River, Billâwar, Kuñjwâni, Gandhi Nagar
8. *Chara zeylanica:* Kuñjwâni, Tikri stream
9. *Lychnothamnus barbatus:* Surinsar Lake
10. *Nitella acuminata:* Gâdhigarh Stream
11. *Nitella hyaline:* Surinsar–Mânsar
12. *Nitella mirabilis:* Surinsar
13. *Nitella mucronata:* Surinsar Lake

The Fauna of Jammu Province

(Animals in Schedule I are the most endangered, while those in Schedule IV are in the safest category of conservation. Schedules II and III come in between).

Mammals

Found almost everywhere

Schedule I: Common Leopard *Panthera pardus*; Leopard Cat *Felis bengalensis*

Schedule II: Jungle Cat *Felis chaus;* Jackal *Canis aureus;* Common fox *Vulpes bengalensis*; Rhesus monkey *Macaca multta.*

Schedule IV: Common Indian hare *Lepus nigriculis;* Mangoose *Herpestes edwardsi.*

Schedule V: Common fruit bat *Rousettus leschenaulti.*

Found in the higher altitudes

Schedule I: Brown bear *Ursus urctos;* Wolf *Canis lupus;* Himalayan lynx *Felis lynx isabellina;* Ibex *Capra ibex;* Markhor *Capra falconeri;* Musk deer *Moschus moschifreus.*

Schedule II: Common langur *Presbytis entalus;* Himalayan black bear *Selenarctos thibetanus;* Wild dog *Cuon alpinus;* Marten *Marten fania intermedia;* Red fox *Vulpus vulpus.*

In the Kishtwâr area

Schedule I: Snow Leopard *Panthera uncia* (at higher altitudes only); Kashmir stag *Cervus elaphus hangul;* Himalayan thar *Hemitragus jemlahicus.*

In the subtropical area

Schedule I: Goral *Goral nemorhaedus;* Pea fowl *Pavo cristetus.* Schedule III: Barking deer *Muntiacus muntjak;* Sambar *Cervus unicolor;* Wild boar *Sus scrofa;* Hog deer *Axis porcinus.*

Schedule IV: Indian Porcupine *Hystrix indica.*

Jasrota Wildlife Sanctuary (Kathua)

Schedule III: Spotted deer *Axis axis.*

The plains of Jammu region

Schedule III: Nilgai *Boselaphus tragocamelus.*

Birds

Recorded from different areas of Jammu region

Schedule I: Black partridge *Francolinus francolinus;* Common swallow *Hirundo rustica;* Common teal *Anascrecea crecea;* Large carmorant *Phalacrocorax carbo niger;* Little cormorant *Palacrocorax niger;*

Monal pheasant *Lephophorus impejanus;* Paradise flycatcher *Terpsiphone paradisi;* Pea fowl *Pavo cri;* Purple Moorhen *Porphyris porphyrio;* Western tragopan *Tragopan.* (Rup Lal Bharti, the Chief Wildlife Warden of the state, adds, 'Pheasants are monal, kalig and jungle fowl. All three are found in Jammû province).

Schedule IV: Bar headed goose *Anser indicus;* Blue rock pigeon *Columba livia;* Cattle Egret *Bubulcus ibis;* Cattle egret *Bubulcus ibis;* Common coot *Fulica atra;* Common myna *Acridotheres tristis;* Common rose finch *Carpodacus erythrinus;* Common shrike *Lanius* sp.; Cuckoo *Eudynamys scolopacea;* Gadwal *Anas strepera;* Green bee-eater *Merops orientalis;* Grey heron *Ardea cinerea;* Grey partridge *Francolinus pondicerianus;* Hoopoe *Upupa epops;* House sparrow *Passer domesticus;* Indian pipit *Anthus* sp.; Indian pond heron *Ardeola grayii;* Indian robin; *Erithacus* sp.; Indian roller *Coracias* sp.; Indian Treepie *Dendrocitta vagabunda;* Jungle crow *Corvus macrorhynchos;* Jungle owlet *Glaucidium raidatum;* Kalij pheasant *Lophura leucomelana;* Kingfisher *Halcyon smyrnensis;* Lapwing *Vanellus indicus;* Little brown dove *Streptopelia seneglanensis;* Little grebe *Tachybaptus;* Magpie Robin *Copsychus saularis;* Northern shoveler *Anas clypeata;* Owl *Bubo* sp.; Pariah Kite *Milvus migrans;* Pied bush chat *Saxicola capratta;* Porcupine *Hystrix indica;* Purple heron *Ardea purpurea;* Purple sunbird *Nectrina asiatica;* Red jungle fowl *Gallus gallus;* Red vented bulbul *Pycnonotus cafer;* Ring dove *Streptopelia* sp.; Rose-ringed parakeet *Psittacula krameri;* Ruddy shelduck *Tadorna ferruginea;* Rufus turtle dove *Streptopelia* sp.; Scarlet minivet *Pericrocotus flammeus;* Spotted dove *Streptopelia chinensis;* Tit *Parus* sp.; Vulture *Gyps* sp.; Water hen *Gallinula chloropus;* Weaver bird *Ploceus philippinus;* White browed fantail flycatcher *Rhipiduri aurela;* White cheeked bulbul *Pycnonotus leucogenys;* Woodpecker *Piciodes dinopium;* Babbler *Turdoides caudatus;* and Black drongo *Dicrurus adsimilis.*

Reptiles

Found in the sub-tropics and plains of Jammu

Schedule I: Python *Python molurus.*

Schedule II: Chameleon *Chameleo calcaratus;* Cobra *Naja naja;* Monitor lizard *Varanus bengalensis;* Spiny-tailed Lizard *Uromastix hardwickii.*

Schedule III: Krait *Bangarus sp.;* Pit Viper *Agkristodon himalayanus;* Russel's Viper *Viper russelli.*

Fish

Found in the Mansar and Surinsar Lakes

Traditional species: *Channa punctatus; Rasbora rasbora; Punctius conchonius; Danio rerio; Esomus daurica.*

Introduced by the government: *Cyprinus carpio communis; Cyprinus carpio specularis.*

Turtles

Found in the Mansar and Surinsar Lakes

Lessemis punctata; Trionyx gangeticus.

Chapter- 3

The Rivers of Jammû

The Tawi

The river originates mainly at the Kaplas Kund in the Bhaderwâh area. From there it descends to Sudh Mahâdev. After that, from Chenainî to Udhampur, it runs along National Highway 1A. At Udhampur it turns south and heads towards Jinganu. It then goes through low hills and turns north-west to reach Jandrah. It proceeds to Nagrotâ and then to Jammû. It enters Pâkistân at 30°45'N 74°38'E.

Kaplas Kund, Bhaderwah

Asaf Mahmud, who has explored the Tawi in some detail, observes: "Surprisingly, some rivulets and seasonal nallahs in this region, which are in no manner related as tributaries of the Tawi, carry its name".

Rafting: The first known run of the river for adventure purposes was conducted in June 1991. Mahmud, who was the captain of the team, reports, "The river was explored in an inflatable canoe from the Sidrah Bridge, on [the Jammû bypass] to Tawi Bridge in [the] city. The run of 6-7 [nautical kilometres] was completed in one hour. The Sea Eagle 340 used for the first time was quite comfortable in riding the waves, without shipping water".

"The river in this section is a classic drop and then long pools. The drops have some interesting standing waves, few upto 100 metres long. The river is [said to have a] 'ferocious' flow during rains in its catchment areas and flood conditions in monsoons. In the winter the water just trickles".

"At this time of exploration, the discharge of the water made the river a mild grade of I and II. As stated by the natives [sic] this situation remains almost constant for several months. Under the conditions mentioned above, the river can be used for imparting basic training in kayaking and raft handling".

"Small ponds formed by oozing water in the depressions away from mainstream in the river bed can be used for elementary paddling techniques".

"Low volume rotational moulded PVC kayaks with complete gear would be suitable for this operation. Adventure rafts will have the tendency to get grounded with rated tonnage aboard".

The Chenâb

The Bârâ Lâchâ pass (4,891m; Himâchal Pradésh/ HP) has the best claim to being the origin of the glacier-fed, perennial Chenâb. Actually two rivulets originate from there: the Chañdr, which flows down south, and the Bhâgâ, that goes north.

A motorable road runs along the river from Khoksar to Tandi/ Tindi (HP). (Manali is 26 km. further south). In all, there are 107 kilometres of road near the river during its sojourn in HP.

A BRO Signboard showing the height of Baralacha pass (16500 feet/5029m.)

In J&K there are motorable roads near the river in the stretches between Atholi and Malhori, Peerah and Râmban, and Kauthan and Jauriâñ. There are pony tracks along other stretches. As everyone who has travelled on the Jammû-Srînagar National Highway knows, the road is often one or two hundred feet above the Chenâb.

The Chañdr and the Bhâgâ join to form the Chañdrabhâgâ. Tandi (2,825m). claims to be the point where this union takes place. So does Bhandarkot (Dodâ district). The word 'Chandrabhâgâ' later contracts to become 'Chenâb'. This happens when it joins River Marau at Bhandarkot. (Hence Tandi's claim is correct).

The ancients knew the river as Asikni.

Dodâ is enormously rich in forests. Contractors fell trees and float them on the Chenâb, which carries the timber downstream. This timber is a hazard that river rafters must take into account.

The river then travels to Réâsî, where it has been dammed at Salâl for a hydro-electric project. As a result, a 30 km. reservoir has been created upstream. In September 1992, there was enormous rainfall at and above the Salâl dam. Massive quantities of timber had accumulated in the reservoir. The timber had to be removed from the dam immediately or the dam might have burst.

Had that happened, Jammû and Akhnoor would have suffered considerable damage but downstream Pâkistân would have been flooded completely. The dam was saved, but the timber piled up at the historic Akhnoor bridge and, a few hours later, wiped out that sturdy, stately structure.

The ice-cold Ranbîr Canal branches off from the Chenâb near Akhnoor and irrigates Jammû district. The river then enters Pâkistân and Pâkistân occupied Kashmir. It has the same place in the folklore and literature of the sub-continent that perhaps the Teestâ has in the Beñgâls. Sohni and Mahiwâl, ill-fated lovers much-mourned in Punjãbî literature, had drowned in the Chenâb near Gujarât (a district of West Punjâb, now in Pâkistân).

Rafting: The first known attempt to run the Chenâb was made in 1985 by an American team in kayaks. They were successful, as was a Delhi-Kashmir team in rafts and K-1s in 1988. However, another raft expedition, also in the 1980s, failed.

River rafters will naturally keep in mind that the level of the Chenâb varies wildly with the season. The waters rise and therefore flow speedily in summer. But in the process they conceal countless boulders below the surface and create deep troughs and what Asaf Mahmud calls 'long surging waves'. In winter there is much less water in the river. The same boulders rise above the river and rafters have to navigate their way around them. During the monsoons the river is, naturally, in spate. However, since the Indian territory that it flows through is almost entirely on a slope, it causes relatively little damage here.

The stretch above Râmban, as well as the segment above Salâl, is dangerous for rafting purposes. However, as Asaf notes, "The section between Salâl and Talwârâ Bridge below [Réâsî] appears to promise good prospects for rafting and kayaking operations".

There are several stretches throughout the course of the river that local people have traditionally plied their country boats on.

The Ranbîr Canal

Water is drawn for this canal from the left bank of River Chenâb near the Akhnoor Bridge (32°54' N, 74°45' E), almost 35km. from Jammû town. This fast-flowing water remains chilly even at the peak of the Jammû summer. The canal mainly runs along the Jammû-Akhnoor road. It goes underground for two brief stretches and has to be carried over troughs by aqueducts. There are several bridges over the canal, some for pedestrians and others for vehicles as well. It crosses River Tawi and has been named after Mahârâjâ Ranbîr Siñgh (1857-1885).

Rafting: It is felt that kayaking might be possible, but not all through the year because water levels vary considerably.

The Râvî

River Râvi constitutes the boundary between Jammû & Kashmir and Himâchal Pradésh (and briefly between J&K and the Punjâb). Its name *The Gazetteer* notes, "The Râvî is fordable throughout the winter season, but the bed is full of quicksands".

Of all the towns and villages of J&K, Basohli has the most special relationship with the river. Till the early 1980s, there used to be a makeshift ropeway between Basohli and the opposite bank (in HP). A trolley hooked

A panoramic view of the Ravi as it flows past Basohli

to the rope was used to move materials and, sometimes, men. Daring Basohliites would swim across the river (minimum discharge: 2,700 cubic feet), balancing themselves on 'cushions' made of inflated sheepskin. The huge reservoir formed by the then Dam has changed all that. Now the easiest way to go across is by ferry.

The Râvî merges with the Chenâb.

Rajouri District

Many little rivers flow through the district. Among the important ones are the Sukh Tawi, the Jamola, the Darhal Tawi, the Ans and the Khandli.

The 17th century Emperor Jehangir wrote in his memoirs that the water of a river that flowed through Rajouri 'became poisoned' during the rainy season. As a result, the people suffered from goitre and became yellow and weak. He did not name the river. It could have been the Munnawar Tawi, the quality of whose water has often been suspect.

Udhampur and Reasi District

Rivers and Lakes

The mighty Chenâb, the Ans, the Tawi and the Ujh rivers flow through the district. They often flow in deep troughs more than sixty or seventy feet below the nearest flat land, making their waters difficult to utilise. The Devika flows through Udhampur town and its waters are incredibly good for digestion.

The Mansar lake is at the south-eastern extremity of the district, while the Sanasar was drained of its waters in the 1980s. An artificial lake has been created because of the Salal 'dam' (Hydroelectric Project). I inaugurated a tourist cafeteria next to it in 1992, but the café has not been a commercial success.

Kashmir

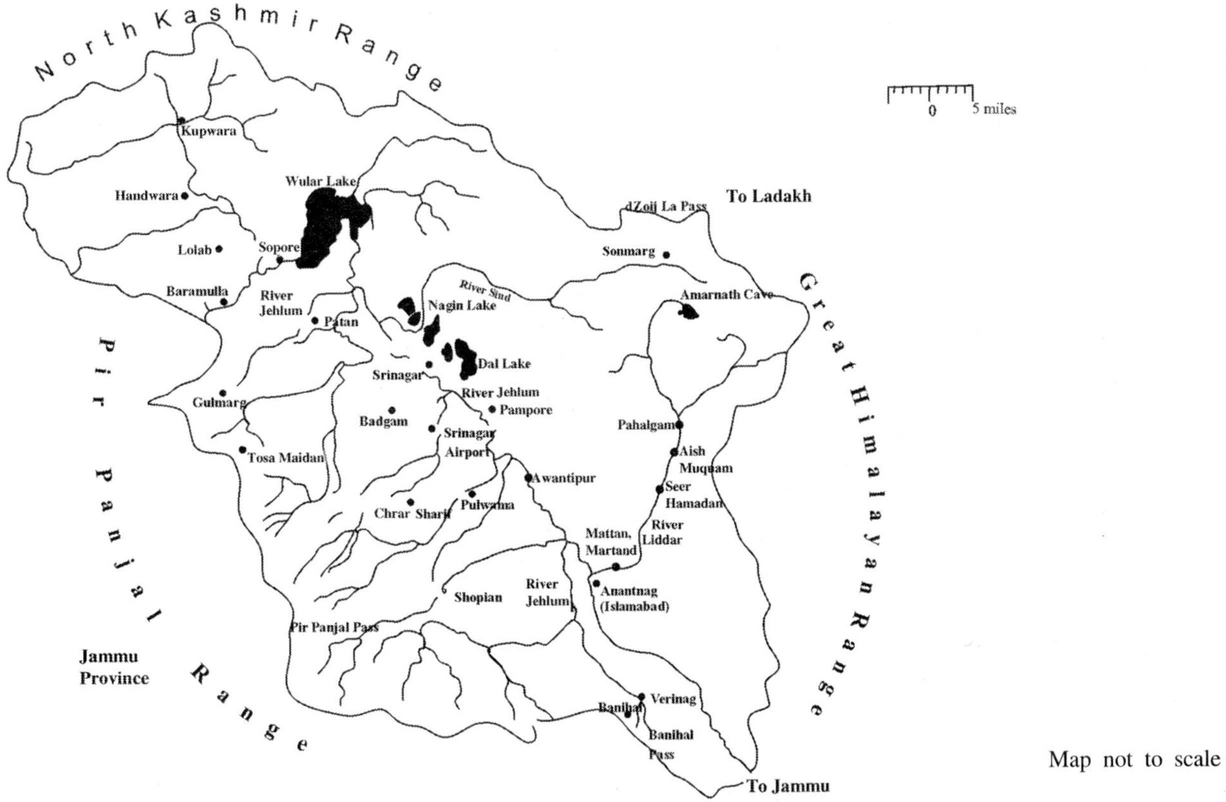

The Valley of Kashmir

Chapter- 4

Flora

In the beginning Kashmîr was a gigantic lake. Several thousand years later the mountain near Bârâmullâ came falling down and an opening was created in the direction of Muzaffarabâd ('AJK'). Most of the waters of that great lake poured out of Kashmîr into what is now 'AJK'. However, a lot of water remained in the Valley. The large number of lakes that dot Kashmîr are the most obvious example of this water. Marshes and 'wetlands' rank next in the hierarchy. And then comes Kashmîr's huge reserve of underground water. The water table not just in Bârâmullâ district but also in the poshest neighbourhoods of Srînagar is so high that it is almost embarrassing. (Let us skip the details. Suffice it to say that in a normal year you just have to dig for a foot or two to find water). As a result, Kashmîr is extremely fertile. All kinds of trees, fruit and flowers grow here. This much is a scientific fact.

After God smashed a passage through the mountain between Bârâmullâ and Muzaffarabâd, and thus drained the Valley, He is supposed to have sent His angels to Kashmîr. These 'Bekdarat' scattered seeds of many kinds to dry the soil. The seeds later grew into the incredible variety of vegetation that we find in the Valley today.

Almond: It Ripens in autumn. The *Gazetteer* (1890) observes, "The sweet almonds are considered dry and warm remedies, and are used in headaches and debilities. Oil is made of them. A branch of the tree is said to keep flies out of the room…"

Apple: There are several varieties, some of which start ripening as early as in June and July. Most, however, ripen in September. The crop is so plentiful that much of it falls off and rots on the ground. In the past (till the 1960s) apples (and several vegetables and fruits) were dried in the sun and stored for the winters. However, with the advent of modern storage techniques, and the availability in winters of fresh vegetables from Jammû and the rest of India, this tradition of drying (dehydrating) produce is on its way out but still not totally gone.

Ambri: The unique tasting ambri apple grows only on Kashmîrî soil and is a rare species heading for extinction. These apples ripen in late autumn. They also yield the largest crop per tree and are most valued for eating. The name of this sweet smelling fruit, M.Y. Taing feels, is derived from the Sanskrit-Persian scent called 'amber' which is obtained from a sea fish. The ambri tree is grown by grafting a branch of an ambri tree on the sapling of a wild apple tree. It starts bearing fruit in twelve to fifteen years. It lives for almost a hundred years. At its peak it yields almost a thousand apples, is tall and has a wide girth. It bears fruit even when it grows old. It is valued as fuel because its flame is strong and its embers smoulder for a long while. Flowers blossom on the tree in late April.

The wood of all apple trees is hard and used for cog-wheels and gun-stocks. Apples have also been grown in Ladâkh and on the banks of the Chenab since mediæval times. The Basohli variety, too, has been grown for several centuries now and marketed in the plains.

The apple in Kashmîrî history: The fruit is called *tsonth* in Kashmîrî. Some theorise that apples are not indigenous to Kashmîr but were brought in from elsewhere. However, the fact that several wild species are found in the forests indicates the depth, and antiquity, of their association with Kashmîr. In any case, the *Râjâtarañginî* tells us that when Queen Didda (AD 980-1003) grew old and started worrying about who would succeed her, she summoned the sons of her brother Uday Raja. She placed a heap of apples before them and said that she would select as her heir the prince who brought her the largest number of apples from the heap. The princes all jumped on the heap and began to fight against each other to grab the most apples. Only Prince Sangram Raja stayed away from the fray. At the end of the day Didda noticed that the number of apples that Sangram brought to her were about the same as what the others had, but there wasn't a scratch or wound on them and that he hadn't battled against his brothers to obtain the fruit.

This impressed her and Sangram succeeded Didda. (He went on to prove quite an inept king. Perhaps his behaviour with the apples indicates why).

The next available reference to Kashmîrî apples dates to Mirza Haidar Dughlat's 16th century '*Târikh-e-Rasheedi*', in which Dughlat praised the fruit.

Apricot: It is grown extensively in Kargil, where the harvested fruit is left to dry on rooftops. (Since the 1970s it is also being dried on curved metal sheets, which concentrate the rays of the sun on the fruit because of the curvature). The kernels yield an oil (*stigumur* in Ladâkhi) which is valued in Leh. The tree yields a soluble gum. Its wood is hard and used for the 'hardcovers' between which Ladâkhi manuscripts and books are bound. It ripens in the early summer.

Birch: Betula tartarica. The *bhojpatr*—bark of this tree is what all ancient manuscripts of Kashmîr were written on. (Some survive in the archives). It is used as a waterproof material on roofs, for the tubes of the *hukka* (tobacco pipe), and for umbrellas.

Cherry: Cherry is locally known as 'glass'. There are two varieties, habshee (dark) and surkh (red). In some parts the bird-cherry is also grown. It ripens in the early summer.

A grove in Kashmir Valley

Chinâr: This majestic tree (Plantanus orientalis) is believed to have been brought to Kashmîr from Farghana (Central Asia), Iran or Turkey. But by whom? By the Mughals? Certainly not. Because when Jehangir came to Kashmîr he could 'go inside' a particularly large tree while 'riding on a horse, with five other saddled horses and two eunuchs'. So, Chinârs were widespread in Kashmîr well before the Mughals. Apparently, some Mughals saw the reddened leaves of a Chinâr grove in October and thought that the forest was on fire. 'Chee nâr ast?' ('What flame is that?') a Mughal is said to have exclaimed. The name stuck.

I once came upon a 15th century miniature. It was painted almost one hundred and fifty years before the Mughal conquest of Kashmîr. It shows the Shankarâchârya hill and temple—and several chinârs.

And it is not just in the Valley that you find the Chinâr. It is *native* to several parts of Jammû province, too, including Sudh Mahadev and the low altitude Chirhai Muttal (both in Udhampur), apart from having been grown forcibly (with stunted results) in Jammû town and even in Delhi. So, clearly the Chinâr is indigenous to Kashmîr. What the Mughals (especially their much loved governor Ali Mardan Khân, 1642-1657) did was to get a Chinâr-cum-poplar grove planted in every village of the Valley. (It is very difficult to grow a Chinâr. Barley is planted around the sapling to speed up its growth).

Where do you get to see a Chinâr? Everywhere in Kashmîr, even though it's still quite a rare tree. Its best grove in Srînagar is the Naseem Bâgh where the University campus now is (next to Hazratbal). A kilometre from Radio Kashmîr and the Tourist Reception Centre, Srînagar, is an elite school called Burn Hall. Opposite the school is a cricket stadium inside the city's second best Chinâr grove. The leaves are 'aflame' in October and the first fortnight of November.

The Dogrâs declared the Chinâr a 'royal' tree, a protection which continues to this day. This means that you'll be jailed for felling a Chinâr tree. Its girth is normally around 12 metres (less than 40'). Its wood, when available, is used in furniture and for the making of papier mache boxes.

Historian G.M.D. Sufi writes, "The Chinâr trees make delightful camping grounds, where they afford a cool and very welcome shade in the hottest part of the day".

Chîr: See 'Pines' below.

Currant: Grows wild in some parts of the Valley and is cultivated in Baltistan (POK).

Cypress: Locally called the sa-roo. Its wood is common but valued because it is durable. Grows in many parts of the state, including the Shyok valley (Ladâkh).

Daphne: Grows between 5,000' and 8,000' and is called *sanarkat* in Kashmîrî. Fibre yielded by its bark is utilised in making high quality ropes. The bark is also used in the making of paper.

Deodar trees: (The Himâlayan cedar). Grows between 7,000' and 12,000' (that's theoretical; up to 9,000' is more realistic). Attains a height of 100 to 200 feet (30 to 70 metres) and a girth of 20 to 40 feet

(6 to 12 metres). Its timber is so durable (and thus valued in the construction of buildings) that bridges made of it have survived for more than 400 years. Gives a dark, strong-smelling, medicinal oil.

Elm trees: The small-leaved elm is found in the lower valleys of Kashmîr and in Tagar (in Nubra). Its wood is more open-grained and less valued than English elm.

Fir trees: Silver and spruce firs grow in Bhaderwâh and Padar (both in Doda, Jammû) between 8,000' and 11,000'. Its wood is not much valued. Grows up to heights of 100' and diameters of 5'.

Gulmarg literally means the 'Meadow of flowers'

Flowers: There are major meadows in almost every district of Kashmîr. There are wild flowers on these meadows and cultivated and wild flowers elsewhere. Many places in all three regions of the state take their names after flowers: Gulmarg (the meadow of flowers), Gulabgarh ('the fort of the rose' or 'the fort of King Gulab'), Poshiana, Posh Pathri (posh means flower), even the Siachen glacier.

Flowers found in the state include the anemone, aquilegia, crocus, daisy, gentian, geranium, iris-purple and white, marsh marigold, poppy-blue, potentialla, primula, rose, and saxifraga.

Fruit: It is not my hopeless infatuation with Kashmîr which makes me assert that it is the best place in India better than even Hyderabad for fruit lovers because there is a new fruit every five or six weeks. (I have also counted at least four or five blossoms during the course of a year and am trying to put them all together in one garden, for the public to see and share my love).

Lal Ded, the mystic poet, however, was inspired differently by this periodic blossoming of flowers and fruit. She said that signs that Kalyug (in this context, doomsday) had come would be that pears, apples and apricots would ripen at the same time, and that mothers and their grown up daughters would leave their homes together to frolic all day and make merry in the company of strangers.

The 1890 *Gazetteer,* on the other hand, goes even further than I. It says, "Hügel, a sound and well-informed botanist, … considers Kashmîr superior to all other countries in the abundance and excellence of its fruits". Of course, one writer of the Raj placed Kandahar (Afghânistan) higher. Yet others complained, as Girdlestone did, that "it is rare to get any fruits of first-rate quality in Kashmîr, simply because they are allowed to run wild, no heed being given to manuring, pruning and grafting". Things have changed somewhat since. However, the point is well taken. Nature has blessed Kashmîr with an incredibly fertile soil. We humans too should do our bit.

Grapes: At least twenty varieties, of which four are of foreign origin, grow in the Valley and ripen in September. Other varieties are found in particular parts of Kargil. Unripe grapes (*kur*) yield fine vinegar.

Hazel: Found at around 8,000'.

Herbs: The forests of the state abound in herbs, medicinal and other. In officialese they are called MFP (minor forest produce). These include the *kuth* (costus spacious).

Holly: *Kursu* is abundant in Bhaderwâh (Doda, Jammû).

Iris: Four species are found in Kashmîr: the white, the purple (both found in graveyards), the yellow and the mauve. Flowering season: April and May. The root yields medicines and dyes.

Juniper: Called *yettu* locally. Grows at 11,000'. Along with rhododendrons, it provides the only fuel available at that altitude.

A blooming lotus bud - Dal Lake, Srinagar

Lotus: Grows on the lakes of Kashmîr, especially the Dal. Popular species: the *pamposh* (nymphæa lotus) and the Nelumbeum speciosum (Egyptian water lily). Blooms in August and September. After that the plate of the leaf begins to decay. It is boiled till it is tender and eaten as a delicacy. The Hindus revere the plant (because it is the seat of Lakshmi and Saraswati Devi ji, and of Sri

Hanuman ji). The Buddhists even more so because of its association with Lord Buddha. Its bean is eaten unripe. (See also 'Waternut'.)

Lucerne: Grown in Ladâkh and used as fodder for cattle.

Mango: Grown in Jammû, especially in the Basohli area.

Mulberry: Eight different varieties grow in abundance in Kashmîr and parts of the Indus valley. In such abundance that the fruit rots on the tree and is mostly eaten by bears. Its wood is hard and used in furniture and boats. Its leaves are considered the best fodder for cattle.

Oak: Grows between 8,000' and 11,500'. Officers of the British Raj observed the curious fact 'that on the south side of the Kashmîr valley [Ânañtnâg?], one does not see the oak and rhododendron, although the elevation of the ground corresponds to that where, on the other side of the Panjab [Jammû-i.e. Doda?] hills, these trees are abundant'. All Himâlayan species are evergreen. Their timber does not float. One species is locally called kray-oo.

Olive: Grows in the Chenab valley. Its wood is strong and heavy, and used as tool handles and for other mechanical purposes.

Peach: Ripens in the early summer. There are two principal varieties, sweet (*modur tsunum)* and sour (*tyut tsunum*).

Pears: There are two main kinds, the hard and the juicy, the *nâkh* and the *baggu-goshâ*. The *Gazetteer* says that 'the *nak* pear has the preference, both for eating and preserving'. I suppose tastes vary. Many of us prefer the fruit 'when overripe and decaying, like the European medlar', as the same *Gazetteer* puts it elsewhere. And it is the *baggu-gosha* that gets 'overripe' and succulent. Both ripen in the late summer.

Its wood is good for carving; that of the wild pear is brown and compact. Printing blocks in Ladâkh are made of pear wood.

Pines: Grows most commonly between 3,000' and 4,000'. At lower altitudes (as low as 1,400') it is stunted. Sometimes found at 5,500'. Exudes sweet smelling resin and turpentine, yields pine needles and its bark is good for charcoal.

Plum: Does not grow wild in Kashmîr – only when cultivated. The fruit is very popular, especially baked into the famous plum cakes of Jee Enn Bakery (on Maulana Âzâd Road in the heart of Srînagar). Ripens in the early summer.

Pomegranate: 'Dân' in Kashmîrî, there are three principal varieties, which ripen in September. The rind is used in tanning and as a medicine, the husk in dyeing and the fruit, too, in medicines.

Poplars: The Valley has two varieties: the local Kashmîrî poplar and the Kabul poplar. In Nubra (Ladâkh) poplar is common till the south side of Shyok.

Quince: Known locally as the *bam-tsunt,* and ripens in October. Its seeds are used as medicines.

Rajma(sh): The vegetarians of Jammû and Punjab like nothing better for their Sunday lunch than well-cooked red beans (râjmâ). These are grown in many parts of Jammû province. The best rajma comes from Bhaderwâh. The rajma of Banni is a close second. (Banni and Bhaderwâh are neighbours). The longer this kidney-shaped bean the better it is supposed to be. Bhaderwâh beans are the longest of the lot.

This is a hard lentil (pulse), the hardest of all lentils eaten in India. It takes much longer to cook than other lentils. It is also that much more difficult to digest. Therefore, it is eaten over lunch so that it gets more time to be digested. Most people cook enough rajma at a time to last two or three meals. The leftovers are kept in the fridge and reheated when needed. They taste better with each subsequent reheating, because this hard bean takes several reheatings to absorb the spices. It also grows softer when stored overnight in a cooked form.

Raspberry: Grows in some parts of Kashmîr.

Rhododendron: Grows at high altitudes, around 11,000', known locally as *tâzak tsun*, its wood is brown and brittle and useful only for fuel. Its flowers are made into a jelly. To be found aplenty trekking between Marbal and Singpur.

Wild Rhododendrons

Rice: Jammû grows the finest *basmati* rice in India, much superior to that of Dehra Dun. Within Jammû the best basmati is grown in R.S. (Ranbir Singh) Pura, in Jammû district. Bishnah, also in Jammû district, too, grows good basmati. The rice is harvested and stored for a year or two before it is eaten. 'Old basmati' tastes infinitely better. Therefore, basmati from the most recent harvest is always the cheapest in shops.

The Kashmîrîs do not use basmati in their cooking. They prefer a thick, inexpensive, coarse variety, because of its odour, flavour and ability to blend with their rich cuisine.

Saffron Harvest

Saffron: The 19th century scholar Dr. King observed that it took 7,000 to 8,000 flowers to yield 17.5 ounces of fresh saffron, which by drying is reduced to 3.5 ounces. This is why saffron is the world's most expensive botanical product, making it among vegetables what caviar is to the animal kingdom. Spain and Iran are the only other saffron growing areas in the world.

History: As its botanical name (*Crocus sativus*) suggests, saffron was first grown in Croycus (now known as Korghoz), near Syria. The Arabs took it to Spain in AD 961. It is believed to have been brought to Kashmîr in the reign of King Lalitaditya (AD 725-753). (According to a newspaper article, saffron was brought to Kashmîr in 500 B.C. The article does not substantiate its claim, therefore I tend to go along with the Lalitaditya theory).

Areas where grown in the state: Within J&K saffron is grown mostly in Kashmîr, and within the Valley mainly in Pâmpore and Parihâsporâ. However, the Mughal royals preferred the saffron of Kishtwâr [Doda district, Jammû province], which still produces fine saffron. Kishtwâr saffron doesn't smell as sweet but has a stronger dye.

Why can't this very expensive product be grown everywhere? For one it can only grow on clayey soil – a 'light ferruginous clay' to be precise, between 1,500 and 2,400 metres above the msl. The place must receive between 30 and 40 cm. of rain and be covered with snow in winter. The temperature must be subtemperate. Only well-drained loamy soils can grow saffron. Tracts of land that have such alluvial soil are known locally as *karewas*. There are five saffron-growing *karewas* in the Pâmpore area, 12-20 km. from Srînagar, all on the right bank of the Jehlum. The national highway goes right through saffron fields. So, if you travel between Srînagar and Jammû or between Srînagar and Pahalgâm, there's just no way you'll miss these fields.

Despite the best efforts, it has not been possible to significantly increase the number of areas where saffron is grown. Government attempts in the 19th century to grow saffron on the nearby Damodar wudar, in the Yech pargana and near Martand, all failed, though the soil and climate were similar to Pâmpore. However, the government has been successful in growing saffron with profit in parts of Budgâm district, which are close to Pâmpore and where the soil is similar.

Appearance and Uses: When sold saffron looks like little pieces of straw, red-coloured, around an inch or two long and as thin as straw.

The flower whose stamens saffron is made of is called *kong* or *kong-posh* in Kashmîrî and *Crocus sativus* in botany. In Arabic-Urdu-Persian the final product is called 'zâf-rân' and in Hindi 'kay-sir' (rhymes with 'fir').

The flower has six petals and six stamens. Three yellow stamens surround three red stamens. Red (and white) stamens alone are used in the final product; yellow stamens are given to the cattle. Each of the stamens/ stigmas used has a style that is around 5cm. long.

Genuine vs. Fakes: Journalist Amit Gupta writes, 'Genuine saffron forms a loosely matted mass of dark, reddish brown, flattened stigmas with a strong characteristic odour and bitterish taste. The stigma is tubular, about 25mm. in length, narrow at the base but broadening towards the upper extremity'.

Varieties: Three categories of saffron are sold in shops: shahi, mongra and lachha. The three types have been listed in the order of quality and price.

Uses: Saffron is eaten, smelt and valued for the strong colour it discharges. It is used for the preparation of Ayurvedic and Unani medicines, Roman perfumes and the exotic *qehwa* (herbal tea). Many Hindus smear a paste, the *tilak,* on their foreheads after the morning prayers. The paste contains some saffron.

Saffron is also used as an ingredient in expensive foods, e.g., certain kinds of *pulao* (pilaf) in central India and in some Kashmîrî meat dishes.

The Ladâkhis have traditionally bought saffron in large quantities (1,600 pounds a year), not to mention Hindus from Kashmîr to Kerala.

Saffron is supposed to be a diuretic, a stimulant and even an aphrodisiac. It is also said to be good for people suffering from diseases of the brain, heart, liver and stomach. What this author can vouch for is that drinking saffron *qehwa* generates considerable heat within the body. It thus provides an internal shield during Kashmîr's cold winters.

How saffron is grown: Saffron grows from bulbs, not seeds. The plant is so short, rising hardly six inches above the earth, that one has to sit on the ground to pluck the flowers.

The land is ploughed and divided into squares of roughly 2.5 × 2.5 metres. These squares are called *kingwâri* and 72 tolas of bulbs are planted, in July or August, into each. The corms are dormant during the summer. The bulbs are placed about 6 inches (15 cm). apart, at a depth of around 10 inches (25 cm)..

Put another way, 5 lakh (0.5 million) corms of the correct size are planted on one hectare of land. Together, these 5 lakh corms weigh 40 quintals. A corm should weigh around 10 grams and have a diameter of between two and five grams to be considered suitable for planting.

Having planted the bulbs/ corms, the farmer can relax for the next ten or even twenty years, that being the life of each bulb, because no fresh planting needs to be done every year. Besides, you can neither irrigate nor add fertilizer/ manure to the soil where saffron is grown. However, the surface soil needs to be dug up three or four times a year. The crop is good if the soil has just the right moisture (too much is bad) and if the rains had been plentiful in April and May.

The yield is low in the first year, better in the second year and best from the third to thirteenth years after which it starts going down again. (I am assuming a 15 to 20-year variety. Regardless of type, yield is best from the third year onwards).

After the soil has yielded saffron for 10 to 20 years it has to be left fallow for eight to twelve years. (If saffron was yielded for only six years depending on the variety, then that land is left fallow for just five years).

Yield: In Spain, one hectare of land yields as much as 16 kilograms of saffron. The yield in Kashmîr is just two to four kilos per hectare.

For that reason some Kashmîrîs believe that their saffron is superior. On average, a corm yields six daughter corms every year.

Bloom: The flowers bloom for about three weeks from mid-October to the first days of November. To see them during the day is nice. But seeing (and smelling) them on a moonlight October night is an experience emperors would crave for. Take the 17th century Emperor Jehangir, for instance. He wrote, "I accompanied my father [Emperor Akbar] to this spot [obviously Pâmpore] during the season of flowers…The appearance [of the flowers] is best at a distance, and when they are plucked they emit a strong smell. My attendants were all seized with a headache, and though I was myself at the time intoxicated with liquor, I felt also my head affected." This connection with midnight is rooted in botany, not romantic poetry. The flowering of saffron takes place between 1 and 5a.m.

Plucking starts in October and continues till early December. The flowers have to be picked in the early morning, before the dew evaporâtes and before the sun starts getting hot. Apparently the flowers contain some fragrant oils which are volatile. These oils are damaged when exposed to sunlight.

Honey: There is some – no, not much – snob value attached to honey produced by bees that have fed on saffron. A 1945 publication of the state government wrote, "Nectar is found in saffron flower at the base of the style and droplets of a sweet liquid ooze out from the peduncle after the flowers have been cut. Bees collect this liquid. The old bee-keepers of the Valley believed… that no honey is ripe for removal from the hives till the bees have collected their harvest from the saffron flower".

Sandalwood: On the authority of Elmslie, the *Gazetteer* states that "there is said to be a forest of sandalwood *(tsandum)* in Wama Divi, in the Kuthar *paragana*, beyond Islâmabad [Ânañtnâg]".

Sycamore: These are found in Padar (Doda), to the north of River Chenab.

Strawberry: Grown in Guréz and, increasingly, in the hot plains of Jammû, including Jammû city. Ripens in Kashmîr in the early summer and in the plains in the winter.

Vine: See 'Grapes' above.

Walnut: Walnut seeds are sown in March and germinate by May. In seven years they grow into trees that yield fruit. However, the annual yield is at its best after the tenth year. Their fruit ripens in the middle of September, when the trees are beaten and the nuts, four to six thousand per tree per year, fall to the ground. The green outer rind falls off in the process and is used to yield dyes (for cloth and walnut wood), ranging from green to almost black. The tree grows mostly between 5,500 and 7,500 feet above the msl.

Walnut oil is used in cooking but does not burn by itself, unless mixed with other oils, such as linseed. The four principal types of fruit bearing walnut are: *kâghazi* (i.e., paper-like), the yield of which is the lowest but the fruit of which is the best and the tree of which has the finest shade; *burzal,* which is not as good as kâghazi; *bulbul dun*, which has such a soft shell that nightingales peck holes through it; and *wânt*, which is the most common variety and the fruit of which is the most plentiful.

After a few years of high yield, the amount of fruit a tree produces in a year starts tapering off. Now these trees start sprouting leaves and branches in abundance. Two or three years of a good yield are followed by as many years of no fruit. Walnut wood is hard and darkens with age. It is used to manufacture furniture, especially cabinets, gunstocks and handicrafts.

The bark of the walnut tree is one of the finest Indian tooth-cleaners, serving as brush and paste rolled into one. In India walnut trees grow in Jammû and Kashmîr alone.

When trade with Tibet was possible, walnut oil was exported from Kashmîr in large quantities. Funnily, the fruit has traditionally been considered 'useless' (e.g., by Sir Walter Lawrence, and by the market). The Kashmîrîs mostly used the fruit to crush oil out of it, and would export the bark (as *dâtun*) to the Punjab. It was only in the 20th century that the fruit itself began to be valued as an 'export'.

Waternut, horned: (singhârâ) Locally known as gâree, goroo and gor. 60,000 tons of it grow at the bottom of the Wular lake. Ripens in October. It is dried and ground into a flour of which cakes are then eaten, especially by Pandits during their fasts, who say that the Goddess Lakshmi brought this fruit to Kashmîr.

Willow: (Salix alba) Two kinds are found in the Valley: The *muska veer* (musk willow) and *vota veer*. The weeping willow is rare, but found at half a dozen places in Srînagar city itself, including the Civil Secretariat. Probably an import from Britain. However, the weeping willow has always been a native of Rattan Peer, which is to the south of the Panjal range. Also grows in Ladâkh. Grows up to 10 metres (30').

Yew trees: Found plentifully between 9,000' and 10,500'. Its bark is sometimes used as a tea in Ladâkh. Not very tall, though with a thick, 'naked' trunk.

Chapter- 5

Wildlife, Sanctuaries, Fishing

Birds

Jammû, Kashmîr and Ladâkh are located on the 'flyway route' of birds migrating from Siberia to the plains of India. Because the state has a large number of lakes and rivers, it plays host to many of these birds. In all it sustains almost 300 species of birds. Several birds visit Kashmîr in summer in order to breed.

Within the state, in winter most birds come down from the high mountains to places like Srînagar City, which are at a relatively low altitude. For that reason, the 'best viewing seasons' mentioned elsewhere in this chapter are normally in winter as far as birds are concerned.

The following is a listing of some of the important species native to or found or seen in the state:

Baldcoot: Breeds on the banks of lakes in Kashmîr.

Bee-eater: Visits Kashmîr.

Bulbul: Seen in the lower altitudes in winter.

Chakor: Found in Kashmîr.

Chough: The *chunka* is common in villages.

Crane, black necked: Also found in the state.

Crane, gigantic: Frequently found in the marshes.

Crow: Two species are found in Kashmîr. One is totally black. The other has a whitish neck. "It is said that the white-necked crow is eaten in parts of Kashmîr, the flesh being considered especially nutritious in cases of bronchitis". (*The Gazetteer*, 1890)

Cuckoo: Called the *byal kuk* in Kashmîri. 'Byal' means 'seed'. Kashmîri farmers plant seeds only after the cuckoo's singing indicates that it is time to do so.

Dabchick: A water bird found in Kashmîr.

Dipper: Visits the state.

Duck: Found in several parts of Kashmîr, certainly in almost every corner of Srînagar city. Near lakes, on lakes, on drainage channels, crossing the roads. Also found on the lakes of Jammû, especially the Mansar. "Many of the ducks are destroyed by eagles, who take up their residence in the neighbouring mountains for the purpose of preying upon them". (*The Gazetteer*, 1890)

Duck, wild: A water bird found in Ladâkh near the Rupshu lakes. Ducks are even more likely to be found near the bigger rivers.

Duck, white-eyed: Found in Kashmîr.

Eagle: Found in Kashmîr.

Finch: Visits Kashmîr.

Flycatcher: Visits the state.

Fowl: The common domestic fowl, along with ducks and geese, is plentiful in Kashmîr. Capons (*kheys kokar*) are bred in the Lolab valley. The domestic fowl is reared in Leh and Nubra.

Kingfisher: Seen in the state, especially in the Dal Lake.

Gadwall: A water bird found in Kashmîr.

Goose, bar headed: Found in the state.

Gull: Seen in the state.

Grebe: A water bird found in Kashmîr in autumn and winter.

Grosbeak, black and yellow: It comes down to the lower valleys in winter.

Hawk: Found in Kashmîr.

Heron: 'One of the three species found here is the same as in England. It is considered important [because it yields] the feather-tufts worn in the turbans of the chieftains of rank. Each heron has two feathers, which grow downwards from the back of the head; and these in the moulting season are carefully collected by men who watch the heronries for this purpose. The birds are often netted, and, after their feathers have been plucked, are set free. A fine is inflicted for killing one... The feather-tuft, the badge of dignity [is] fixed in a funnel shaped stem, covered with gold wire and often richly jewelled. Numerous herons may be distinguished at their [favourite] fishing stations, and the common king-fisher is seen at every corner of the lake, breasting the sun for an instant, and then dropping into the water like a falling emerald'. (*The Gazetteer*, 1890)

The Eastern Grey Heron is one of the species found in the state.

Hoopoe: Common in Kashmîr.

Moorhen: (dabchick) Breeds near the edges of lakes in Kashmîr.

Nightingale: The *bulbul* is found in Kashmîr.

Oriol(e), golden: The *poshnul.* A summer-bird, comes down to the lower valleys in summer. Commonly found.

Parrot: Not indigenous to Kashmîr but common in Jammû, including the city.

Partridge, grey and snow: Found in Kashmîr.

Pelican: According to *The Gazetteer*, a small kind of pelican is found in the marshes.

Pheasant: Varieties found include the snow pheasant, *koklas*, *kullich* and the Argus. In Kashmîri poetry and idiomatic language it is high praise to say that a woman walks like a pheasant.

Pheasant, monal: The male is brilliantly coloured. Comes down in winter.

Pintail: A water bird found in Kashmîr.

Pochard: A water bird.

Raven: The large raven (*porok*) is very frequently found in villages.

Quail, common: Found in Kashmîr.

Shoveller: A water bird found in Kashmîr.

Snipe, jack: A water bird found in Kashmîr.

Sparrows, cinnamon: Seen in the lower valleys in winter.

Stork: Seen in the state.

Starts: They visit Kashmîr.

Swallow: Visits Kashmîr.

Swallow, sea: See 'Terns' below.

Terns: They gather by the thousand in and around the Wular lake, right up to the Jehlum.

Thrushes: They visit the state.

Tits: They visit Kashmîr.

Vultures: Species found in Kashmîr include the Bearded Vulture.

Waterfowl: Every species of waterfowl is to be found in Kashmîr, and in plenty, in winter when they come down from the colder Yarqand and Mughalistan. They leave when spring begins.

Water hen: Found in Kashmîr.

Woodcock: Found in Kashmîr.

Woodpecker: Visits Kashmîr.

The birds (avifauna) of Dâchîgâm[i]

Family : Ardeidae

Grey heron *Ardea cinerea*

Pond heron or Paddy bird *Aredeota grayii*

Little egret *Egretta garzetta*

Family : Anatidae

Pintail *Anas acuta*

Widgeon *Anas penelope*

Common Pochard *Aythaya ferina*

Family : Accipitridae

Black-eared kite (large) or Indian Kite *Milvus migrans lineatus*

Sparrow-hawk *Accipiternisus nisosipnilis*
Short-toed eagle *Circaetus chrysactos*
Black eagle *Ictinaetus melayensis*
Golden eagle *Aquila chrysaetos*
Shikra *Accipiter badius*
Himâlayan griffon *Gyps himalayensis*
Bearded vulture or lammergeier (or lammergeyer) *Gypaetus barbatus*

Family : Falconidae

Kestrel *Falco tin nunculus*

Peregrine falcon *Falco peregrinus japonensis*

Family : Phasianidae

Monal pheasant or Impeyan *Lophophrous impejanus*
Chukar partridge *Alectoris chukar*
Koklas pheasant *Pucrasia macrolopha*

Family : Charadixidae

Common sandpiper *Tringa hypoleucos*
Woodcock *Scolopax rusticola*

Family : Columbidae

Blue rock pigeon *Columba livia*
Wood pigeon *Columba palumbus*
Rufous turtle dove *Streptopelia orientails*
Indian ring dove *Streptopelia decaocto*
Slaty-headed parakeet *Psittacula Himâlayana*

Family : Cuculidae

Pied crested cuckoo *Clamator jacobinus*
Indian cuckoo *Cuculus micropterus*

Cuckoo *Cuculus canorus*

Small cuckoo *Cuculus poloiocephalus*

Family : Strigidae

Barn owl *Tyto alba*

Little owl *Anthene noctua*

Family : Apodidae

Alpine swift *Apus melba*

Family : Alcedinidae

Lesser-pied kingfisher *Ceryle rudis*
Common kingfisher *Alcedo atthis*
White-breasted kingfisher *Halycon smyrnensis*

Family : Meropidae

European bee eater *Merops apiaster*

Family : Coraciidae

European Ruller *Coracias garrulus*

Family : Upupidae

Hoopoe *Upupa epops*

Family : Picidae

Wryneck *Jyna torquilla*

Scaly-bellied green woodpecker *Picus squamatus*

Black-naped green woodpecker *Picus canus*
Himâlayan pied woodpecker *Picoides himalayensis*
Brown fronted pied woodpecker *Picoides auriceps*
Yellow fronted-pied woodpecker *Picoides mahrattensis*

Family : Laniidae

Grey-backed shrike *Lanius tephronotus*
Rufous-backed shrike *Lanius schach*

Family : Oriolidae

Golden oriole *Oriolus oriolus*
Maroon oriole *Oriolus traillii*

Family : Dicuruidae

Grey or Asy Drongo *Dicrucus leucophaeus*

Family : Sturnidae

Starling *Sturnus vulgaris*

Common mynah *Acridotheres tristis*

Family : Corvidae

Yellow-billed blue magpie *Cissa flavirostris*
Jackdraw *Corvus monedula*

Jungle crow *Corvus macrorhynchos*

Carrion crow *Corvus corone*

Raven *Corvus corax*

Black throated jay *Garrulus lanceolatus*
Yellow billed or Alpine cough *Pyrrhocorax graculus*

Family : Campehagidae

Scarlet Minivet *Pericrocotus flammeus*
Longtailed minivet *Pericrocotus ethologus*

Family : Pycnonotidae

White checked Bulbul *Pycnonotus leucogenys*
Black bulbul *Hypsipetes madagascariensis*

Family : Muscicpaidae

Variegated laughing thrush *Garrulax variegatus*
Paradise flycatcher *Terpsiphone paradisi*
Redbilled babbler *Stachyris pyrrhops*
Sooty flycatcher *Muscicapa sibirica*
Rufous tailed flycatcher *Muscicapa ruficauda*

Kashmîr red-breasted flycatcher *Muscicapa subrubra*
Black-caped sibia *Heterophasia capistrata*
Streaked laughing thrush *Garrulax lineatus*
Little pied flycatcher *Muscicapa westermanni*
White browed blue flycatcher *Muscicapa leucomelanura*
Slaty Blue flycatcher *Muscicapa leucomelanura*
Grey-headed flycatcher *Culicicapa ceylonensis*

Sub Family : Sylviinae

Large-billed bush warbler *Bradypterus major*
Plain or yellow browed leaf warbler *Phylloscopus inornatus*
Grey headed flycatcher warbler *Seicercus xanthoschistos*

Tickell'sleaf warbler *Phylloscopus affinis*
Palla's leaf warbler *Phylloscopus proregulus*
Large crowned leaf warbler *Phylloscopus occipitalis*
Gold crest *Regulus regulus*

Sub Family : Turdinae

Himâlayan ruby-throat *Erithacus pectoralis*
Magpie robin *Copsychus saularis*
White caped red start or River chat *Chaimarrormus leucocephalus*

Blue whistling thrush *Myiophonus caeruleus*
Tickell's thrush *Turdus unicolor*
Greywinged blackbird *Turdus boulboul*
Blackbird *Turdus merula maximus*
Plumbeous water redstart *Rhyacornis fuliginosus/fuliginosa*
Little forktail *Enicurcus scoulex*
Black-backed forktail *Enicurcus immaculatus*
Spotted forktail *Enicurcus maculatus*
Hodgson's grandala *Grandala coelicolor*
Dark-Grey Bush chat *Saxicola ferrea*

Stone chat *Saxicola torquata*
Grey headed thrush *Turdus rubrocanus*

Family : Troglodytidae

Wren *Troglodytes troglodytes*

Family : Cinclidae

White breasted dipper *Cinclus cinclus*
Brown dipper *Cinclus pallasii*

Family : Prunellidae

Alpine accentor *Prunella collaris*

Family : Paridae

Grey Tit *Parus major*
Green backed Tit *Parus monticolus*
Crested Black Tit *Parus melanolophus*
Black Tit *Parus rufonuchalis*
Yellow Checked Tit *Parus xanthogenys*
Fire Capped Tit *Cephalopyrus flammiceps*

Family : Sittidae

European Nuthatch *Sitteuropaea nagaensis*

Family : Certhidae

Himâlayan Tree Creeper *Certhia Himâlayana*

Family : Motacillidae

Yellow wagtail *Motacilla flava*

Yellow headed wagtail *Motacilla citreola*
Grey wagtail *Motacilla cinerea*
Pied or white wagtail *Motacilla alba*
Large Pied wagtail *Motacilla maderaspatensis*

Family : Zosteropidae

White eye *Zosterops palpebrosa*

Family : Ploceidae

House sparrow *Passer domesticus*
Cinnamon Tree Sparrow *Passer rutilans*

Family : Fringillinae

Gold-finch *Carduelis carduelis*
Himâlayan greenfinch *Carduelis spinoides*
Common rosefinch *Carpodacus erythrinus*
Pink Browed rosefinch *Carpodacus rhodochrous*
Redmantled rosefinch *Carpodacus rhodochylamys*
Redbrowed rosefinch *Callacanthis burtoni*
Orange bullfinch *Pyrrhula aurantiaca*
Redheaded bullfinch *Pyrrhula erythrocephala*
Black and Yellow grosbeak *Coccothraustes icterioides*
Red breasted rosefinch *Carpodacus puniceus*

Family : Emberizidae

Rock bunting *Emberiza cia*

Grey headed bunting *Emberiza fucata*
White capped bunting *Emberiza stewarti*

Land Animals

The following is a selective listing of species that spend at least part of the year in the state:

Antelopes: Several species are found in the state. The *gural* (Himâlayan chamois) is native to Kishtwâr and the Panjal range. Travels alone or in couples. Its horns grow to around eight inches.

Barhal: An 'enigmatic' mammal, because it is not clear whether it is a sheep or a goat. Found in Kashmîr as well as Ladâkh. (Also spelt and pronounced 'Bharal.' Also called the *napoo*). Has long horns, just under a metre long, and its flesh is considered a delicacy. Also see 'Sheep, blue'. Almost never found below 13,000' even in winter. In summer goes up to 16,000'.

Bears: Found all over Kashmîr, including in Srînagar city itself (in the Pari Mahal-Raj Bhavan-Royal Springs International Golf Course area). Major habitats include the Nowbug and Lolab valleys. They normally do not attack humans unless attacked or irritated first. Of course, when they attack they normally crush the victim to death.

Bears, Himâlayan black: (*Ursus Thibetanus*) Called the 'hâput' in Kashmîri.

They wake up in the spring, after their winter hibernation. They mainly eat herbs and fruits but can be carnivorous as well. To this extent they are infinitely more dangerous than brown bears. They spend the summer at altitudes between 10,000' and 12,000', i.e., near the tree-line. When fruits ripen, they visit the fields and create havoc there, destroying crops and corn-fields. In autumn they ransack maize fields when they come down to the villages in the lower valleys. They move out after sunset. In this author's experience they venture out only when it is fairly dark.

Found at: All over the Northwestern Himâlayas, especially in the Dâchîgâm National Park. These bears are found at altitudes lower than those in which brown bears live, and are smaller than the brown kind.

The Asiatic Black Bear lives on the edges of forests and on steep wooded hills. In winter, it migrates from the high mountains to the warmer hills lower down. It hibernates in winter. The rare black bear that is seen in winter is likely to be weak and sickly.

Most black bears are nocturnal. They start looking for food after sunset and sleep after sunrise. However, in Dâchîgâm and its neighbouring areas, black bears have been seen moving about even during the day. They are expert climbers.

Food habits: Black bears eat wild fruit, berries, wild pears, apricots, maize and nuts. In autumn they mainly eat the resin of pinus because other foods are hard to get. The mating season is in late autumn and cubs are born in early spring.

Bears, brown: Mainly, the *Ursus Isabelina [Kashmîriensis] or Ursus arctos isabellinus)* In Kashmîri they are called the 'gura haput'. They hibernate in winter.

Where found: Reddish or brown bears are between six and seven feet tall and live in the lower ranges. In summer they live well above the snowline, on barren, open peaks. In Dâchîgâm, they have been spotted in upper Dâchîgâm, between Dagwan and Nagaberan.

Food habits: In the initial weeks of summer they eat wild fruit, herbal roots and fresh grass. They also hunt marmots and similar animals. As summer progresses, they steal the cattle, sheep and goats of the recently arrived Gujjars and Bakerwâls. In autumn, they eat berries, wild fruit, apricots, peaches, mulberry and nuts.

Mating takes place in the first part of summer. Brown bears try to stay away from men and never kill humans.

Camels: The double-humped Bactrian camel is found in some parts of Leh district. Mahârâjâ Gulab Singh, who seems to have been an absolute visionary in these matters, introduced camels on the Murree-Bârâmullâ route. Remnants of his scheme can still be seen in parts of Jammû district, in the rural areas behind Nagrota.

Cats: Commonly found in the state.

Cat, Jungle- (*Felis Chaus*): This is a common wild cat found almost everywhere, including Dâchîgâm. It prefers grasslands, scrub jungles and the reedy banks of rivers. In Kashmîr, these cats are found near towns, among rocks and in old buildings. The jungle cat is often active during the day. However, it prefers mornings and evenings. It preys on small mammals, birds and on poultry.

Cat, Leopard- (*Felis bengalensis* or *Felis viverrina*): This nocturnal animal is found in the forests of Kashmîr, especially in Dâchîgâm. It preys on small birds and animals. Leopard-cats normally rest in the hollows of trees. Sometimes these cats have been seen moving about during the day as well.

Cattle: Cattle are so abundant in the state that an entire community, the Gujjars, which constitutes more than 18 per cent of the state's population, is mainly dedicated to rearing cattle on a commercial scale. Smaller communities do so, too. Then there is domestic rearing.

Buffaloes have always been in short supply in Kashmîr, as 19th century records indicate. Which is why with all that cattle, milk production is always less than the demand. Buffalo bulls and buffalo cows are not indigenous to Kashmîr but are found in the hills all the same.

Common horned cattle are not at all common in Ladâkh. At most they might be found in the lower parts of Ladâkh. The Himâlayan counterparts of common Indian oxen are widely found in Nubra and the warmer regions of Ladâkh. Yaks, or, more accurately, their descendants, are the type of cattle common to Ladâkh. (See 'Yaks' below).

Deer, barking- Locally called the *khakar*, it barks whenever alarmed, and in the evenings. Found only on the southern side of Kashmîr and on the western and southern slopes of the Pîr Pañjâl range.

Deer, musk- (*Moschus chryogaster*): (Called 'roos' and 'rous' in Kashmîri). This is a rare species, mostly because it has been hunted and killed through the centuries for its musk-pods. There is no real need to kill the animal because in China musk is extracted from the living animal deer without causing it any injury. Its population is also declining because leopards, foxes and yellow throated martens eat it.

This small and shy animal is found in the lower parts of Ladâkh, and in Kashmîr at altitudes around 7,500' (including Dâchîgâm). It is also found in Warhwan valley (Jammû) and Tilail.

The musk deer prefers high mountains, woodland scrub and birch forests. It lives above the zone where pines grow. When it comes down to the lower hills it seeks the safety and protection of dense forests. It likes to be alone and often tries to conceal itself. The musk deer feeds at dawn and dusk and prefers lichens, leaves and flowers. The breeding season is January and the young ones are born in June.

Dogs: In particular the Bakerwâls (shepherds), who live in the mountains, keep large, ferocious dogs that protect them and their flock from wild animals.

Large packs of wild dogs have traditionally roamed about and caused damage in Lâr, Dachinpara and several other parts of the Valley, as well as in Warhwan in Dodâ.

There is a breed of pointer dogs in the mountains near Râjourî. The 19th century British writer Vigne also noticed another breed of very small dogs, somewhat resembling the fox-dog, but smaller. He saw one that stood only eight inches high over the shoulder, but was long in proportion, with a sharp nose and a bushy tail, and covered generally with long white hair. Such dogs are said to have been imported from Chambâ.

Ermine: Found in Kashmîr.

Fish: There is a separate section on fishing.

Fox: A 'large, full-brushed Meltonian' variety is common in Kashmîr, where it is known as the *luhv* or *luhf.* The flying fox, locally known as the *usgagor* is found all over Guréz, especially when the season has just begun. This fox prefers to live amidst brushwood. It frequents cultivated land.

Fox, red (*Vulpes vulpes*): The Red Fox is found in Ladâkh and Kashmîr. It prefers bush woodlands. There it digs a burrow under the ground to live in. Or it might live among rocks or under the cover of dense vegetation. It is a nocturnal animal. Hunger might force the stray Red Fox to come out during the day, though. It is a loner. Its diet changes with the season and depends on what is available. Also on what that particular fox has grown to like. The Red Fox preys on small rodents and birds: pheasants, partridges, marmots and voles. This monogamous animal is said to pair for life. Red Fox couples are known to live in the same place for years at an end. This home is often a burrow with more than one opening.

Goats: The Kashmîris prefer the mutton of sheep to goat-flesh.

Goats, mountain: i) The *surrow* or *buz-e-kohi* lives in the Sind valley and Dachinpura in the Panjal. Not commonly found. ii) The *thar* (known as *kras* in Kishtwâr), too, lives in the Panjal range, in Warhwan, Kishtwâr and Banihal, on rugged and dangerous terrain. It is bigger than the surrow (which is about three feet or a metre high), though both have horns of about fourteen inches (about 35 cm). each. The thar develops a splendid fleece as it grows old.

Hângul: See the section on 'The Hângul' later in this chapter.

Hare, Himâlayan Mouse (*Ochotona roylei*): The Himâlayan Mouse Hare is found all over the Himâlayas. In Kashmîr, good places to find it are the mountains above Dâchîgâm. It lives on open rocky ground above the tree line. There it resides under rocks and heaps of stones. The steep slopes of pine forests are another place where it might be found. In forests, it burrows under the roots of trees. Its diet changes with the season and availability. It eats coarse grass.

Horse, domesticated/ ponies: Kashmîr has always had good horses of its own. Polo has been popular since at least mediæval times. Mahârâjâ Gulab Singh imported stallions, including Arab and Turkish ones, and mares. He earmarked grass reserves for horses and ponies in general, because of their importance as transport in the hills. They carry passengers as well as goods. This dependence has not lessened even in the first decade of the 21st century.

The ponies of the Dachinpara area, on the banks of the Lidder, are considered the best.

Hyenas: Rare in Kashmîr.

Jackal (*Canis aureus*): Jackals have been seen in the Himâlayas. They come out after sunset and retire at dawn. They are also active by day. During the rutting season, they come out looking for water to drink. They also like to lie in the shade of forests. Jackals sometimes hunt in packs for small deer or antelopes.

Kashmîri stag: See 'Hângul' later in this chapter.

Lañgûr, Common: (*Presbytis entellus*) Langurs live on trees. Or, as scientists would put it, they have arboreal habits. Langurs live in unisex groups. They are sexist but not ageist. Their groups consist of langurs of all ages. They tend to live in harmony with other members of the group. Therefore, these groups stay together for years, if not forever.

In winter, there is almost nothing to eat in the snow-bound mountains. This forces most of them to migrate to the plains of the Valley. However, many spend their winters on pines and firs, even though these trees might be enveloped in snow.

Langurs are vegetarians. They live on wild fruit, flowers, buds, shoots and leaves. In winter, they are known to eat climbers, including the Climatus grate and Hedera nepalensis. For this reason they devastate gardens.

As is the case with other relatively weak animals, the size of their groups increases in autumn and winter. Which means that two or more smaller groups merge when they come down to their winter home. This is obviously because the enemy, too, comes down to the plains when it gets cold. The leopard is their main predator. When they see or sense a beast of prey or some other danger, they start making guttural sounds of alarm. This warns other members of their group. This sound is very different from the whoops of joy that they voice when they hop from tree to tree.

The Dâchîgâm National Park is one of their countless winter homes. It is not unusual to find langurs there throughout the year.

Langur, Himâlayan gray: Also comes down to the lower reaches in winter. Goes back to the higher mountains in summer.

Leopards[ii] **:** (*Panthera pardus millardi*) This is an endangered animal and a sub-species of Panthera pardus.

Places where it might be found: Almost everywhere. Leopards don't need forests or dense groves of trees to flourish. They do quite well in the open country, among rocks and scrub. For this reason they come in contact with humans quite often: including in Srînagar city. Other things being equal, they would prefer to live near pastures, so that they can eat cattle.

They kill and eat most kinds of animals. They prey on birds, deer, langurs, monkeys, large rodents and smaller beasts of prey.

I know of at least one instance (which took place in the summer of 2001) when they killed a human, a BSF soldier, who had gone to the rocks above Srînagar's Pari Mahal for his early morning ablutions. The Wildlife Department of the State has recorded a leopard attack on women in Dâchîgâm, one November day in the 1990s, when the women were walking through a dense grove.

Leopards tend to walk on roads, paths and tracks beaten through forests by other animals. They breed throughout the year. In Kashmîr they are found in the Dâchîgâm National Park, lower Dâchîgâm and on the road from Panzgam to Phalipora, especially in winter, even more so when there is snow.

My own sightings of leopards (and bears, and 'near sightings' of hanguls): It was around 9 pm on a September evening in 1997. Two friends, Gautaman Bhaskaran (of *The Hiñdû*) and Chandâ Nârang (a filmmaker and chîrû-goat/ shahtoosh expert), and I had walked down from the Raj Bhawan[1] to the Dal Lake. We were sitting on the embankment known as the Cheshma Shahi ghât. By day this is an extremely busy intersection, and even at 9pm there is some traffic. A jeep came from behind and parked itself right behind us. We found that a bit of a nuisance. After a while an officer got out and said, "We were wondering if you knew that there's a leopard right across the road".

We had been planning to walk back, but now we gratefully accepted the officer's offer of a lift. The leopard was less than a hundred metres from the Boulevard. So, what had brought him there? The bones and other leftovers of the meat that BSF (Border Security Force) soldiers camping near the Boulevard had eaten.

A year before, in the summer, Dr. Mridu Rai and I were walking up from the Cheshma Shahi to the Nehru Guest House. There is a dry nallah (stream) between the two. It was quite early, just after sunset, and the sky was still fairly bright. A large leopard came hurtling down the nallah just as we got there.

1. Gubernatorial palace. I was His Excellency's Principal Secretary (chief of staff) then.

It was running so fast that it didn't notice us. In case it had you wouldn't have had to suffer much of this book (it was much slimmer in 1996).

The next time that Mridu came visiting, we decided that it was too risky to go to those woods in the fading light. So this time we resolved to return to the Raj Bhawan by 5.30 pm. As we were walking down from Pari Mahal, just when the densest part of the woods came to an end, we saw a BSF soldier walking uphill in our direction. 'I suppose that you know that there's a leopard right above you, on that rock near the electric pole', he said.

Our blood froze. The Raj Bhawan was still almost two kilometres away. The leopard, on the other hand, was ten or twelve feet above us. Getting a lift in a vehicle was not even a possibility. We just prayed hard and slinked away. (Poor you: for I lived to complete this chapter).

I have spent almost nine 'years' in the Cheshma Shahi-Raj Bhawan-Pari Mahal woods of Srînagar. (By nine 'years' I really mean four full-years and five half-years, May to October). This is an exclusive area because the Governor lives in the Raj Bhawan. Casual visitors have not been allowed into these woods since 1990. As a result the greenery has been left untouched and there are more trees and shrubs than ever before. This has led to a noticeable increase in wildlife. A family of four leopards and a group of black bears, also four—live there, the bears throughout the year and the leopards in the cooler months. One hangul has sometimes been spotted in the area. So have been several foxes, countless jackals (well-fed ones at that), some wolves and several snakes, including poisonous ones. Perhaps there are some hyenas, too.

During these nine years I have sighted leopards six or seven times. On four of these occasions my guests and I were within a leap or two of the leopard. This is a fairly easy animal to sight, even in spring and autumn. If I haven't seen leopards more often, it is purely because I walk through those woods only when I have guests.

Animals are supposed to be scared of fire. Once when we got really delayed in those woods, and it was very dark, I passed this nugget of information on to my friends Mustafa Quraishi and his sister Sarah. None of us smokes. So we neither had matches nor a cigarette-lighter. Mustafa was a photographer with *The Indian Express*. He very brightly informed us that he had a flash-gun with which he would scare all animals away. When we reached the densest (and darkest) part of the woods, I told my friends that this was where there had been a leopard right above Mridu and me. So, Mustafa promptly clicked his powerful flash-gun. The light blinded all three of us. We could no longer see the black road. Once again prayer and guesses about where the road was, got us through.

Bears are much easier to sight than leopards (and even easier to hear). They spend all their lives in an area that is four miles square. I have seen their nocturnal movements for so long that I have developed a system on how to spot them. In a nutshell, their movements vary with the length of the day, and the weather. In June, when days are the longest and it is quite warm, bears come out later in the night than, say, in October when days are shorter and colder. Or, to make it simpler still, I have noticed that bears reach the woods across the road from the Nehru Guest House between 9.30 and 10 at night during the two warmest months. If you follow this system and have patience, you are almost guaranteed a sighting of bears within two days.[2]

Foxes are the other animals that you will almost certainly see in this area at night: and very close to the Boulevard at that. I haven't yet spotted a hangul in the wild. But there is one that ravages gardens near the Nehru Helipad (which is near the Palace Hotel and also close to my hut in the Raj Bhawan) and then proceeds to the Royal Springs Golf Course at night. The next morning we see signs that the killjoy had been there, unfortunately when we were sleeping.

But I haven't told you about the fourth time that I came very close to a leopard. This was in February 1994, when there was snow all around. I was looking out of the window of my Raj Bhawan office around noon when I saw the sweetest little leopard cub on the hill slope a few feet from the window. You know how human toddlers are when they gingerly take their first steps: they seem lost in some deep, but happy, thought as they take each hesitant step. That's exactly how that leopard cub looked, even

---

2. Is that a big deal? I assure you that it is. A group of us went to Thekkady in Keralâ (South India) to sight something as obvious as an elephant. At the sanctuary we saw several glorious species of birds but not a single elephant, despite a four- day wait. Nor did any of the other groups there. I believe that the probability of such sightings can be predicted mathematically, because during the day-long drive through the woods between Munnar and Thekkady a herd of wild elephants suddenly rushed past us.

   Similarly, some British friends spent several days at Dâchîgâm without managing to see a hangul outside the enclosures.

   I believe that if you study the behaviour of animals like bears (who have set habits) and certain birds long enough, you can develop a system that greatly improves the chances of a 'sighting'.

though with four legs it did not have the same fear of falling down. There was the same smile on its face as wordless human babies have when they gleefully take their first steps. And its eyes had the same faraway look.

Leopard, Snow: (*Uncia Unica*) Also known as the white leopard, the snow-leopard is called the 'shena seh' in Kashmîri. It is an elusive animal, very difficult to spot. (Two Germans spent an entire winter with me in Zâñskâr trying to photograph this hard-to-get mammal. We spotted some rare ibexes instead: but even those not close enough to photograph).

This is an endangered species. It has been called a 'survivor from the frigid Pleistocene era'.

Places where it might be found: The snow-leopard is found throughout the Himâlayan range: the higher mountains of Kashmîr and Ladâkh being more favoured than most of the other Himâlayan areas. People have 'sighted' it quite often in the Suru, Warhwan and Nubra valleys. It is believed to live in Zâñskâr, too. More likely places to spot it are the Hemis High Altitude Park (Ladâkh), the Dâchîgâm National Park, Overa, and the mountains of Kishtwâr (Jammû) and Chângthâng (Ladâkh). Within these areas, look for relatively narrow and steep ridge valleys.

In summer, it lives amidst rocks and cliffs, above the tree line. In winter, it comes down to the villages of the lower valleys and hills, when its prey does the same.

An indicator of the health of an ecosystem: The snow-leopard hunts at night and eats the ibex, barhal, markhor, wild goats, sheep, musk deer, hare, marmots and large birds.

The presence or absence of snow (or other) leopards in a Himâlayan forest tells us a lot about how good or bad the ecology of that area is. Or, as scientists would put it, this animal is a 'natural indicator' of the ecological health of that 'ecosystem'. If you have actually read the entries in this chapter so far, especially those on the hangul, the musk deer and the langûr, you might have noticed that a) leopards eat them all, and b) when these 'prey' animals come down from the cold mountains in winter, so does their predator, the leopard. They are the leopard's food. Therefore, the leopard follows them wherever they go.

So, if there are plenty of leopards (snow or otherwise) in an area (all right, 'in an ecosystem') it means that the animals that it eats ('the prey species') must also be there in good numbers. Now, these 'prey species' are mostly vegetarians ('herbivores'). If there are many of them in an area, this indicates that there are plenty of trees and shrubs of the right type in that 'ecosystem.' And if males and females of these species are found in more or less equal numbers in an area, this would suggest that their population is likely to remain the same or even increase. Or, as scientists would put it, this means that 'normal reproduction' is a 'predominant feature' of that 'ecosystem.'

You might have also noticed in this chapter that while other animals eat each other (or vegetables), no one eats the leopard. Thus, the leopard is at the top of the food-chain. That is why it is the 'apex carnivore' in most Himâlayan forests.

Lynx: Called 'patsalov' in Kashmîrî. Lives in Kashmîr and Ladâkh. Seeks shelter in forests, and amidst tall grass and reeds.

Markhor: Called Raphoche in Ladâkhi. This 'serpent-eater' is a very large goat. The markhor of Astor (now in POK) has huge, flat horns, which rise with just one sweep. The type found in the Pîr Pañjâl has horns that are much smaller and rise upwards with two-and-a-half or three twists (the third twist might be incomplete). Also lives in the Kâzinâg range.

This migratory animal moves around the Behram Gala pass (in Poonch) and in the middle mountains between the Kishan Ganga and Jehlum rivers. It lives on 'dangerous ground' but not on the high mountains where the ibex does. Prefers dense birch and pine forests. Grazes on the grassy glens of these forests. Rarely goes above the snow-line.

Markhors travel in herds. They feel most secure from attack when housed amidst precipitous crag and rock. In December the older ones join the females and younger males. In spring they break company again.

Marmot, docile, Marmot, Himâlayan (*Marmota bobak*) and **Marmot, Longtailed** (*Marmota caudata*): Marmots are found in the higher Himâlayas, especially in Ladâkh and the mountain ranges to the North of Kashmîr, especially near the holy Amarnâth ji cave-shrine. (Also in Garhwal in the north Indian state of Uttarakhand) The Himâlayan and Longtailed Marmots are found at different altitudes.

This cat-sized animal lives in groups in large colonies. It hibernates in deep underground burrows all through the winter. During much of summer it is too groggy to react to hunters. Its responses are rather slow. Hence the epithet 'docile'. Even a child can walk up and grab a marmot, especially for its attractive golden-brown skin. However, don't even try. You'll be causing major offence to religious sentiment in Ladâkh if you do. It's considered most sinful to kill a marmot. You can see why.

A species called *drin, dring* or *pua* in Kashmîri is frequently preyed upon by the eagle. It makes a loud noise when in danger. Found only at high altitudes (8,000' to 14,000'), amidst rocks. It is dull yellow in colour, with a darker stripe on its head, back and tail.

Marmots eat grasses, leaves, roots and the seeds of plants.

Marten, Beech (*Martes foina*) **or Stone:** In India, apart from Sikkim (north-eastern India), beech martens are found only in Kashmîr. They have sometimes been seen in lower Dâchîgâm, and even less frequently in Upper Dâchîgâm.

Stone martens live in the temperate and alpine parts of the Himâlayas. They live above the tree line, in forests as well as on barren mountains. They nestle in the hollows of trees, under logs, in holes in the ground and amidst rocks. In the higher mountains they prey upon voles and the mouse hare. In forests they hunt squirrels and attack birds. They also eat cherries. Stone martens mate in February. Their offsprings are born in late April.

Marten, Yellow-throated (*Martes flavigula*): This Himâlayan animal lives in temperate forests: preferably those that are below the tree line. (It also inhabits sub-tropical and tropical forests, e.g., the east Indian state of Assam). The yellow-throated marten hunts by day as well as night, but prefers the hour immediately before dawn. It scours the ground for prey. However, trees are its preferred hunting 'ground'. That's where it finds squirrels and the birds' nests. It scans nests for eggs and young birds. It also eats hares, partridges, pheasants, rats and mice. It has a special talent for jumping from one branch of a tree to another.

Mice: Commonly found in the state.

Monkeys: In Kashmîr they are found in the Lolab valley, in the forest near Gulmarg and in the lower portion of the Kishan Ganga valley. Commonly found in Jammû City.

Mongoose: Found in Kashmîr.

Mules: Mules, whether in the areas bordering Kulu, Kâñgrâ and other parts of HP, or those in regions neighbouring Yarqand, have proved to be the sturdiest animals in the mountains when it comes to carrying loads.

Otter, common: (*Lutra lutra*) Locally called the *uder*. The Kashmîris also call it the *kula oddur*. Found in most of the rivers of Kashmîr, often under bridges. In summer, when fish, especially carps, migrate upstream to spawn, otters too travel up torrents and streams. They eat fish. Therefore, they have to go wherever their prey does. In winter they come back to the streams of the lower mountains.

They live amidst boulders and rocks. Also under the roots of trees that grow by the banks of rivers. They are often found lying in fern brakes, reed beds and bushes. Given a choice they would live in a cold place: in the hills and mountains, or near high-altitude streams and lakes.

In the Dâchîgâm National Park they are found all over River Dagwan and the nallâh (stream). They frequently attack the fish of the Fisheries Breading Farm at Dâchîgâm. Otters hunt at night. They also eat crabs, frogs, rodents and water fowls. Their skin is much valued.

Ovis Ammon: See 'Sheep, wild'.

Ovis Orientalis: Known as the 'shapoo' and 'urial' in the Punjâb. In the areas of Kargil under Pâkistâni occupation (Baltistan, Astor, Bunji) it is called the 'oorin'. Found in most parts of Ladâkh, mainly along the Indus. It lives on steep, grassy, hill-slopes above forests.

Panther: Known as the 'seh' in Kashmîr. Found in forests as well as in inhabited areas. In the forests panthers hang around the paths commonly taken by other animals. They go to villages to eat up dogs and other domesticated animals.

Pigs: Mahârâjâ Gulab Singh introduced them in Kashmîr. Because of the Muslims' aversion, his descendant (perhaps Mahârâjâ Pratap Singh) got rid of all pigs from Srînagar. However, some pigs escaped into the woods and are found there in a wild state.

Porcupine, Indian: (*Hystrix indica*) Found in some regions of Kashmîr; also in Kishtwâr. In the Dâchîgâm area it has been seen in Phaliphora in February, at Waskar at other times and in big numbers between Drog and Kavnar.

The porcupine lives on the rocky sides of hills. It thrives on all kinds of lands and topography—moist as well as arid, open land as well as forests. During the day it nestles in caves, amongst rocks or in burrows. The porcupine is essentially a vegetarian. It eats fruits and grains. However, it also chews the bones of dead animals and the horns that deer have shed. From these it obtains the calcium and lime that it needs to make its quills grow.

Rat, Common House: (*Rattus rattus*) Commonly found in the state.

Serow: (*Capricornis sumatraensis*) This is a 'goat antelope of the genus *Capricornis,* of [the] mountainous regions of eastern Asia, [and has] short horns and a dark coat'.[iii] It is called Ramu, Halj and Salabhir in Kashmîri. It lives throughout the Himâlayas between 6,000' and 10,000' and in Assam at lower heights.

The serow seeks protection from the weather in shallow caves and amidst boulders on the slopes of thickly wooded gorges. It eats grass, herbs and shrubs. Its mealtimes are around sunrise and sunset. The serow is a loner, but is very energetic. In the Dâchîgâm National Park, a serow was once seen in a group of hanguls.

Sheep, blue: See 'Bharal' above.

Sheep, domesticated: The Bakerwâls (who live throughout the State), the Chopâns (Kashmîr only) and the Gaddis (Jammû and Himâchal Pradesh) are the three principal communities that rear sheep on a commercial scale. Kashmîr used to 'export' sheep to Jammû and other regions till the early part of the 20th century. Meat consumption zoomed after the 1950s. Since then Kashmîr has been a net importer of sheep. The Kashmîris eat only sheep meat. (Goat mutton is the norm in most of the rest of India).

Squirrel, Kashmîrî Flying-: (*Hylopetes fimbriatus*) Found in Kashmîr.

Stag, Kashmîri: See 'Hângul'.

Stone marten: See 'Marten, stone.'

Vole, royles: (*Alticola royelei*) Found in Kashmîr.

Weasel, Himâlayan: (*Mustela sibrica*) Found in the state.

Wolves: Common in Kashmîr, in the barren higher mountains but not in the plains of the Valley. Also found in Ladâkh. They eat sheep, to the distress of shepherds for whom this is a huge economic loss.

When the nomadic shepherds move uphill to the mountain pastures in summer, so do the wolves. In winter they come down and move about in the lower valleys, fairly close to the plains. In summer they live amidst thickets of reeds and scrubs. In winter they seek shelter in caves and amidst rocks.

Reptiles and Insects

Bees: Farmers in Kashmîr often maintain several hives, sometimes as many as ten each, in their houses. When rural houses are built, cylindrical cavities are left in the walls of one of the floors to house the hives. These hives are removed every year in late September or early October.

Frogs: Found all over Kashmîr. In Srînagar city they live in the Dal lake.

Lizards: Numerous in Kashmîr.

Mosquitoes: 'It is probable that (between July and September) in no country in the world are mosquitoes found in such swarms as on the lakes of Kashmîr and in their vicinity; any part of the body which may be exposed to their attacks becomes literally black with them... The only way to obtain even partial relief is to sit between pans of burning horse-dung, the fumes of which drive them away'. That was *The Gazetteer* writing in 1890. Their numbers have lessened considerably since, and wire mesh windows and chemical repellants have done away with the dung. However, if you are ideologically hostile to chemical lotions you know what to look for instead.

Sand-flies: Common between July and September.

Scorpions: The *puhur*. Plentiful in the Cheshma Shahi-Pari Mahal-Raj Bhawan area of Srînagar city, also in the Dachinpura and Lâr areas. Their bites can be fatal.

Snakes: The snakes of the *kandi* (semi-arid) parts of Jammû and Kathuâ districts in particular (and Jammû region in general) are extremely poisonous and cause many deaths every year. Probably, that is why snakes are worshipped (propitiated might be more accurate) in that area.

Snakes are almost unknown in Ladâkh. (A few non-poisonous species have been found). Kashmîr has several species of snakes (*har*). It is said that *none* of them is poisonous. This is not correct. Those in the Sind valley certainly are. Some areas beyond Pahalgâm are known for the *gunas* snake. In Srînagar City, snakes are found outside the municipal limits, in the Cheshma Shahi-Pari Mahal-Raj Bhawan area, for instance.

The deadly Harwan Krait is to be found in this belt. Many of the other snakes of Kashmîr are not venomous.

The Kashmîris say, "There are no snakes in any place from which the peak of the Nanga Parbat is visible". This essentially confirms what I said about Ladâkh. You can see the Nanga Parbat only from places that are at fairly high altitudes. There it will be too cold for snakes to survive. But what about places not that high?

There are instances of the cobra having been seen in Kashmîr. Also the boa-constrictor, according to the 19th century traveller-writer Vigne. However, other writers feel that the Kashmîri *ajdâ*, mistaken for a boa-constrictor, is really an overgrown rock-snake.

Either way, I suppose you've got my point: there are several types of dangerous snakes in Kashmîr. The *gunas*, common to the Lâr area (and in the rocky eastern parts of Kashmîr), is one such. The Dachinpura area has venomous snakes. The Kashmîri *gulawut* (throat-catcher) is believed to lunge at a man's throat.

Parks and Sanctuaries

It is advisable to wear khaki, green or camouflage in all these sanctuaries and national parks. Please do not disturb the animals with loud noises, radios, music playing systems, motorboats (if there's a river or lake nearby), diesel generators, etc. (I am thought of as a Luddite, an enemy of progress, because of my refusal to allow motorboats at many tourist destinations). Please don't leave behind non-biodegradable garbage. Flash photography can irritate some animals into violence, and scare others needlessly.

National parks are a 'higher' category than sanctuaries.

National Parks

Dâchîgâm National Park: This is the prima donna of the parks and sanctuaries of the state. Dâchîgâm means 'the ten villages', that being the number of villages which had to be acquired and resettled in order to create a wildlife sanctuary here. It covers an area of 141 sq. km. In the first half of the twentieth century it was the exclusive hunting preserve of the Mahârâjâ of the state. In 1951, it was converted into a national park. Entrance to various parts of the park is still strictly regulated. (Please contact the Chief Wildlife Warden, whose office is in the TRC, Srînagar).

The flora of the park includes a silver-birch forest and conifers. It is the main home of the hângul, an endangered species of antler deer, akin to the European red deer, an endangered species. (See below). The hângul (Kashmîri stag) has huge antlers and a white patch on its rump. The park has around twenty species of mammals in all, including black and brown bears, the musk deer and leopards. In addition it has more than 150 species of avifauna. There is also a trout (fish) farm in the campus.

The Drâphâmâ Guest House, where Prime Ministers Pt. Nehru and Indira Gandhi used to stay, is not available to tourists. However, theoretically it is possible to rent a hut in the Panzgam, Laribal, Gratnar or Sangargulu villages for an overnight (or longer) stay. A Tourism Department leaflet from the 1960s says, '[The park is] open throughout the year [and] there is no prime viewing season'.

Biosphere Reserves and Wildlife Sanctuaries

('Biosphere Reserve' is the category that ranks after 'National Park').

The Overa-Aru Biosphere Reserve: 76 km. from Srînagar; close to Pahalgâm. Animals that live here include the musk deer, the brown bear and the leopard. There are many types of birds as well. This reserve begins at 3,000 metres (i.e., more than 9,500 feet) above the sea and goes right up to 5,425 metres. A government publication says, 'Prime viewing time for the upper areas is from May to August. In the lower areas, for bird viewing the best time is March to May and for animal viewing from September to March'. Self-catering holiday cottages can be booked through the Chief Wildlife Warden, TRC, Srînagar, who also authorises entry into the reserve.

The Overa Wildlife Sanctuary: Spread over 32 sq. km. More than a dozen species of mammals (best season: September to April) and eighty types of birds, notably several species of pheasants live here. (Best bird watching is between March and August).

The Gulmarg Biosphere Reserve: 48 km. from Srînagar. This reserve covers an area of 180 sq. km. It is at 2,400 metres above the sea (around 7,500 feet) at its lowest and climbs up to 4,300 metres (almost 13,000 feet). Mammals: the Himâlayan musk deer, bears – both brown and black—and the red fox. Best season: September to March. Birds: highland species, migratory as well as resident.

The Gulmarg Wildlife Sanctuary: This was declared a sanctuary in 1987. Its boundaries: In the north are the Butapathri/ Bâbâ Réshî

Forests; to the south is the Poonch Forest Division; the eastern boundary consists of the Bunadawas/ Drang Forests; and in the west are the Khanpathri Forests and the Poonch Forest Division. The sanctuary is spread over 139.25 square kilometres. It is more or less rectangular. It falls between 33°.55' and 34°.06' North (latitude) and between 74°.17' and 74°.29' East (longitude).

There is a majestic mountainous range, with moderate to steep slopes, around the sanctuary. Among the important peaks in this range is the Affarwat Peak (4143 metres). The area drains the Ferozpora Nallah as well as several smaller streams that join it.

The sanctuary aims to protect, conserve and multiply the endangered musk deer as well as the Himâlayan Brown Bear, the Leopard and other animals and birds found in the area.

Flora: The vegetation in this area is both diverse and pretty. It contains coniferous forests as well as ornamental 'ground flora.' The main types of forests within the sanctuary are[iv]:

Sub-alpine: Forests make up more than 80 per cent of the sanctuary. The species that grow here include the Silver Fir (*Abies pindrow*), Kail (*Pinus wallichiana*), Spruce (*Picea smithiana*), Yew (*Taxus baccata*), Maple (*Acer pictum*) and Haan or Horse-chestnut (*Aesculus indica*). Birch or bhoj patr (*Betula utilis*) grows in the 3000-3500 metre zone.

Alpine Forests: Above the tree line (10,000 feet) is a vast expanse of green alpine pastures. This is a series of lush meadows (*margs*). A rich variety of grasses and flowering herbs and shrubs, dotted with junipers and rhododendrons, grows on them.

Fauna: The Musk Deer: The Gulmarg Wildlife Sanctuary is the home of the musk deer (roos, in Kashmîrî) *Moschus moschiferus*. This is a 'critically endangered species.' Legally speaking, it is an animal protected under Schedule I of the Wildlife Protection Act. The climate and forests of this sanctuary make it an ideal habitat for the musk deer. This animal is found in the 2400-4300 metre zone. It lives in several types of high-altitude forests, where the juniper, rhododendron and skimmia grow. In winter it can sometimes be seen at altitudes below 2100 metres.

Mammals: The Gulmarg Wildlife Sanctuary is also the home of many kinds of mammals. These include the Leopard (*Panthera Pardus*), the Leopard Cat (*Felis bengalensis*), the Red Fox (*Vulpes vulpes*), the Yellow Throated Marten (*Martes flavigula*), the Himâlayan Brown Bear

(*Ursus arctos*), the Himâlayan Langûr (*Presbytis entellus*), the Rhesus macaque/monkey (*Macaca mulatto*) and the Himâlayan Black Bear (*Selenarctos tibetanus*).

Avi-fauna: The Gulmarg Wildlife Sanctuary also has a rich population of birds. It is the breeding ground for many rare species of resident pheasants and a number of summer migrants from other parts of the Indian sub-continent. The birds that visit or live in the sanctuary include Himâlayan Monals, Common Koklas, Himâlayan Snowcocks, Hoopoes, Woodpeckers, Crows, Nut-crackers, Bulbuls, Fly-catchers, Warblers, Chats, Thrushes, Dippers, Tits, Creepers, Wagtails, Sparrows, Pipettes and Owls.

The Hângul (*Cervus elaphus hanglu*):

This Kashmîri stag, a type of red deer, is close to extinction. The hângul is a variety of the 'barâsinghâ'.

Viewing season: The hângul is a forest animal. It changes its feeding grounds with the season, which means that it goes from one forest to another looking for good grazing grounds. Like many other animals, it lives in the lower hills in winter and goes uphill in summer.

The hângul sheds its horns in late March. It then climbs up to the top of the forest-line, where it still is winter. In contrast it is spring in the plains of Kashmîr. By autumn (sometimes by late-August) the horns are likely to have sprouted again. By then the lower hills of Kashmîr would have started cooling, too. So the hângul returns to them. This is when the hângul starts feeling horny. (I swear the pun crept in all on its own. Maybe that's how the word was derived).

This is called the rutting season among male deer (and among goats and rams). The stags start calling out to their females, but this alerts hunters as well. Hânguls are trapped or killed when they are found outside the sanctuaries. In winter, too, they tend to get completely 'legged in the snow', which makes it easier to catch them.

Rutting: This is 'an annually recurring condition or period of sexual excitement and reproductive activity in male deer'.[v] For hânguls it begins around mid-September and ends in the middle of October. During the rut, adult males separate from other males, while females form groups. (Sounds familiar?) The fawns are born in May.

Viewing time: The best time at Dâchîgâm is around sunrise and well after sunset. This is partly because during the day cars move about near the hânguls' favourite oak patch. The hânguls, naturally, find these cars a nuisance: and a danger to their lives.

The horns: The decorative rims of Kashmîrî saddles are made of these horns.

Habitat/ Places where the Hângul is found[vi]*:* This endangered species lives only in the moist temperate forests of Kashmîr Valley, and some neighbouring areas. Holloway and Schaller noticed that this dear was found only in a region that was 65 km wide. This area is to the north and east of the Rivers Jehlum and Lower Chenab. It stretches from Zahurah in the north to Ramnagar (Jammû) in the south. The only place outside the state where a few Hânguls might be found is Siyabehi in neighbouring Himachal Pradesh.

The hângul spends the summer at high altitudes. It is found mainly in north Kashmîr and, theoretically, in Kishtwâr and Bhaderwâh. (See also 'Dâchîgâm National Park'). In the Valley it is supposed to live in Bandiporâ, Nowbug, Dandwar and the Sind valley. Some stray groups of hânguls have also been seen in the Dârâ [Forest] Reserve, the Brain Reserve, the Khonmoa Reserve, the Shikargah Reserve, Lolab, Desu and the Overa Wildlife Sanctuary. In the 1990s, it was also sighted in the Raj Bhawan campus in Srînagar. It occasionally visits the erstwhile Srînagar City Forest (now the Royal Springs Golf Course). Hângul tracks have been found on snow at Waskar.

The best place to look for hânguls is the Dâchîgâm area. So is the corridor between the Dâchîgâm National Park and the Overa Wildlife Sanctuary.

Social behaviour: Hânguls move about alone as well as in groups of up to twenty-five members. In winter, bigger groups of as many as forty hânguls have been seen in Dâchîgâm, especially near Drâphâmâ in the Nagpur oak patch. Hânguls go to oak patches to rest because these groves provide the best cover in winter. Groups break up in spring. Part of this segregation is along gender lines. Co-ed groups are hardly ever seen in the summer. (That's how stag parties got their name). The hânguls are a matriarchal lot. The hinds [female red deer] look after the young, with no help from the stags. Mother-fawn relationships last only till the fawn can look after itself. Mature stags do not live with the hinds except during the rutting season.

Female hânguls form small groups during the summer. These sororities consist of between twelve and sixteen members. Stags move alone or in smaller groups of between two and nine.

Why do they form groups at all? Protection from predators is an obvious reason. In summer they feel more secure, so their groups are smaller. In winter even the predators come down to the lower hills. The weather, thus, is an important factor. Food is a third. Members of a group inform each other about where the best grazing grounds are.

Hânguls are quite territorial. Each group and, within a group, each member has its grazing territory. Like the human nomads of the state they have a winter territory in the lower hills and a summer territory in the higher mountains. A well-defined route (or 'corridor') invariably connects the two. Interestingly, just as the human nomads of the state think of the winter camp as their 'real home,' so do the hânguls. This is why Dâchîgâm is so popular with the hânguls. Most of them consider Dâchîgâm their 'real home' and repair to this sanctuary for the winter.

What the hângul eats: The plants that the hângul likes most are Fraxinus hookeri, Jasminum humile, Haemerocallis fulva, leaves of Morus alba and Salix. Its favourite fruit are Aesculus indica and Quercus robur. It also eats the Smilax vaginata, Dioscorea deltoidea, Rumax patientia, Colchicum lutecum and Polygonum amplexicaule.

Population/ An endangered species: The population of hânguls in Dâchîgâm has been declining rapidly since the 1940s. Both Hindus and Muslims eat hângul flesh. So do leopards and black bears.

In 1940, there were around 3000 hânguls (according to A.R. Wani and Holloway). In 1947, this population was estimated at 2000 and in 1950, at 400 (Gee). In 1969, Schaller conducted a census during the rut. He felt that only 180 hânguls were left. Holloway (1970) counted just 140-170 hânguls.

And then, because of the government's efforts, the hângul population began to grow again. In 1971, Owen of the World Wildlife Fund did a detailed census and concluded that there were as many as 320 hânguls. At the time the J&K Wildlife Department was putting the number at 550. In March 1980, everyone agreed that the figure was at least 347.

In March 1983, the hângul population was estimated at 550. According to the Wildlife Protection Department in 1986 the number was 605. By 1988 it was as high as 860 (Mir Inayat Ullah).

And then came militancy. The decline resumed. In the early 1990s, the hângul population dropped to somewhere between 140 and 170. The Government stepped in again. By 1995, the population had risen to 290 (Rouf and Rashid). The 1999 census estimated that there were between 270 and 325 hânguls in Dâchîgâm proper, and between 435 and 520 hânguls in and around the Dâchîgâm National Park. The census of March 2000 estimated that there were 350-470 hânguls in the Park.

Predators: Leopards, black bears and snow leopards prey on the hângul. Of these, snow leopards very rarely visit Dâchîgâm. However, leopards and black bears live in and around the Park. During the initial years of militancy (the early 1990s), some humans camping in those woods were without doubt responsible for the rapid decline in the hânguls' population. However, also because of militancy the average human has been too scared to go into the woods. Therefore, there has been an increase in the number of leopards and black bears in the area: right up to the Shankar-acharya hill, with Cheshma Shahi and the Pari Mahal in between. (The upside of this is that because humans have reduced their visits to this area, the illegal felling of trees, too, has declined sharply. The Zabarwan Mountains have much thicker forests now. And if your sympathies are with wildlife in general and not just with hânguls, there is much to celebrate).

The hângul is one of the few mammals available for leopards to eat. Therefore, too, they have been disappearing fast. (So have been the dogs maintained by the Indian para-military forces in that area).

References

i. This and some other entries in this chapter are based on a 'Checklist' given to me by Mian Javed Husein, Regional Wildlife Warden, Kashmîr. I have followed the spellings used in the 'Checklist,' changing them only where I was certain.

ii. Some details in this entry, too are based on the 'Checklist' given to me by Mian Javed Husein, Regional Wildlife Warden, Kashmîr.

iii. *The American Heritage® Dictionary of the English Language.*

iv. Details about the Gulmarg Wildlife Sanctuary are courtesy Mian Javed Husein, Regional Wildlife Warden, Kashmîr.

v. *The American Heritage® Dictionary of the English Language, Third Edition* © 1996 by Houghton Mifflin Company.

vi. Several of the details about the Hangul given in this section are courtesy Mian Javed Husein, Regional Wildlife Warden, Kashmîr.

Chapter- 6

The Rivers of Kashmîr

The Jehlum

Kashmîrî Muslims call the Jehlum by the names Veth, Vyeth and Behet. The Kashmîrî Pandits call it the Vitast(a) and Vyatast. The ancient Greeks knew it as the Hydaspes and Bidaspes. The rest of the sub-continent (and, officially, even J&K) refers to this great river as the Jehlum. Maharaj K. Koul calls it 'The Great Artery of Kashmîr' while Arora has named it 'The Great Waterway of Kashmîr'.

Origin: It originates in Verinag, at the feet of the Panjal mountains in Ânañtnâg district in southern Kashmîr. Some 203 km. (or 195.2 km., depending on what you count) later, it leaves Kashmîr Valley at Kichhama near Bârâmullâ town.

Verinag – water spring and garden

The Kashmîrî Pandits believe that the river really begins at Vethvatru, a small spring near Verinag. It combines with streams at Ânañtnâg town (Islâmabad). The river flows into the Wular lake. Here the river deepens and widens considerably. It then leaves for Bârâmullâ town. At this point the river is about 10' deep and roughly 100 metres/ yards wide. After that the river travels to Uri and finally Kichhama.

Delta, plateaux: The Jehlum's delta in Kashmîr is the huge Wular lake. On the wular's southern side are plateaux. These are alluvial in origin and about 300m. higher than the river bed.

Towns on its banks: On its banks several important towns were founded over the centuries, as were famous shrines and temples. The more important of these towns are Srînagar, Bârâmullâ, Sumbal, Hajan and Sopore. The Bamba tribe has traditionally lived on the river's right bank.

Dimensions: Maharaj K. Koul estimates that 'in its course from Khânabal to Banyari, the point where it enters the Wular, the fall of (the) Jehlum is 165 feet in the first 30 miles and 55 feet in the next 24 miles. From the point where it leaves the Wular to Bârâmullâ town, its fall is very slight. During winter, when the river is at its lowest, the average breadth is 210 feet and its mean depth is 5 feet'. He adds that 'the catchment area of the valley (is) 116 miles long (and between) 40 and 75 miles (wide). So, the Jehlum receives the rainfall of some 3,900 sq. miles'.

The river winds its way gracefully through Srînagar city for almost seven kilometres. There used to be as many elegant bridges over it in Srînagar. The number seven is considered lucky everywhere, and in the case of Srînagar the sobriquet 'the city of the seven bridges' had been around for centuries. So, when, in the 1950s, an eighth bridge had to be built, rather than jettison the figure seven, this bridge was simply named the Zero Bridge, a name it retains to this day when the number of bridges has crossed ten. The average width of the Jehlum while in the city is about 65 metres. Its deepest point in the city is at Batyar (near Ali Kadal), where it is almost eight metres deep in the summers and five metres deep in winter.

Tributaries: Many mountain streams and rivulets join the Jehlum during its journey in the Valley. Above Khânabal these include the Sandrin, the Brang, the Arpat from Kothar, the Kokernag and the Achâbal. Below Khânabal, the Lidder, a major river in its own right, comes down from the Târsar lake, collects the melting snows of the Lidder valley and merges with the Jehlum.

As the Jehlum continues its course, it is joined by the waters of the Arpal Nag spring, and the drainage from the Wasterwan and the mountains of Trâl.

At Shadipura the biggest merger – 'marriage' (*shadi*), to use the local expression – of them all takes place. At this point the Sind (Indus) empties itself into the Jehlum. The expanded river then passes through the gigantic Wular Lake after which it is joined, at Doabgam ('the village of the two waters') by just one more major stream, the Pohru, which brings with it the excess waters of the Lolab valley and water from the slopes of Kajinag. Parts of the Pohru (as those of the Sind and the Vishu) are navigable. The Ramshi stream is another tributary.

Tributaries that meet the right bank of the Jehlum are: i) Major tributaries: the Lidder and the Sind; ii) Minor ones: Arrah, Bandipur, Erin, Harbuji and Pohru.

Rivulets and streams that join the Jehlum on its left bank are i) the Veshau/ Vishu/ Vishav from Kokernag which meets it below Bîjbehârâ; ii) the Rembiara from the Pir Panjal; iii) the Doodh Ganga from Ludarmarg, which merges with it south of Srînagar; and iv) the Sukhnag from the Gulmarg area. These tributaries drain the Pîr Pañjâl and are smaller than many of the tributaries that join the right bank.

Quality of water: The waters of the Ningal, the Sukhnag and the Sind streams are much favoured for drinking. Abdullah Khân, a medieval Governor of Kashmîr, insisted on getting his drinking water fetched from the Ningal to Srînagar everyday. (The Ningal empties itself into the Wular, while the Sukhnag and the Ferozepur streams end in a marsh near the Jehlum).

Rafting: Till the beginning of the 20th century boats used to ply on the Jehlum.Till then, this, the biggest river of Kashmîr, was also its main 'highway'. Boats plying on the Jehlum would carry men and materials from one end of Kashmîr to the other. It picks up considerable speed between Bârâmullâ and Kohala. It is navigable from Khânabal to Khadinyar, a village five km. ahead of Bârâmullâ town.

However, in winter, beginning around November, the waters of the river recede, making navigation difficult, especially in the stretch just above Srînagar city. I have been trying to revive this tradition. In the stretch within Srînagar there were points where the bottom of our boat would hit hard objects, especially the remnants of old bridges.

Time taken: The Jehlum travels for 75 km. between Ânañtnâg and Srînagar. (The road distance between the two is only 56 km). Boats travelling downstream cover the distance from Khânabal/ Ânañtnâg to

Srînagar in around twenty hours. Upstream from Srînagar is different. Houseboats take four days. 'Light doongas' do it in around 2½ days.

A 'light doonga' will take half a day to travel from Bârâmullâ to Sopore. It's another day and a half from Sopore to Srînagar, using the Nuru canal. In case you take the route through the Wular, add another two days.

The downstream boatride by 'doonga' is much faster. The Srînagar-Wular journey takes about 20 hours. You can do Srînagar-Nuru-Sopore in roughly 22 hours. Sopore-Bârâmullâ will take six hours. Downstream journeys by shikara will take half as much time.

Timings vary according to the time of the year and, thus, the level of the water.

The rafting route: The stretch on which boats can ply, from Ânañtnâg to Bârâmullâ, is about 130 km. long. As we have seen they can sail upstream as well as down. After Bârâmullâ the river enters a gorge and is extremely unsafe because its waters acquire great velocity. At the other end, in most months the journey starts at Khânabal. The short stretch between Ânañtnâg town and Khânabal is normally too dry to permit boating.

The route is as follows:

- Ânañtnâg
- Vazir Bagh (fine groves on both banks)
- Khânabal (has a Dogrâ era rest house)
- Bîjbehârâ (six km. from Khânabal; old Hindu temple ruins near the bank)
- Sangam bridge (a mob burnt the old bridge in 1931)
- Avantipur (grand temple ruins; the Tral valley is above this village)
- Payech (Hindu temple ruins)
- Kakapur
- Ladoo (somewhat away from the banks are some Hindu temple ruins)
- Khunmoh
- Pampore (13 km. before Srînagar; Woyin and Khrew are nearby)
- Pantha Chuk (the old stone bridge is about eight kms. from Srînagar)

- Pandrethan (three km. from Srînagar; temple)
- Srînagar/Munshi Bagh
- Srînagar/Chhatabal
- Shadipur (25 km. north of Srînagar. From Shadipur to Sopore the route is normally through the Wular. However, when the level of the water is high, the Wular can be more or less bypassed by taking the Nuru canal, which connects Shadipur with Sopore).
- Sumbal (five km. from Shadipur).
- Andarkot (1.5 km. from Sumbal).
- Hâjan (35 km. from Srînagar)
- Banyari (River Jehlum meets Lake Wular here).
- Sopore
- Dubgam (11km. from Bârâmullâ; a village on the right bank; River Pohru, which comes down from Lolab, meets the Jehlum here)
- Bârâmullâ
- Sheeri
- Gântmul
- Bunyâr (Hydro electric power plant)
- Uri
- Lalpul (The last village under Indian administration. After that the river flows into the occupied Kashmîr).

Hydel power: Today, the 105 megawatt Lower Jehlum Hydel Power Project, the Valley's biggest, is fed by this river. The 480 MW Uri Hydel Project also draws its energies from the Jehlum.

Floods: The Jehlum overflows almost every third or fourth year. The plains of Ânañtnâg and Pulwâmâ districts, and thus parts of the National Highway to Srînagar, get submerged. Crops are destroyed and road traffic to and from the rest of India ceases till the flood abates two or three days later. Koul notes, "Many disastrous floods are noticed in the vernacular histories, but the greatest was the terrible inundation which followed the slipping of the mountain at Khadanyar below Bârâmullâ town in 879 AD. The channel of Jehlum was blocked and a large part of the valley was submerged. In 1841, there was a serious flood, which caused much damage to life and property. The flood of 1893 was also a great calamity... At the time of floods more than 45,000 cusecs is the daily discharge of the water excluding the breaches. In former times the villages lying along the river were obliged to keep the artificial embankments in repair (and) flood-gates existed... For many years this obligation had not been enforced, and under the supervision of Sir Walter Lawrence, the State Settlement Commissioner, the embankments below Srînagar city were repaired, and the floods of 1892 were kept in check".

The funny thing is that to an extent these floods are necessary. From 1998 to 2002 rainfall was very insufficient. Garbage piled up on the banks of the river. Several people actually started praying for a small flood. Their prayers were answered in 2003. Floods also moisten land and add to the subsoil water and the mini-floods of early 2003 were a relief.

Taming the floods: The Kashmîrîs have for centuries tried to prevent floods in the Jehlum. Suyya was the chief engineer of King Avantivarman (AD 855-883). He deepened the gorge ahead of Bârâmullâ. In 1902, the Dogrâ Mahârâjâ employed European civil engineers to try to do the same again. They failed. Later in the Dogrâ era, perhaps in the 1920s, electrically powered dredgers were employed, this time with great success. The grand remnants of this large boat can still be seen grounded near a bank of the river in Bârâmullâ town.

The Sind River

The dZoji La Pass

This is a tributary of River Jehlum. It has two sources. The northern one originates near the dZoji La when the snow accumulated there melts. The other stream comes from the Dachinpara area. The two streams merge at Baltal to become the Sind. It now begins to flow with considerable speed and ferocity over large rocks. The gorge below Sonamarg is narrow and rocky. This stretch is dificult to navigate. Till Gagangir it mainly flows down a slope. The stretch above Gagangir freezes over during the coldest part of winter.

A few kilometres after Sonamarg the valley begins to open up, and the river begins to widen.

As it proceeds westwards, through the Sind valley, several tributaries join it. The Kanknai stream merges with it near Kajipura village (in the Lâr area). The stretch between Shadipur and Ganderbal is navigable.

The Sind 'marries' (i.e., merges with) the Jehlum at Shadipur.

The Sind Valley: This is the largest of the many valleys that exist within the all-encompassing Valley of Kashmîr. The old trade route between Kashmîr and Central Asia went through this valley, much along the present National 'Highway.' The valley begins near Baltal and ends at Ganderbal. It is thus around 90 km. long.

After the green meadows of Sonamarg, we enter a gorge that is thickly wooded on both sides. Several rocky hillfaces here are used to train people in rock-climbing. The landscape then gives way to a pleasant, open river valley. Between Koolan and Gagangir (7,200') the river mainly flows over flat land. Here the river widens greatly, in part because of the centuries-old islands of *alluvium* that have formed inside it. Fir trees grow on these islands. The flat part of the valley begins shortly after Gund (6,500'). For a long while we remain in the river valley. Then, around Ganderbal, we enter a short wooded stretch.

Treks through this valley have been listed in the chapter on 'Trekking.' The best time to trek in most parts of the Sind Valley is June. July to mid-August is next best. However, snow on some treks does not melt till early July: the Lidder-Kûlan trek, for instance.

The Lidder River

The sources of River Lidder ('the yellow river') are the glaciers of the mountains of Pahalgâm. Its tributaries include the Aru and Chandanwari 'nallahs'. Its waters are treated at Bumzoo and are the main source of drinking water for Ânañtnâg town and the villages around it. It flows into the Jehlum north of Ânañtnâg/ Islâmabad town. The great King Zain ul Abedin got constructed a canal by which the waters of the Lidder were conducted to the semi-arid Martand plateau near the town. The areas in and around Pahalgâm are known as the Lidder valley and include fascinating lakes like the Shesh Nag.

The Lidder valley: The valley is about 60 km. long. It begins at the glaciers of Kolâhoi and Shrî Amarnâth jî and ends near Aish Muqâm, which is in the fertile plains. Western visitors have traditionally preferred Gulmarg as a resort. However, as a region the Lidder valley has been their favourite, especially for trekking. This is mainly because of the beauty of the place: with forests, meadows, glaciers and tall mountains.

The Brang and the Sandrin

These rivulets have their origins in the Kokernag and Kapran areas respectively, both in Ânañtnâg district. They irrigate agricultural land, provide drinking water and play host to a large variety of fish, including the trout.

The **Brang** (also spelt Bring and Brengi) is one of the headwaters of the Jehlum. It takes its rise at the feet of the Brari Bal. It is known as the Tansan stream till it reaches Woyil (Woylu). There it is joined by a much larger stream which brings the waters of the Nowbug valley. As it goes further west and reaches Hillar, the waters of the Kokernag spring combine with it. Then just west of Ânañtnâg the whole stream unites with the Arpat and Sandrin rivers at village Harnag, west of Ânañtnâg.

The Brang is fordable throughout the year upto the Woyil. After that it is fordable mainly in winter. However, when the melting snow flows into it, the Brang becomes a large and somewhat difficult stream. Since mediæval times there has been a *kadal* (bridge) over it near Urigam.

The **Sandrin** (or Sandran), is one of the sources of the Jehlum. It rises in the mountains near the Nandmarg pass and flows through the Shahabad valley to Harnag. Its bed dries almost completely between Kut and Tamman. In any case its bed is broad and, therefore, not very deep. The melting snow makes it a vast torrent. The waters of the Vettarittar Nag merge with it.

The Veshau/Veshav/Vishav

'The river of Vishnu', is one of the sources of the Jehlum. It originates at the feet of the Panjal range from the Konsa Nag spring in south-west Kashmîr.

The *Ain-e-Akbari* says that the Veshau is a stream that 'issues picturesquely from an orifice in the mountain, and at the same place is a declivity down which the waters tumble from a height of 18 yards with a thundering roar'. It adds that 'Hindu devotees throw themselves down from [the] summit [of this mountain] and with the utmost fortitude sacrifice their lives, in the belief that it is a means of securing their spiritual welfare'.

In the beginning the river flows north. Then near Kangwattan the Chitti Nadi merges with it. A few kilometres later the Versini, flowing from the Budil pass, too, joins it. A little ahead, near the cataract of

Arabal, the Veshau cuts through the rock and majestically flows down to the plains of Kashmîr.

Thereafter, the Veshau flows south-east along the hills for two or three kilometres, before turning north. The clear stream with a bed of shingle goes through loam and in due course becomes a dirty but very wide (50 metres) river. That this was almost always so, and not the result of 20th century deforestation, is clear from the 1890 *Gazetteer*. A part of the Shopian area receives water from two branches of the Veshau. Wargama and Abulwana are watered by the Tougur branch. The Burni is the other stream. The Veshau meets the Rembiara stream at Nowana village. Together they pour into the Jehlum through the Sadarinaji 'nallah'.

The Kishan Ganga

Known in 'AJK' as the Neelum, this river originates in Drass (Kargil). Its waters are extremely cold and play host to large quantities of trout. It meanders through the hills of Tilail, Gurêz, Keran and Arnah, before emptying itself into the Jehlum at Domel (lit.: 'where the two meet'). Its waters have, even in centuries past, rarely been clear, carrying as they do detritus from the brittle mountains that they pass through.

The route: The river gathers strength in the Tilail valley. Therefore, some British Raj surveys place its origin there. It then flows west. After a while it is joined by the Raman Sind, which comes from the south. It then meets the wide Burzil stream, after which it bends towards the north-west towards the Gurêz valley and the Dawar area. Thereafter, the river goes towards the south-west and pours its waters into the Jehlum near Muzaffarâbâd in POK. From start to finish the river is almost 290 km. long.

During the winters the upper part of the river, above Gurêz fort, gets frozen almost completely.

Through most of its course the Kishan Ganga is either rough or has a very strong current or keeps dropping off heights, making it almost impossible to navigate. However, towards its end, near Muzaffarâbâd its velocity softens somewhat and, briefly, makes it navigable. From September to April, when its waters are low, it is fordable near Gurêz fort and remains so till Sirdari village. The valley that it creates (shortly after Kanzalwan) is at most places too narrow and steep to permit cultivation or even human settlement. However, the same qualities make the course of the river rather nice to look at.

The road from Kashmîr to Skardu (in 'AJK') begins at Kanzalwan, near the source of the Burzil stream. It goes through the upper part of the Kishan Ganga valley. Indo-Pak relations being what they are, the road is in disuse. However, even when the state was united, the road would get snowed under in winter (as is the wont of most roads at those altitudes in Ladâkh and Kashmîr) and the Dogrâ Mahârâjâ's troops would need to repair it afresh every year around May.

Main tributaries: The Kishan Ganga receives the waters of countless little streams. Its more important tributaries are i) the Raman Sind, which joins it from the south of the Tilail valley; ii) the Burzil stream of north-east Guréz; iii) the largish Matsil stream which brings the waters of the northern parts of the valley of Kashmîr; iv) the Kel Dara, which brings the waters of the region south of Chilas and Astor. The Kel river flows in the opposite direction and rushes towards the Kishan Ganga till it collides with the latter at a right angle with such velocity that for a moment it halts the Kishan Ganga and creates a large whirlpool just above the point where they meet; v) the Kankatori or Samgan joins the Kishan Ganga in north Dawar, opposite Sharidi; vi) at Titwal it is joined by the Jagran river, which contains the waters of the Shamshabari and Kazi Nag streams as well as the drainage of Karnah valley.

Fish: The river abounds in fish. However, as in the rest of Kashmîr people of the Kishan Ganga valley are not very fond of eating fish. The roe of the fish (i.e., the mass of eggs in its ovarian membrane) is poisonous and causes illness.

The rivers and streams of Budgâm district

- Sut Haran
- Nârâ Nâg
- Sukh Nâg
- The Ahij branches into several streams such as the Mala Kol, the Lar Kol and the Sona Maen Kol, which irrigate the Beerwah area.
- Pushkar Nag
- Gandhak Nag

The other major streams of the district are the **Shaliganga Nallah** and the **Ferozporâ Nallah**.

Ladakh

Leh, Zanskar, Suru Valley

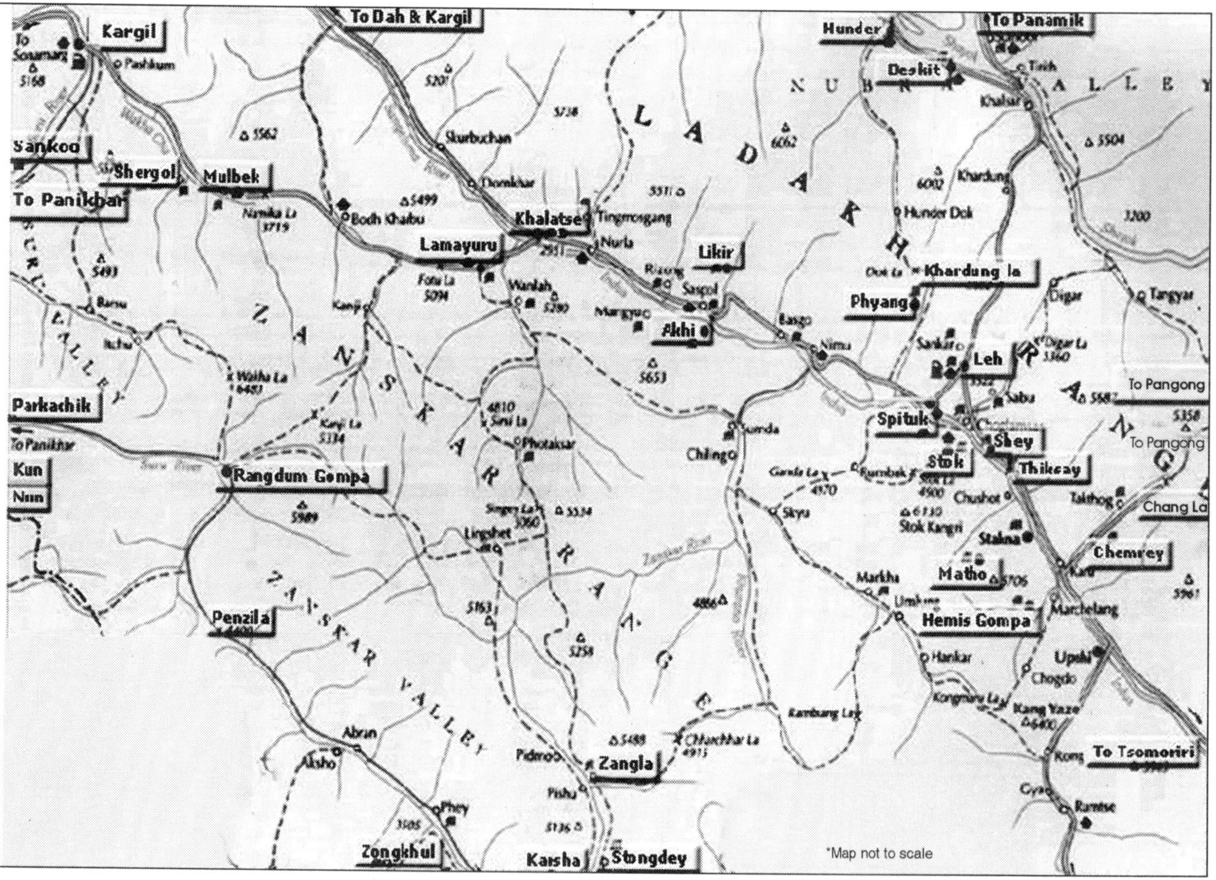

*Map not to scale

Chapter- 7

Places where wildlife might be found

Some mountains were formed when two drifting continental plates collided. The relatively young Himâlayan range was born when the Indian and Asian plates rammed into each other. As a result, the Himâlayas have fauna from the oriental as well as palearctic regions. Ladâkh is in the northern part of the Himalayan range. Therefore, most of it is in the palearctic rather than oriental region.

Ladâkh is an arctic desert. It has hardly any shrubs, and other than at riverbanks and places where humans live, no trees or natural forests either.

The slopes of the lower mountains have very little vegetation. However, as the mountains rise higher, towards the snow line, their slopes start playing host to herbs, wild roses and willows. This is the alpine zone.

Trees and plants grow wherever the soil, wind, availability of water and 'exposure' are good. In Ladâkh not only is water very scarce and the ground rocky, the place is incredibly cold. As we go higher up the mountains, it gets chillier. Greenery becomes even more difficult to find. Amateur visitors assume that so does wildlife.

However, this is not true. Some animals have adjusted magnificently to these harsh conditions, including the biting cold, the insignificant amounts of greenery, the rocky earth and the lack of protective shelters. Almost all ungulates, and the majority of other animals, go down to lower and, thus, warmer altitudes in the autumn, and spend the winter and early spring there.

However, other animals, notably marmots and the brown bear stay on in the upper reaches, where they hibernate. We humans are not the only ones to be affected by "mountain sickness" in Ladâkh because of the shortage of oxygen. So are other animals. Their system responds to this problem by causing the number of red blood corpuscles in their body to increase, as does their blood acidity.

Nature has given some of the bigger mammals warm, shaggy coats for the winter.[1] That, according to the Department of Wildlife, Government of Jammu and Kashmîr, is perhaps why more species of goat and sheep live in the 'open country' in Ladâkh than anywhere else in the world.

Ladâkh is the highest inhabited region in the world. It is located where three 'zoogeographic' zones meet. Therefore, Ladâkh plays host to an incredible array of wildlife—over a hundred and fifty species of bird and more than a dozen major mammal species. Many of these animals are found only in Ladâkh, having become extinct elsewhere. One of the highest densities of ungulates in the region, thus, lives in the Karakoram-West Tibetan Plateau Alpine Steppe.

Parks and sanctuaries

It is advisable to wear khaki, green or camouflage in all these sanctuaries and national parks in Ladâkh. Please do not disturb the animals with loud noises, radios/ music playing systems, motorboats, diesel generators, etc. (I am thought of as a Luddite, an enemy of progress, because of my refusal to allow motorboats at many tourist destinations, whenever I am in a position to do so). Please don't leave behind non-biodegradable garbage. Flash photography can irritate some animals into violence, and scare others needlessly.

National parks are a 'higher' category than sanctuaries.

The Hemis High Altitude National Park: This park covers an area of 600 sq. km. The dozen-odd species of mammals that live in this area include the snow leopard, the ibex and the great Tibetan sheep—the bharal and the shâpû. They are best seen between September and May. Rare birds, too, pass through the park. For example, the Himalayan snow cock. Best viewing season is March to May and September to December.

---

i In summer we humans shear this coat and use the hair as wool.

The Hemis park is spread over the catchment areas of two valleys, both of which drain into the Indus river. There are several camping sites in the park, which you can drive to from Leh. Permission to visit/ camp can be obtained from the Wildlife Warden, Leh.

Himalayan blue sheep in the Hemis National Park

Châñgthâñg[i] is an upland plateau in east Ladâkh. It borders Tibet and is a southwest extension of the Tibetan plateau. Châñgthâñg is best known for its large brackish water lakes, the Pangong, Tsomo Riri and the Tso Kar. If you actually manage to go through this book, you will notice repeated mention of this plateau in connection with some of the most exciting forms of wildlife in the world, including the black-necked crane, the Brahmini duck, the chîru goat, the kyâñg wild ass and the marmot. Sightings of the latter two are almost guaranteed, unless you are plain unlucky.

The reason why there are so many rare species in this area is that Châñgthâñg has a unique combination of huge marshes and sandy plains, flat deserts and lakes and streams (tributaries of the River Indus), some snowfall (unusual for a desert), some rainfall (60mm. to 70mm. a year), chilling temperatures (minus 40°C in winter) and very high altitudes (between 4,000m. and 7,000m)..

In 1993-94, I was able to get the three lakes opened for tourism but, fortunately, not the 4,000 square kilometre Châñgthâñg Wildlife Sanctuary. Tourists can't go to the sanctuary because it is close to the areas that the Chinese army has occupied illegally. China had invaded the area some time before 1962. This (and the subsequent response) has greatly upset the ecological balance of the area. I now regret my enthusiasm of 1993-94 to allow tourists into the area. They have further damaged the very tender ecology of Châñgthâñg. Therefore, it is just as well that tourists aren't allowed into the sanctuary. The area was notified as a wildlife sanctuary in 1987.

It is not as if tourists (and the border situation) are deliberately killing the kiângs (wild asses). What we humans do is that we construct buildings and roads on pastures and wear the scanty grass out by walking or driving on it. This reduces the amount of grass that the asses can eat. We have also been disturbing the animals of Châñgthâñg through noises that were never heard before in that quiet desert (including the sounds of vehicles and helicopters). We have at times taken away the places in which these animals, especially the kiâng, used to live. All this has naturally led to a depletion of the kiâng (and other animal) population in Châñgthâñg.

In 1995, the Zoological Survey of India observed that the highest density of kiângs was in the 'undisturbed' Dungti-Tsaka La sector of the Châñgthâñg Wildlife Sanctuary. The density, as well as absolute numbers, was low in the 'disturbed' sectors of Nyoma-Loma and Loma-Hânlé. Regions that were moderately disturbed, for example, Tsaka La-Chishul and Chishul-Lol Yogma, had moderate populations.

There were an estimated 188 kiangs in the sanctuary.

There, thus, is a direct correlation between disturbances and the number of kiângs (and other animals) in an area.

The flora of this desert region mainly consists of low thorny scrub (Loricera spinoide, Hippophae rhamnoides), Tibetan furze (Caragana sp). and a number of grasses (Festuca sp., Carer sp)..

Protected areas in the Ladâkh-Baltistân-Gilgit region

The following areas have been 'protected' in the region, on both sides of the line of control, by declaring them as wildlife sanctuaries (WS) or game reserves (GR, a Pâkistâni category).

Antelopes in the Karakoram

Snow Leopard, K2 National Park

Kârâkoram, 1,790 square kilometres; Hemis National Park/WS, 1,400 square kilometres; Hemis National Park/WS, 3,890 square kilometres; Khunjerab II, 2,269 square kilometres; Gya-Meru WS, 80 square kilometres; Tingri WS, 50 square kilometres; Lungnag WS, 940 square kilometres; Rupshu WS, 190 square kilometres; Naltar WS, 210 square kilometres; Kargah WS, 240 square kilometres; Chassi/Bowshdar GR, 480 square kilometres; Naz Bar GR, 410 square kilometres; Sherqillah GR, 130 square kilometres; Danyor Nullah GR, 160 square kilometres; Pakura Nullah GR, 140 square kilometres; K2 National Park, 2,330 square kilometres; Nar Nullah GR, 160 square kilometres; Astore WS, 750 square kilometres; Baltistân, 330 square kilometres; Askor Nullah GR, 150 square kilometres; Kanji WS, 90 square kilometres; Bodh Kharbu WS, 100 square kilometres; Rangdum WS, 280 square kilometres; Agram Basti, 270 square kilometres.

The Wetlands of Ladâkh

Ladakh has three of the world's highest wetlands. These are the Tsomo Riri, Tso Kar and Pangong Tso lakes. Almost three hundred and seventy species of rare birds have been sighted in the area. They are the only places in India where the bar-headed geese breeds, the most important sites in Ladâkh for the waterfowl to breed and the only place outside

China where the black-necked crane breeds. Mammals like the wild ass (kiâng), snow leopard, lynx and Himalayan blue sheep live in the vicinity.

Reference

i. Sources of information for this set of entries include JM, Julka, JRB Alfred, HS Mehta and R Paliwal of the High Altitude Zoology Field Station, Zoological Survey of India, Solan, Himachal Pradesh; and the Zoological Survey of India, 'M' Block, New Alipore, Kolkata-700 053.

Chapter- 8

The Land (and some other) Animals of Ladâkh

The following is a selective listing of species that spend at least a part of the year in Ladâkh (and, in a few cases, the rest of the state, especially the occupied areas). In some cases local names have been mentioned after the common English name but before the scientific name, for example in the headwords <<Antelope, Tibetan (Chiru, Tosh/ Pantholops hodgsoni)>>, Chiru and Tosh are the local names.

Mammals etcetera

Antelope, Tibetan *(Chiru, Tosh/* **Pantholops hodgsoni***)*: An ungulate. Conservation status: Critical. A considerable population of the Tibetan antelope lives in the Changchenmo area. It prefers to stay at altitudes between 14,500' and 19,000'. It is about a metre high and its horns are normally half a metre in length. Male antelopes vastly outnumber females. Bot worms live under the skin of these antelopes, and in considerable numbers.

This is a little goat that lives in the steppes of Kânji Nâlâ, a 'Tibetan' plateau. It also lives in Aksai Chin. At both it prefers altitudes above 5,000 metres. In summer it migrates in herds to the Dopsang Plains and the Changchenmo valley. The chîru has beautiful horns that can be as much as 69 cm. wide.

This delicate animal, described by some naturalists as 'strange,' often feels itchy when the weather is hot. It then rubs its woolly body against thorny bushes, where it leaves wisps of its extremely rare, and, thus, expensive wool. People go from bush to bush looking for these wisps, which involves great effort and cost. Shahtoosh shawls are made of these wisps.

Would it not be simpler (and infinitely less expensive) to simply catch hold of a chîru, kill it and pull out all its hair for shawls? No. That would be killing the goat that lays the 'golden', in this case, hair. The hair of chirus curl up as soon as they die and, therefore, cannot be used in shawls.

The ban on shahtoosh shawls is, thus, totally misguided. The chiru is rare and perhaps endangered but shawls are not the reason.

Argali, Tibetan: (*Nyan*/ Ovis ammon hodgsoni) An ungulate. Conservation status: Critical. Found in parts of the Ladâkh-Balâwaristân region.

Argali

Asses: Found in several parts of the state, including Ladâkh.

Ass, Tibetan wild: (Equus Kiang Moorcroft) An ungulate. Conservation status: Vulnerable. Known as the kiâng in Ladâkh, the Tibetan wild ass is, morphologically, more of a horse than an ass. Its ears, for instance, are longer than those of a horse but much shorter than what an ass would normally have.

Physical appearance: The kiâng is the biggest wild ass found in Africa and Asia. It is a sleek, handsome animal and is about '13 hands' tall. It normally is reddish-brown (rust coloured) all over and white on the stomach. In winter it turns dark brown. Its tails, like those of a zebra, have a long tuft of hair at the end.

Like a horse, its tail tuft is large and its hooves are broad. However, like other wild asses, its mane is short and upright. Along the back there is a black stripe, from one end to the other, from nape to tail. This is a characteristic of wild asses.

Habitat: The kiâng lives in the Hânlé valley, near the Pangong and Rupshu lakes, and in Changchenmo. It mostly lives above 14,000' and, therefore, tolerates the cold the way few animals can. It prefers the open sandy tablelands near the Tibet border and altitudes between 3950 and 4850 metres.

Kiângs live in herds in which there are adult males and females as well as their foals. The number of kiângs in a herd varies between two and nineteen. Some herds have as many as forty-five members, a few even more. (The Zoological Survey of India found a herd consisting of 84 members in September, 1994). Occasionally the ZSI also came upon some solitary adult males.

I have seen a report which says that in the higher plains of Rupshu you can sometimes see herds of as many as a hundred. In view of the ZSI's very meticulous survey I wonder if the figure of a hundred is a carefully considered one, or a casual observation. Ditto for my own encounter with kiângs, mentioned below.

There probably are 1,500 wild asses in all of Ladâkh, local experts feel. (The Zoological Survey of India[1] estimates the population at around two thousand, which seems more realistic considering the large numbers that this author saw at Hânlé alone).

I had gone to Hânlé in 1995, in connection with the setting up of an observatory. I had the privilege of giving those pioneering scientists some humble assistance by way of land and clearances for that project. Our helicopter flew extremely low, which was possible because there were no trees, poles, mounds or other obstructions. This, unfortunately, caused some panic among the kiângs and made them run very fast. But we must have seen at least two, maybe even three, hundred wild asses in that single day.

However, all of us accept that the wild ass of the Indo-Tibetan Himâlayas is an endangered species. It mainly eats Festuca sp., a sturdy grass that grows in very, very small quantities.

There might be some kiângs in the Spiti region of neighbouring Himachal Pradesh and north Sikkim.

The kiâng is found in large herds on the highest flat grounds between the Kuenlun and the Kârâkoram. Wild asses like to live near fresh water lakes. The Tso Kar lake is particularly favoured.

1. In August 1995, the ZSI studied an area of 490 square kilometres, located at about 220 km south-east of Leh and covered the following sectors: Nyoma-Hânlé, Loma-Chishul through Tsaka La, Chishul-Lol Yogma, and Chishul-Mane along Pangong Tso.

Outside India, the kiâng lives in Tibet and the Tsinghai and Szechuan regions of China. To and fro migration takes place between Ladakh and the neighbouring Tibetan areas.

Sub-species: There are three sub-species of kiâng. They differ from each other in terms of colour and size, and live in different parts of the Himâlayas. The polyodon is the smallest of the three and is found in south Tibet and north Sikkim. The sub-species kiang is native to the Changthang area of east Ladakh and west Tibet. In terms of size it stands in the middle. The holdereri is the biggest sub-species and lives in east Tibet and Szechuan.

An easy slay: The kiâng does not run away from men, unless irritated by gesture or sound. In fact, wild asses come up to within 150 metres of visitors to give them the once over. (Yes, man is not the only curious species). The Champas eat their flesh. (See also the section on the Changthang Wildlife Sanctuary on pp. 117-118).

Bears: They normally do not attack humans unless attacked or irritated first. Of course, when they attack they normally crush the victim to death.

Bears, Himalayan black: (Ursus Tibetanus) They waken in the spring, after their winter hibernation. These bears are found at altitudes lower than those in which brown bears live, and are smaller than the brown kind. They mainly eat herbs and fruit but can be carnivorous as well. To this extent they are infinitely more dangerous than brown bears. They move out after sunset. In my experience they venture out only when it is fairly dark. When fruits ripen, they visit the fields and create havoc there, destroying crops and corn-fields.

Bears, Himalayan black (medium-sized): (Selenarctos tibetanus) This bear lives in forests at altitudes of around 4,500 metres in the summer. It sets up home in dug-out hollows and caves. This predator eats almost everything, from ripe corn and fruit to deer, goats, sheep and, yes, termites. Three or four black bear couples have been sighted in the inhabited parts of Kargil/ Zanskar in July-August when the apricot and apple fruit ripens.

Bears, brown: (Mainly, Denmo/ Ursus arctos; also the Ursus Isabelina) A large carnivore. Conservation status: Low Risk. The Ursus arctos lives at higher altitudes than its black cousin and is more capable of adjusting to difficult living conditions. There are some two hundred such bears in Ladâkh, mostly in Zanskar but some twenty in the rest of Kargil.

Bharal: (Napo/ Pseudois nayaur) An ungulate. Conservation status:

Low Risk (also spelt and pronounced 'barhal'). This is an 'enigmatic' mammal because it is not clear whether it is a sheep or a goat. It has some morphological traits of sheep and some traits of goats. It is found in Kashmîr as well as Ladâkh. In Ladâkhi it is called nâ or snâ.

Bharal

This species of blue sheep is the most commonly found type of sheep in all Ladakh. Unlike the shâpû/ urial, the bharal is found in abundance. Its brownish-grey exterior is part of the reason, because its colour camouflages the animal and thus protects it to an extent. Bharals often stand absolutely still, which makes it very difficult for hunters to see them. When frightened, bharals run extremely fast to safe places.

The bharal is small and lives wild almost throughout Ladâkh, especially Zâñskâr, Tiri and Changchenmo, up to altitudes of around 15,000'. It has long horns, just under a metre long, and its flesh is considered a delicacy. The bharal is almost never found below 13,000' even in winter. In summer bharals go up, in large herds, to alpine meadows at 16,000', in fact, even higher. Some zoologists have spotted herds at between 18,000' and 19,000', on meadows where the summer grass is plenty.

Camel, Ferral Bactrian (*Nabong*/ Camelus Bactrian): An ungulate. The double-humped Bactrian camel is found in some parts of Leh district.

Cattle: Common horned cattle are not at all common in Ladâkh. At most they might be found in the lower parts of Ladâkh. The Himalayan counterparts of common Indian oxen are widely found in Nubra and the warmer regions of Ladâkh. Yaks, or, more accurately, their descendants, are the type of cattle common to Ladâkh. (See 'Yaks').

Deer, musk: This is a rare species, mostly because it has been hunted and killed through the centuries for its musk-pods. It is found in the lower parts of Ladâkh, especially in western Ladâkh.

The musk deer lives above the zone where pines grow. It prefers birch forests. When it comes down to the lower hills it seeks the safety and protection of dense forests.

Deer, Tibetan ravine: Called the goa locally and mainly found around Hânlé (Leh). Its horns are different from those of its mainland Indian counterpart and can be up to 35 cm. (14 inches) long.

Dogs: In particular the Bakerwals (shepherds), who live in the mountains, keep large, ferocious dogs that protect their flock as well as themselves from wild animals.

The 'toy-dogs' of Zâñskâr (Ladâkh), in particular those bred by the erstwhile royal family of Zangla, are much in demand outside Ladâkh. Apparently they even manage to survive in the much hotter plains of central India (perhaps with air conditioning).

Also found in Ladâkh is the Tibetan mastiff, which is considered an 'ill-tempered' shepherd's dog.

Dog, Wild (*Phara*/ Cuon alpinus laniger): A large carnivore. Conservation status: Critical.

Fox: There is a fairly big population of the foxes in Ladâkh. Western Ladakh is the best place to look for the fox. If you travel at night on the national highway between Kargil and Mulbek, or in the Suru valley, you are likely to drive past foxes with thick, bushy tails. Regrettably, many red foxes are trapped for this very fur, which is then smuggled out.

Fox, red (*Watse*/ Vulpes vulpes or Vulpus vulpus): A large carnivore. Conservation status: Low Risk. The Red Fox is found in Ladâkh. It prefers bush woodlands. There it digs a burrow under the ground to live in. Or it might live among rocks or under the cover of dense vegetation. It is a nocturnal animal. Hunger might force the stray Red Fox to come out during the day, though. It is a loner. Its diet changes with the season and depends on what is available and also on what that particular fox has grown to like. The Red Fox preys on small rodents and birds—pheasants, partridges, marmots and voles. This monogamous animal is said to pair for life. Red Fox couples are known to live in the same place for years at an end. This home is often a burrow with more than one opening.

Gazelle, the Tibetan: (*Gowa*/ Procapra picticaudata) An ungulate. Conservation status: Critical. This small animal can be found in the steppes of the Kânji Nâlâ, a 'Tibetan' plateau. It normally moves in herds of five to ten. On some rare occasions it has been seen on the eastern fringe of Ladakh. Its horns typically measure 36 cm.

Goats: In Ladâkh goats have two important uses (other than meat): to transport materials on and, more commonly, for their wool. That is why the second kind are called 'shawl-goats' and are bred in Nubra, Zâñskâr

Gazelle

and Rupshu. The latter are shorn once a year. The best hair is used for shawls and is called lena. Common wool is called bal. Hair is separated from the wool, is used for blankets, tents and ropes, and is called spu.

Hare: Common in Ladâkh, where its ears are larger than those of its British counterpart and where it is bluish grey in colour.

Hare, mouse: Found in Ladâkh.

Horse, domesticated/ ponies: Ladâkhi horses, that's right, horses, not ponies, are short but sturdy. The ones from Zâñskâr are among the best. In Leh they have traditionally been weaker. Horses and ponies from Drâss and Kargil are great load carriers. The Ladâkhis, too, play polo.

Horse, wild: Found in Ladâkh.

Ibex: (Capra ibex. '*Skin*' or '*sekin*' in Ladâkhi). This goat can be found in the Suru and Warhwan (Doda, Jammu) valleys, Basgo, and POK's Astor and Baltistân regions. There are around 250 ibex in the steppes of Kânji Nâlâ, a 'Tibetan' plateau.

The size of ibex herds varies between ten and sixteen. In summer this gregarious animal moves from place to place grazing on grass, which, in that season, is everywhere. Their breeding season begins in November, and they deliver in late June, after a six-month pregnancy.

Ibexes prefer altitudes above the tree line. They thus climb to heights that are considerably higher than the ones that smaller wild goats go to. That is because they like to live amidst black precipitous rocks and cliffs. They seek shelter and security amidst sheer cliffs and ridges. In winter they come down to lower altitudes for food and shelter. Therefore, winter and spring are when it is easiest to find ibexes.

Ibexes are afraid of dogs. In Baltistân (POK), and in some other parts of the region, human hunters send dogs to drive ibexes up rocks. Thereafter the humans come over and shoot the ibexes.

Physical appearance: This is the best looking goat in all of Ladâkh. Besides, it cannot be mistaken for any other kind of goat. It has a pair of elegant spiral horns. The biggest ibex horns on record measure 147 cm. The animal is large and stocky.

Ibex, Siberian (Skin/ Capra ibex sibirica) An ungulate. Conservation status: Vulnerable.

Leopard, snow: (*Shan*/ Uncia uncia) A large carnivore. Conservation status: Endangered. Also known as the white leopard and ounce, this is an elusive animal. It is very difficult to spot. Two Germans spent an entire winter with me in Zâñskâr trying to photograph this hard to get mammal. We spotted some rare ibexes instead, but even those not from close enough to photograph.

The snow leopard is a 'survivor from the frigid Pleistocene era,' as a government publication puts it. It is found throughout the Himalayan range, i.e., the higher mountains of Kashmîr and Ladâkh being more favoured than most of the other Himalayas. It has been sighted often in the Suru, Warhwan (Kishtwar, Jammu) and Nubra valleys. The snow leopard is believed to live in Zâñskâr, too. It eats the ibex, the bharal and the markhor.

The snow leopard also lives in Central Asia, and within India, in the Himâlayan mountains of Arunachal Pradesh, Sikkim, Uttar Pradesh and Himachal Pradesh.

In summer this solitary animal lives amidst rocks and cliffs, above the tree-line. It comes down to the villages in the lower valleys and hills in winter, when its prey does the same.

Physical appearance: The chest and under parts of this awesome animal are cream in colour. It has a thick coat of gray on which there are black rings or rosettes. This colour scheme camouflages it against rocks and the snow. But why would this supreme predator need to camouflage itself? Actually this is an offensive camouflage. The snow leopard does not want its prey to see it coming.

The snow leopard has large nostrils, because oxygen is scarce in the high mountains where it lives. Its limbs are short and its chest muscles well-developed so that it can climb mountains the better. The snow leopard's hair is long and dense. Its tail is almost three feet long (that being equal to 75-90 per cent of the length of its head and body measured together).

Its prey: In summer, while camping at high altitudes, it eats goats, the ibex, blue sheep and the shâpû. It follows its prey when they migrate uphill in spring and also when they come down in autumn. It also eats pikas (Ochotona spp)., hares (Lepus spp). and gamebirds (chukar partridge and snowcocks). In winter, it terrorises domestic stock. It normally hunts in the early morning and late afternoons.

Population: It is estimated that there are some two hundred snow leopards in Ladâkh. A government website comments, 'With almost 40-50 skins smuggled out of Ladakh in the 1950s, 30-40 in the 1960s and 10-15 still [in the 1990s and '00s] being slipped out, the main enemy of this animal is, undoubtedly, man'.

The Chinese use the bones of snow leopards in their medicines as a substitute for tiger bones. Fur coats made of the skins of snow leopards are sold in China and Taiwan. Trophy hunters, however, remain the main threat.

Khunjerab II in Pâkistân Occupied Kashmîr and Taxkorgan IV in Occupied Tibet are the only two protected areas in the snow leopard's 'range' where viable populations (i.e., at least fifty breeding adults) of the animal can live. (A range is a region in which an animal can live. Most of Ladâkh-Balâwaristân and Tibet are within the snow leopard's range). Eighty five to ninety per cent of the areas in which the snow leopard lives are unprotected.

Lynx: (Felis lynx/ Lynx isabellina. Called eeh in Ladâkh). A large carnivore. The lynx looks a bit like the wolf because its ear tufts stick out equally conspicuously. It is fawn and white in winter and somewhat darker in summer. Its tail is short and dark. The lynx eats marmots, snowcocks and hares.

This isabelline cat seeks shelter in forests and amidst tall grass and reeds. This good looking animal lives in the remoter parts of Ladâkh at altitudes of around 4,400 metres.

Markhor: (Capra falconeri) Called *Raphoche* in Ladâkhi. This 'serpent-eater' is a very large goat. The Astor (now POK) markhor has huge, flat horns, which rise with just one sweep. This migratory animal lives on 'dangerous ground' but not on the high mountains where the ibex does. Prefers dense birch and pine forests. Grazes on the grassy glens of these forests. Rarely goes above the snow-line.

Markhor

Markhors travel in herds. They feel most secure from attack when housed amidst precipitous crag and rock. In December the older ones join the females and younger males. In spring they break company again.

Marmot, docile: Found in Ladâkh. Just before you reach the Rangdum gompa, travelling down from Kargil, there is a large expanse of land that teems with marmots. This cat-sized animal hibernates in underground burrows all through winter. During much of summer it is too groggy to react to hunters. Its responses are rather slow. Hence the epithet 'docile'. Even a child can walk up and grab a marmot, especially for its attractive golden brown skin. However, don't even try. You'll be causing major offence to local religious sentiment if you do. It's considered most sinful to kill a marmot. You can see why. The docile marmot is plentiful in places like Drâss, right on the highway, especially right after the dZoji Lâ opens (late May/ early June). You are almost guaranteed sightings while driving to Nubra.

Marmot

Marten, stone: (Martes foina) This is a good looking and swift animal. It lives above the tree line, in forests as well as on barren mountains. It nestles in the hollows of trees, in holes in the ground and amidst rocks. Its looks make its fur much valued internationally. Therefore, hunters stalk this normally vigilant animal. It is estimated that four hundred skins of the Stone Marten are smuggled out of Ladâkh every year.

Mules: Mules, whether in the areas bordering Kulu, Kâñgrâ and other parts of HP, or those in regions neighbouring Yârqañd, have proved to be the sturdiest animals when it comes to carrying loads.

Nyan: See 'Sheep, wild'.

Ovis Ammon: See 'Sheep, wild'.

Ovis Orientalis/ Ladakhi *Urial* (*Shâpû/* Ovis orientalis vignii) An ungulate. Conservation status: Endangered. Known as the 'urial' in some parts of the Punjâb and greater Ladâkh. In the areas of Kargil under Pâkistâni occupation (Baltistân, Astor, Bunji) it is called the oorin.

The shâpû is found in most parts of Ladâkh, mainly along the Indus. It lives on steep, grassy, hill slopes above forests.

Urial

The adult urial typically weighs around 85 kg. and the tips of its horns can be as much as a metre apart. (The Jammu and Kashmîr Forest Department's impeccable website very precisely says that the horns measure 99 cm). This is perhaps the smallest sheep in East Asia. It normally is no taller than its horns. Urials live on grassy mountain slopes, normally between 3,000 and 4,000 metres. That, by Ladâkhi standards, is not a very great altitude and the majority of the human population lives in this zone. Therefore, it is quite common for hunters to kill urials.

As a result there are hardly five hundred urials left in the main inhabited areas of Ladâkh. There are another forty or fifty urials in the Markha and Rumbak valleys. For that reason all conservationists must unite to keep this dying species alive: not just by banning hunting but mainly by helping urials breed in greater numbers.

Urials, like most sheep, mate in December-January. Their offsprings are born in or around May.

Predators: In any eco-system there are many docile animals (and many species of docile animals). There also are a few predators (and even fewer species of predators) that eat the gentle ones. In Ladâkh, the number of predators (and predator species) is smaller still because food is more scarce than elsewhere. Ladâkh's best known predators are the snow leopard, the brown bear, the wolf and the lynx.

Sheep, blue: See 'Bharal'.

Sheep, domesticated: In Ladâkh there are two kinds of sheep. i) The huniya has a large, black-face, and is used to transport materials, most notably salt, especially in Châñgthâñg and Rupshu. ii) In Kargil there is a smaller, prettier kind, which is eaten.

Sheep, Marco Polo: (Ovis ammon poli) An endangered species found in parts of the Kârâkoram-West Tibetan Plateau Alpine Steppe. This sheep is the largest of its genus.

Sheep, wild: The nyan is also known as the Great Tibetan Sheep (Ovis ammon). It is found near Shushal (the pass as well as the region), Hânlé and Rupshu. Its horns can be up to a metre and a half long (145 cm. is not unusual) and half a metre in girth.

All sheep, found anywhere in the world, are related very closely to each other. Even when they seem to look different, they are mere modifications of the same species. The nyan looks much like an antelope.

The Ovis ammon is the largest and grandest of all the wild sheep found in Ladâkh. It lives between 14,500' and 19,000' in summer. The nyan has a strong sense of smell, which alerts it if a hunter or an enemy is coming that way. The belief is that the nyan is a very difficult animal to get hold of. This is a view based on the terrain on which the nyan lives and the winds that blow there. However, the 1890 Gazetteer says that such 'difficulties ... are very much magnified'.

If we accept that the difficulties have been magnified, then the low probability of sighting this animal has to be attributed to its rarity. There is a population of some two hundred nyans in the easternmost part of Ladakh. This is an animal that migrates to wherever food and water are available but almost never goes down to altitudes below 4,500 metres. It lives in the wilderness.

The gregarious Ladâkhi shâpû is found near and along River Indus. Its herds are not very big.

See also 'Bharal'.

Squirrel, woolly flying: Some zoologists call this the 'single endemic mammal' found in the Kârâkoram-Himâlayan-Hiñdu Kush ecoregion. It lives at high altitudes in scanty pinus and picea forests.

Stone marten: See Marten, stone.

Ungulates: This is the most widespread set of species in Ladâkh-Balâwaristân. Most of them are endangered. See also the entries on 'Sheep, wild,' 'Sheep, Marco Polo,' 'Argali, Tibetan,' 'Markhor,' 'Ibex' and 'Ovis orientalis.'

Urial: See 'Ovis orientalis'.

Weasel, altai: (Mustela altaica) Found in the Ladâkh-Balâwaristân region.

Wolf, Tibetan (*Shangku*/ Canis lupus chanko) A large carnivore. Conservation status: Vulnerable.

Wolves: (Canis lupus) Some three hundred wolves are found in Ladâkh. They eat sheep, to the distress of shepherds for whom this is a huge economic loss. This makes wolves the most detested predators in Ladakh.

When the shepherds move uphill to the mountain pastures for the summer, so do wolves. In winter they come down close to the lower valleys (and fairly close to the plains). In summer they live amidst thickets of reeds and scrub. In winter they seek shelter in caves and amidst rocks.

There are two broad varieties of wolf in Ladâkh. The kind found in the north are light fawn and brown. The ones in the south are darker. Wolves hunt in pairs and move over very long distances. One kind of wolf regularly moves across a narrow valley at dusk.

Yâk: The yâk is a kind of ox and is the biggest animal found in the cold Himâlayan desert of Ladâkh. Some kinds of yak weigh around a tonne. The tips of its curved horns can be as much as 90 cm. away from each other and can measure 76 cm. over the curves.

There are two kinds of yak.

Yak, domestic: When a yak mates with the common cow, the offspring thus produced is a hybrid called a dzo if male, and dzo-mo if female. The dzo-mo produces more and better milk than the female yak. The Ladâkhis convert most of the milk into butter, rarely consuming it directly, not even in tea (in which butter, rather than milk, is used). The next generation of cow-yak is called dimo in Leh-Zâñskâr and brimo in Kargil and is kept only for its milk.

The domesticated yak is not as tall as the wild variety, it is broad and strongly built, and is useful for carrying loads. However, this placid animal cannot walk long distances. It gets footsore if it does. Therefore, it is quite useless at pulling the plough. The dzo-mo is used for the ploughing of fields as well as for carrying loads.

Nubra, being at a lower height, does not produce good yaks. Their dark hair is cut only when it almost reaches the ground.

Yak, wild: (Dong/ Bos grunniens) An ungulate. Conservation status: Critical. This kind is native only to Ladâkh where it is known as the dong in Leh-Zâñskâr, and brong in Kargil, It is a very rare animal and much larger and more impressive than the domesticated variety. The bulls are considerably outnumbered by the cows.

Wild yaks are native only to the Kepsang and Polrang valleys. Therefore, they might even be seen in the Kubrung and Kepsang nallahs of the neighbouring Changchenmo valley, and in the nearby ravine, left of the Shyok. Indeed, this ravine is called the dongaylak, or 'the wild yaks' summer pastures'. Wild yaks are found in large herds on the highest flat grounds between the Kuenlun and the Kârâkoram. Favoured altitudes are between 15,000' and 16,000', normally the latter. Wild yaks spend their summers at altitudes above 6,000 metres. In winter they migrate in herds to the lakes, marshes and lower valleys.

Because of their inaccessibility to even the common Ladâkhi, wild yaks were first described only as recently as in the 1870s, by the great Russian explorer and horse-expert, Count Nikolay Mikhailovich Przhevalsky (1839-1888).

The Champa tribals eat the flesh of these yaks. Their horns can be thick and up to 77 cm/ 30 inches long. Their tails are greatly valued.

Physical appearance: Wild yaks are evenly black, with parts of the back and head sporting a slight tinge of rust. The tail is bushy, like that of a horse. They have a dense cover of long, shaggy hair, which is slightly grey at the muzzle. They resemble the bison, except that they are bigger.

Reptiles, insects etcetera

Amphibians: There are supposed to be no amphibians in Ladâkh. However, this is not strictly correct. Amphibians of the Bufonidae family have been reported in the Ladakh region. The species reported include:

Bufo viridi

Bufo latastii

Scutiger occidentalis

Annelida: Three species of Annelida from the cold desert of Ladakh were studied and recognised in the 1980s and 1990s.

Bees: The honey bee is not found in Ladâkh, though the black spotted bee, the bonga nakpo, as well as the wasp known as the golden bee (locally, the boni-ser), are. Since at least mediæval times the Ladâkhis have been making honey 'without the aid of bees'. (Which is the kind we'd have for lunch every Wednesday at our CU Green lunches at Cambrîdge University. Honey without cruelty. My fellow Greens would love the Ladâkhis).

Bluebottles: Common in Ladâkh at the peak of summer: July-August.

Fish: Fishing is taboo in the Buddhist parts of Ladâkh (Leh, and some parts of Kargil, especially Mulbek and Zâñskâr). Any attempts on your part to catch fish in the Buddhist areas will cause very deep offence. As soon as you are seen fishing, you will immediately be surrounded by a hostile mob.

Frogs: See 'Amphibians' above.

Ladâkh has few insects other than houseflies (and they are only in July and August) and the insects mentioned in this section. No snakes.

Lepidoptera: Three species of Lepidoptera from the cold desert of Ladakh were studied and recognised in the 1980s and 1990s.

Lizards: There are at least three species of lizard in the region—Agama himalayan (common), Scincella ladacensis (sparse), and Phrynocephalus theobaldi (stone deserts).

Locusts: In Ladâkh found only in Zâñskâr.

Reptiles reported in the Ladakh region, in addition to those mentioned elsewhere in this section, include:

Family	**Species**
Agamidae	Phrynocephalus theobaldis
	Phrynocephalus recticulatus
	Laudakia himalayana
Geckonidae	Crytodactylus montium salsorum
	Crytodactylus stoliczkai
	Crytodactylus lawderanus
Scincidae	Scincella himalanum
	Scincella ladacense
Coluberidae	Coluber rhodorachis
	Elaphe hodgsoni
	Ptyas mucosus

Sand-flies: In Ladâkh found in swarms in Nubra and the lakes, especially the Tsomo Riri, where their huge presence can be uncomfortable for the visitor.

Scorpions: The puhur. Plentiful in the Cheshma Shahi-Pari Mahal-Raj Bhawan area of Srinagar city. Also in the Dachinpura and Lar areas. Their bite can be fatal.

Snakes: There are no snakes in Ladâkh, where the only reptile is a small lizard. It is said that Ladâkh is too cold for snakes to survive. I've never found one in any part of Ladâkh. British records, too, bear me out. However, the more recently published (around 1990) 'Gazetteer: Ladâkh Region' suggests that some non-poisonous species are found in the region. I still have my doubts.

Chapter- 9

The Birds (avifauna) of Ladâkh

Jammû, Kashmîr and Ladâkh are located on the 'flyway route' of birds migrating from Siberia to the plains of India. Because the State has a large number of lakes and rivers, it plays host to many of these birds. In all 225 species of birds, representing 34 families, have been sighted in Ladakh. Around 110 of these species breed in Ladakh, mainly in the summer.

Very few birds live in Ladâkh throughout the year because the place is so cold and is a desert to boot. However, some parts of Ladâkh have water and others have trees and shelter of kinds. This is more than what some of the neighbouring regions can offer. Therefore, some birds spend some time in those parts Ladâkh. Thus, when we say 'Found in Ladâkh' below, we really mean 'found during the season, and then at particular places in Ladâkh'.

Partridges and snowcocks, pigeons and accentors are the only birds that spend their whole lives in Ladâkh, mainly in the upper reaches.[1] Some birds live in the upper reaches in summer and the foothills in autumn, winter and spring. Most birds move to the warmer parts of the world, after a halt in Ladâkh.

1 However, a senior zoologist asserts, incorrectly, "There are no endemic bird species, and bird richness is low." (Emphasis added.)

Birds seen in Ladakh are those normally found in the a) Palaearctic, and b) Indo-Malayan regions. In turn, they are of four kinds:

i) Those that live in Ladakh throughout the year, in the higher reaches in summer and in the less severe valleys in winter.

ii) Those that spend time in Ladakh in spring (April-May), some to breed there, some on their way across the Himalayas and many because they want to get away from the heat of the plains of the Indian sub-continent. They normally dwell near water or fields. Apart from the Black-necked Crane, birds that breed in Ladakh include the Bar-headed Goose, Brown-headed Gull, Great-crested Grebe, Lesser Sand Plover and Ruddy Shelduck.

iii) Those that spend time in Ladakh in winter (October/ November to April/ May), trying to escape the even more severe winter of the mountains up north. They seek the lower valleys near rivers—the wider the valley, the more sunshine it is likely to receive and the more attractive it will be for birds.

iv) Birds that fly ('migrate') through Ladakh, normally in spring and autumn, mostly the latter, on their way elsewhere. This is the biggest of the four groups but these birds spend less time in the region than the other three. There are more migration routes in eastern and central Ladakh than in the west.

Chukar

Coot

Chiffchaff

Red-billed Chough

The following is a listing of some of the important species native to or found or seen in Ladâkh. In some cases the Ladakhi name of the bird has been mentioned after its zoological name; followed by the average length of the bird, first in centimetres and then in inches.

Black necked Crane

For the sake of convenience, in this chapter I have assumed spring to mean April and May, summer as June to August, autumn as September and October, and the rest to be winter.

Accentor, Alpine (*Prunella collaris*) is a resident of the higher mountains of Ladakh—rocky places like Khardung-La—where it has often been seen in groups of around five.

Accentor, Altai (*Prunella himalayana*)

Accentor, Black-throated (*Prunella atrogularis*)

Accentor, Brown *(Prunella fulvescens)*

Accentor, Maroon-backed (*Prunella immaculata*)

Accentor, Robin (Prunella rubeculoides/ Bangma-tsildir, Tseldir, Bang-tsil/ 18cm/ 7in). has a distinct orange stripe on its chest. Seen amidst trees and shrubs in Zanskar, Markha and Nubra, in winter and elsewhere in the summer.

Accentor, Robin: (*Prunella rubeculoides*) Found in the Ladâkh region. Interestingly, it 'winters' in this region.

Accentor, Siberian (*Prunella montanella*)

Avocet, Pied (*Recurvirostra avosetta*/ Khamchuganlok/ 43cm/ 16in). has a white plumage and a black back and wings. It seeks water, mainly near Tso Kar but occasionally also in the Upper Indus Basin.

Bee-eater, Blue-cheeked (*Merops persicus*)

Bee-eater, European (*Merops apiaster*)

Bittern, Great (*Botaurus stellaris*)

Bittern, Little (*Ixobrychus minutus*)

Blackbird, Eurasian (*Turdus merula*): Solitary birds have been spotted near Hanle in early October.

Bluethroat *(Luscinia svecica)*

Brambling (*Fringilla montifringilla*)

Bunting, Chestnut (*Emberiza rutila*)

Bunting, Grey-necked (*Emberiza buchanani*)

Bunting, Little (*Emberiza pusilla*) has, on rare occasions, been seen near Hanle, in June.

Bunting, Ortolan (*Emberiza hortulana*)

Bunting, Pine (*Emberiza leucocephalus*)

Bunting, Red-headed (*Emberiza bruniceps*) has, on rare occasions, been seen near Hanle in October.

Bunting, Reed (*Emberiza schoeniclus*)

Bunting, Rock *(Emberiza cia)*

Buzzard, Long-legged (*Buteo rufinus*): Solitary birds have been seen in the Hanle area between June and August.

Buzzard, Upland (*Buteo hemilasius*/ Nyllsy Muoqpo/ 71cm/ 28in). has a white head with brown streaks, and visits the open spaces of Fukche, Hanle, Loma, Puga and Tso Kar in summer.

Chakor: The rekpa/ skekpa variety is found in LadâkhSâbû in Ladâkh is a sanctuary for chakors. This is a village half way between Leh and Choglamsar. To reach Sabu a detour to the left (east) needs to be take from the main road. Chakors fly in and out of people's houses because in Ladâkh the killing of chakors (and most other animals) is taboo. The chakor is also found on the way from Leh to Nyoma and Upshi.

Chiffchaff, Common (*Phylloscopus collybita*)

Chiffchaff, Mountain *(Phylloscopus sindianus)*

Chough, Red-Billed (*Pyrrhocorax pyrrhocorax*/ Chunka-Khamar/ 40cm/ 16in). has a long, thin, red bill that curves downward. It is seen around cliffs and pastures of the lower valleys of east Ladakh, Leh, Nubra and Zanskar.

Chough, Yellow-Billed (*Pyrrhocorax graculus*/ Chunka-Kasher/ 39cm) is seen in the upper reaches, rocky mountains and grasslands of east Ladakh, Leh, Nubra and Zanskar.

Chough: The *chunka* is common in the villages. Choughs are birds of prey. They go wherever humans and other animals go. They have been sighted at altitudes of as much as 6,150 metres.

Chukar *(Alectoris chukar)* See 'Partridge' below.

Coot, Common *(Fulica atra)*

Coot, Common (*Fulica atra*/ Hanta Chanluk/ 38cm/ 15in). This greyish-black bird with a white bill and green legs can be seen near water in the Indus Basin, east Ladakh, Shey and Tsigul Tso.

Cormorant, Great (*Phalacrocorax carbo*)

Cormorant, Little (*Phalacrocorax niger*)

Crake, Baillon's (*Porzana pusilla*) spends late August and all of September in Ladakh, mainly Lalpari and the marshes of Tso Kar.

Crake, Corn (*Crex crex*)

Crake, Spotted (*Porzana porzana*)

*

Crane, Black-necked (*Grus nigricollis/* Cha Thung Thung Karmo/ height: 135cm/ 54in). Count Nikolay Mikhailovich Przhevalsky (1839-1888), a great Russian explorer, ornithologist (and much more, including horse expert), was the first to study the black necked crane in 1876. The bird has still not been researched adequately.

The male is only a little bigger than the female. Much of the bird (its head, neck, tail, legs and less important feathers is black), its plumage a greyish white, its bill green, and the crown on its head red. BNCs have long necks.

ORIGIN*:* There are fifteen species of crane in the world. Cranes, in general, were in existence sixty million years before man. They now seem to be headed for slow extinction, some scientists feel. Other ornithologists, who met in Moscow in 1982, felt that the BNC was in no immediate danger. This optimism is partly based on the hunch that China has a big BNC population but is not letting the world know (or doesn't know itself). More important is their observation that since 1960 the BNC population visiting Ladâkh has remained exactly the same: three breeding BNC couples a year.

However, Pfister's sightings indicate that the view that only three or four breeding pairs of BNCs visit Ladakh every year might be an underestimate. In 1997 he recorded 38 birds in eastern Changthang, of which 24 were breeding. He found three breeding pairs in Hanle in one year and 'two pairs fighting for territories, plus a loner' in another. During a single season he spotted eight cranes in Chushul, including a breeding pair; three birds at Tso Kar, including a breeding pair; one breeding pair in Harong, Tangtse valley; and one breeding pair in Lalpari in each of two years.

Migration, Breeding and Routine Life while in Ladâkh: BNCs have been seen between June and October in the wetlands of Chushul, Hanle, Puga, Staklung and Tsokar.

Most cranes are migratory and travel thousands of miles every year. The black-necked crane flies up to very high altitudes to nest. It breeds only at altitudes that are between 3500 metres and 5500 metres. Three places in Ladâkh fit the bill.

In summer the BNCs, worldwide, are found in two distinct groups. The western group of BNCs goes to eastern Ladakh and the eastern group to southern Tibet. These are two extremes of the Tibetan plateau. At other times BNCs have been spotted in Asian lands as far apart as Bhutan and India's Arunachal Pradesh in the west and Szechwan, Yunan and Vietnam in the east. If each of their winter homes is a dot on a map and all these dots are joined together, they will form an arc.

The BNC that we find in Ladâkh likes to live in open marshlands, wet plains, prairies and, sometimes, sandy flats.

Every year three BNC couples—sometimes more—come to Ladâkh, through the Indus valley, in mid-April or early May, normally the latter. They fly along the banks of River Indus as they head for marshes where they build their nests. BNC nests are large cushions of dead aquatic vegetation placed on shallow water up to two feet deep, or even on open meadows. BNCs, thus, are 'ground nesting' birds. They prefer marshes because humans and other mammals can't reach there easily.

Apparently, BNCs need lots of space when they breed because these three couples live very, very far apart from each other. One BNC couple builds its nest in Chushul, one in Hânlé and the third near Tso Kar. Even as the crane flies there might be as many as ninety or a hundred kilometres between each of these three places. If there is a fourth (or fifth) breeding couple in any particular year it would normally be only passing through.[2]

If snowfall had been poor in the immediately preceding winter, the marshes might be dry. In that case, BNCs have no option but to build nests on dry land: where their eggs are in great danger.

Roughly three weeks after settling in the nest, the female lays an egg and then, 12 to 24 hours later, another. This generally happens in May. The size of each dull-white or brown egg is around 10cm. by 6cm. It weighs around 200 grams.

Predators try to eat these eggs. Humans collect them to sell to tourists. (You can help save the BNC from extinction by refusing to buy BNC eggs. All of us together should ensure that water is not diverted away from the marshes. We should also ensure that marshes are not 'developed' into pastures for cattle).

If a unit of the Indian Army happens to be posted nearby they sometimes post a guard or two near the nesting sites to ward off both kinds of poachers.

Brahminy ducks and BNCs share the same marshes. Therefore, they don't always like each other. The ducks normally arrive a few weeks later. BNCs see the ducks as intruders and male cranes often chase them away with their large wings (64cm/ 25in. wide). Cranes are particularly aggressive if they find the ducks going near their nests. They don't stop at merely shooing the intruder away. BNCs might chase the intruder for almost an hour till he leaves the pond altogether. For that half-hour or more the incubation process gets disturbed because both parents leave the nest for the while that there is an intruder around.

Both parents take turns to sit on the egg to incubate it. Naturalists of the Wildlife Department of Jammu and Kashmîr have observed that there are around ten such shifts during the course of a day. Each shift, thus, is of around two and a half hours.

After an incubation of eighteen to twenty-four days,[3] one live chick is born. (The other one always dies, even though more than two-thirds of

2. Ladâkh is not the main breeding ground of the BNC worldwide. It has breeding places for just three to five BNC couples. Tibet attracts a far greater number.

3. Twenty-eight to thirty-six days, according to another study.

the eggs hatch successfully. If it does not die a natural death, its other newborn sibling pecks it to death).

The chicks are brown or gray and are very pretty when they are born. They start swimming within hours of their birth. In a day or two they are fairly developed.

Army guards remain around till the chicks are strong enough to defend themselves.

Towards the end of October or early November, the BNCs leave Ladâkh and fly away, with their newborn chicks, to eastern Tibet or South China.

Adult cranes keep these chicks with them for nine or nine and a half months in all, i.e. till the next mating season. After that they shoo their own children away. The young form a peer group and fly together till they are old enough to breed, which might be when they are three to five years old. Some precocious cranes start mating at two.

Physique: The black-necked crane is big, majestic and very good looking. Typically, it is four feet tall. However, its height can vary between two and five feet and its wingspread can be around seven or eight feet. Its body is pale gray, almost white. Its neck, head, feet and 'secondaries' are black and its bill green. There is a red patch on its beak.

Like other cranes, its legs are long and its bill and neck are long and straight. Its hind toe is raised. Apparently, this toe does not support any of the BNC's weight when the bird walks.

Cranes' windpipes are coiled, a bit like the coils of a trumpet, and for the same reason. As a result, cranes emit loud, throaty sounds that, on a quiet day, can be heard for miles. These notes can be quite musical and nice to the ear.

The BNC's Flight: When the BNC flies, its head and neck point straight ahead. At times BNCs fly as high as five kilometres above the earth, and well above the ground even the rest of the time. Once up there they form a large 'V' and go around in fascinating circles. BNCs glide only when they descend.

Food: BNCs are enormous eaters and eat all kinds of berries, fruits, worms, insects, reptiles and, sometimes, birds. They rarely eat fish.

Song, Dance and Mating Rituals: BNCs perform stylish dances in most months of the year, but more so during the breeding season. Sometimes entire flocks—including baby cranes—join in. (Yes, at times there are flocks).

As in Spanish flamenco dances, the courting couple walks stiffly around each other, in brisk, stilted steps. Also as in flamenco, as they do so, they spread their wings only partly and hold their legs elegantly below them. They might even bow low. Then they might jump into the air, six to nine feet above the ground, as loud cries go out all around. Just one crane might do this, or a pair might, or even the whole flock might.

Scottish bandmasters toss their batons into the air and catch them on the way down. Cranes likewise toss twigs into the air with their bills and catch them also with their bills.

The cranes' 'unison calls' are another fascinating ritual. when the entire flock squeals as one.

*

Crane, Demoiselle (*Grus virgo*)

Crane, gigantic: Found in the marshes.

Crane, Siberian (*Grus leucogeranus*)

Crow, Carrion *(Corvus corone)*

Crow, House *(Corvus splendens)*

Crow, Large-billed *(Corvus macrorhynchos)*

Cuckoo, Eurasian *(Cuculus canorus)*

Cuckoo, Eurasian (*Cuculus canorus*): Solitary cuckoos have been spotted by Pfister between June and early September in Hanle, Hundar and Raar, on grassy land and in orchards.

Cuckoo, Pied Crested (*Clamator jacobinus*)

Curlew, Eurasian (*Numenius arquata*)

Dipper, Brown *(Cinelus pallasil)*

Dipper, White-Throated (*Cinclus cinclus*) is frequently seen in the upper Indus valley and near Ganad-La, Rumbak, Sumdo and Tsomo Riri, throughout the summer and early autumn, normally near gurgling brooks where the water rushes down slopes.

Dipper, White-throated *(Cinelus cinelus)*

Dove, Eurasian Collared (*Streptopelia decaocto*)

Dove, European Turtle- (*Streptopelia turtur*) A solitary bird was spotted amidst poplars in Hundar in September.

Dove, Little Brown or Laughing (*Streptopelia senegalensis*) A solitary bird was spotted by Pfister with a group of Hill Pigeons in Hanle in October. It is mainly found in the lower valleys.

Dove, Oriental Turtle- (*Streptopelia Orientalis*/ Kamru, Gondil/ 33cm/ 13in). can be seen around orchards and fields near Leh town, Nubra and the Suru Valley. Predominantly brown, the adult bird has a grey to pink underbelly.

Dove, Red Collared (*Streptopelia tranquebarica*)

Dove, Spotted (*Streptopelia chinensis*)

Drongo, Black (*Dicrurus macrocercus*): Solitary birds have been spotted between June and October in the Hanle and Mahe areas.

Duck, Brahminy (*Tadorna Ferruginea*/ Muru / 25in./ 64 cm): Called surkhaab and surkhwâb in Hindi-Urdu and Ruddy Shelduck/ Ruddy Sheldrake in English, this is a reddish-orange duck with a fair head and neck. It breeds in Pangong Tso and brackish water lakes, and is found in the wetlands of east Ladakh and the Indus basin between Demchok and Likche. The male acquires a slim black collar on the lower neck during the breeding season, which it later sheds. Often quadruple chicks are born, which are reared by both parents in equal measure. Perhaps the most vigilant of birds, it cries out as soon as it senses danger.

Duck, wild: A water bird found in Ladâkhnear the Rupshu lake. Ducks are even more likely to be found near the bigger rivers.

Dunlin (*Calidris alpina*) has, on rare occasions, been spotted near water in Lalpari, in late September, and just one or two birds at a time.

Eagle, Golden (*Aquila Chrysaetos*/ Laknak, Nele, Gyab-Lak/ 90cm/ 36in). This big bird can be seen in Changthang, Drass, Leh, Nubra, Suru valley and Zanskar. When it flies its long wings rise above in a V.

Eagle, Greater Spotted (*Aquila clanga*): Solitary birds have, on rare occasions, been seen in places like Hanle in late September/ early October.

Eagle, Lesser Spotted (*Aquila pomarina*)

Eagle, Pallas's Fish(ing)- (*Haliaetus Leucoryphus*/ Nyallak/ 84cm/ 33in). This fish- and water-bird- eater is found near rivers and lakes in the Chumur, Hanle, Shey and Stakmo areas. Its head and tails are white and its wings brown.

Eagle, Short-toed Snake- (*Circaetus gallicus*)

Eagle, Steppe- (*Aquila Nipalensis*/ Lhak, Rewgyab/80cm/ 31in). can be seen in the countryside around Chumur, Hanle, Shey and Stakmo.

Egret, Cattle (*Bubulcus ibis*) has on a few rare occasions been seen near Tsomo Riri, where a pair or two might go to breed, in summer.

Egret, Large (*Casmerodius albus*)

Egret, Little (*Egretta garzetta*)

Falcon, Peregrine (*Falco peregrinus*) is a rare visitor to Ladakh, where solitary birds have sometimes been seen near the swamps of Lalpari in late September.

Falcon, Saker (*Falco cherrug*)

Falcon. Laggar (*Falco Jugger*) has been spotted on rocks in the Hanle area—normally solitary birds—in summer.

*

Finch: The varieties that visit Ladâkh include:

Finch, Brandt's Black-headed Mountain-*(Leucosticte brandti)*

Finch, Crimson-winged (*Rhodopechys sanguinea*)

Finch, Hodgson's Plain Mountain *(Leucosticte nemoricola)*

Finch, Mongolian (*Bucanetes mongolicus*, sometimes spelt *mongolica*) visits Hanle, Leh town and Loma between May and August, often to breed.

Finch, Plain-backed Snow-*(Pyrgilauda blanford)*

Finch, Streaked Great Rose-*(Carpodacus rubicilloides)*

Finch, Tibetan Snow-*(Montifringilla adamsi)*

Finch, White-rumped Snow-(Pyrgilauda taczanowskii)

Rosefinch, Common *(Carpodacus erythrinus).*

*

Fish-Eagle, Pallas's (*Haliaeetus leucoryphus*)

Flycatcher, Asian Brown (*Muscicapa dauurica*)

Flycatcher, Red-throated (*Ficedula parva*)

Flycatcher, Rusty-tailed (*Muscicapa ruficauda*): There have been a few sightings near Zinchan in the early summer.

Flycatcher, Sooty/ Dark-Sided (*Muscicapa sibirica*) has been spotted on a few rare occasions by the stream near Mahe.

Flycatcher, Spotted (*Muscicapa striata*): A rare summer visitor, it has been seen inside groves in Hundar and Panamik.

Forktail, Little (*Enicurus scouleri*)

Fowl: The domestic fowl is reared in Lehand Nubra.

Gadwall (*Anas strepera/* Jugnagma/ 50cm/ 20in). This water-loving bird has sometimes been seen near Nyoma, Shey, Yoye Tso and east Ladakh in late September-early October in small groups of between three and five.

Garganey (*Anas querquedula/* Sikkar/ 40cm/ 16in). visits the water bodies of east Ladakh, Shey and Nubra in spring (April-May). It has broad white stripes on either side, and a white abdomen.

Godwit, Black-tailed (*Limosa limosa/* Thingril Jogṅak/ 41cm/ 16in). likes shallow water bodies. On some occasions one or two birds have been seen near Hanle, Startsapuk Tso (in August and September), Tso Kar and Tsigul Tso. When it flies the broad white stripes on its wings can be seen.

Goldcrest (*Regulus regulus*)

Goldfinch, European *(Carduelis carduelis)*

Goose, Bar headed (*Anser indicus/* Nangpa/ 75cm/ 30in). This grey, white and brown bird is found—and breeds—in alpine pastures just below the snowline. That's because insects, which this frequent summer guest eats, are plentiful in those meadows. It also likes wheat and barley. So, by night it flies to grasslands near rivers and lakes to feed. In summer it can be seen at Chushul, Hanle, the country around Mahe, Tso Kar, Tsomo Riri and near the Upper Indus Basin. It starts leaving Ladakh between late August and early October to go to the Gharana (Jammu) and Hokersar wetlands (Kashmir). Both genders look similar. There are two black bars on the mature bird's white head but none when it is growing up. Its long wings cover its tail when it is at rest. It breeds near lakes, both freshwater and saline; marshes; rivers; and the wetlands of Changthang. Lake Tsomo Riri—the north and south banks of the lake and islands within, to be precise—is its biggest breeding colony in India, followed by Lam Tso, Startsapuk Tso, Tsigul Tso, Tso Kar and some minor lakes in Changtang and Rupchu. While still found in groups of several dozen this is an increasingly threatened bird.

Goose, grey: A water bird found in Ladâkhnear the Rupshu lake.

Goose, Greylag (*Anser anser*)

Goshawk, Northern (*Accipiter gentilis*)

Grandala (*Grandala coelicolor*): Solitary birds have been spotted on a few rare occasions near Zinchan in the early summer.

Grebe, Black-necked (*Podiceps nigricollis*)

Grebe, Great Crested (*Podiceps cristatus*/ Changa–rankest/ 49cm/ 19in). visits Startsapuk Tso (where it breeds and nests), Tsomo Riri, Tso Kar and Yoye Tso in summer. It has no tail. A black streak runs from the bottom of its straight, pink bill to its eyes. It builds floating nests and carries the young on its back

Grebe, Little (*Tachybaptus ruficollis*)

Greenshank, Common (*Tringa nebularia*)

Griffon, Himalayan (*Gyps Himalayensis*/ Thankar/ 125cm/ 49in). is found in the mountains near Kargil, Tso Kar, Tsomo Riri, the Upper Indus Basin and Zanskar. Its legs are pink.

Groundpecker, Hume's (*Pseudopodoces humilis*) visits Ladakh in the summer, sometimes to breed. It has been seen in Chumur, in the Hanle region and near Tso Kar between June and August.

Gull, Black-headed (*Larus ridibundus*)

Gull, Brown-headed (*Larus brunnicephalus*/ Nayagar/ 42cm/ 16.5in). normally has a white head which turns brown in the breeding season. It can be seen near the water bodies of east Ladakh and the Upper Indus Basin. This is one of the first birds to reach Ladakh in summer.

Gull, Little (*Larus minutus*)

Gull, Pallas's (*Larus ichthyaetus*/ Towgarma/ 70cm/ 28in) breeds near lakes and is seen near the water bodies of east Ladakh, the Upper Indus Basin and Suru valley.

Harrier, Hen (*Circus cyaneus*)

Harrier, Montagu's (*Circus pygargus*)

Harrier, Pallid (*Circus macrourus*)

Harrier, Western/ Eurasian Marsh- (*Circus aeruginosus*) visits Lhungparma (Tangtse), Nubra, Startsapuk Tso and Tso Kar in mid-August and September and can be seen flying alone or in groups of up to two dozen birds at a time. Has sometimes been seen in June as well and likes swamps.

Heron, Black-crowned Night- (*Nycticorax nycticorax*)

Heron, Grey (*Ardea Cinerea*/ Bainlong/ 94cm/ 37in). can be seen near lakes, marshes and rivers in east Ladakh, the Upper Indus Basin and Suru Valley. Adult herons have white heads and necks, with some black on the sides and abdomens. Their bill and legs turn orange during the breeding season.

Heron, Indian Pond- *(Ardeola grayif)*

Hobby, Eurasian (*Falco Subbuteo*) is frequently seen around swamps near Shey and Rizong in summer.

Honey-Buzzard, Oriental (*Pernis ptilorhynchus*)

Hoopoe, Common (*Upupa epops*/ Hututusay, Utu-tutse, Pupuk-shele/ 30cm/ 12in). is an orange bird with a thin, downward curving bill. Seen in the grassy countryside of lower Ladakh.

Ibis, Glossy (*Plegadis falcinellus*/ Charakpa/ 52cm/ 21in). is a dark bird with a downward curving brown bill, seen near Hanle, Tsomo Riri and some water bodies of east Ladakh.

Ibisbill (*Ibidorhyncha struthersii*/ Tunglakma/ 41cm/ 16in). is a black faced bird seen, two or three birds at a time, between June and October near the banks of River Indus, especially near Shey, which is one of its breeding grounds. Some sightings have been reported in winter as well.

Jacana, Pheasant-tailed (*Hydrophasianus chirurgus*)

Jackdaw, Eurasian (*Corvus monedula*)

Jaeger, Parasitic (*Stercorarius parasiticus*): Pfister spotted a Jaeger—otherwise rarely seen in Ladakh—chasing a Brown-headed Gull in the north-west corner of Tsomo Riri in June. 'It called a loud *crae-craecrae*,' he records.

Jay, Black-headed (*Garrulus lanceolatus*)

Jay, Eurasian (*Garrulus glandarius*)

Jungle, Crow (*Corvus macrorhynchos*)

Kestrel, Common (*Falco Tinnunculus*/ Thha/ 36cm/ 14in). can be seen around the fields and grasslands of east Ladakh, Mahe, Nyoma, Shey and near the Upper Indus Basin. It builds its nest on cliffs. Both male and female kestrels have 'moustache' stripes, which are broader in the case of the males.

Kingfisher, Common or Small Blue (*Alcedo atthis*/ Ngya-Za/ 16cm/ 6in). has frequently been seen, normally alone or in a pair, often near water, in Hanle, east Ladakh. Leh, Nubra and Shey, between June and late October. It lunges vertically into the water for fish, sometimes lingering above the water before doing so.

Kite, Black (*Milvus migrans*)

Kite, Black-shouldered (*Elanus caeruleus*)

Koel, Asian (*Eudynamys scolopacea*) has been seen on sand and rocks near Hanle in June.

Lammergeiers *(Gypaetus barbatus)* are bearded vultures. They are birds of prey. They go wherever humans and other animals go. They have been sighted at altitudes of as much as 6,150 metres. The wingspan of this majestic bird can be a stunning three metres. It is because of these huge wings that they can glide on high powerful upcurrents. Some awestruck rural Ladâkhis believe, incorrectly, that this vulture can scoop up young lambs and carry them away on its gigantic wings. Lammergeiers always live close to mountains.

Lapwing, Northern (*Vanellus vanellus*)

Lapwing, Red-wattled *(Vanellus indicus)*

Lark, Asian Short-toed (*Calandrella cheleensis*)

Lark, East Calandra- (*Melanocorypha bimaculata*)

Lark, Greater Short-toed (*Calandrella brachydactyla*)

Lark, Horned (*Eremophila alpestris*/ Chipa-gut, Up-tshakir/ 18cm/ 7in). breeds in the highland pastures of east Ladakh, Nubra and Zanskar The male has horns..

Lark, Hume's Short-toed *(Calandrella acutirostris)*

Lark, Tibetan/ Long-billed Calandra- (*Melanocorypha maxima*) has been seen in good numbers—more than two dozen at a time—in Chumur between August and mid- September. It reaches Hanle, where it breeds, by June.

Laughingthrush, Streaked (*Garrulax lineatus*)

Laughingthrush, Variegated (*Garrulax variegatus*)

Linnet, Eurasian (*Carduelis cannabina*)

Magpie, Black-Billed (*Pica Pica*/ Katang-putit/ 50cm/ 20in). can be seen near Leh town, and the villages of Nubra and east Ladakh, mainly in orchards and groves. This is a black bird with a white abdomen and sides, and blue-black wings.

Magpie, Yellow-billed Blue- (*Urocissa flavirostris*)

Mallard *(Anas platyrhynchos)*: A water bird found in Ladâkhnear the Rupshu lake.

Martin, Eurasian Crag-*(Hirundo rupestris)*

Martin, Northern House-*(Delichon urbica)*

Martin, Pale *(Riparia diluta)*

Martin, Plain *(Riparia paludicola*)

Merganser, Common *(Mergus merganser)*

Merlin (*Falco columbarius*)

Monal, Himalayan: (*Lophophorus impejanus*) Found in the Ladâkh region.

Moorhen, Common (*Gallinula chloropus*)

Nightjar, European (*Caprimulgus europaeus*)

Oriole, Eurasian Golden (*Oriolus oriolus*) is frequently seen in June and July near Chumur, the Indus, Nubra and Tsomo Riri. It likes vegetation and relatively low altitudes.

Osprey (*Pandion Haliaetus*/ Nyallak Thawo/ 58cm/ 22in). looks like a big gull and is a fish eater found near rivers and lakes in the vicinity of Chumur, Chushul, Hanle and the Upper Indus Basin. It keeps its head down while flying and has big, slim wings. It breeds in the Himalayas.

Owl, Eurasian Eagle- (*Bubo Bubo*/ Ugpa/ 56 cm/ 22in). has been seen at night between June and September in Hanle, Fukche, Lalpari (which is one of its breeding grounds), Nubra, Sumdo and Tangtse, normally atop rocks or near ancient monuments. This brown and white bird has feathers on its legs.

Owl, little—Hutton's and Tibetan (*Athene noctua—bactriana* and *ludlowi* respectively/ Ugpa/ 23cm/ 9in). is a brown bird with streaks on its abdomen and crown. It has been seen between June and September in the rocky parts of Chang La, Chushul, Hanle, Nubra and Tso Kar (frequently seen near the last-mentioned lake, which is a favoured breeding area). It builds nests in the hollows of trees and on rocks. The two sub-species mentioned interbreed.

Owl, Long-eared (*Asio otus*)

Owl, Pallid Scops (*Otus brucei*): Pfister spotted a pair on the branches of a willow tree in Hanle in October after a snow shower.

Owl, Short-eared (*Asio flammeus*)

Partridge: Partridges breed at altitudes of around 5,000 metres. Along with snowcocks they are among the few species that spend their whole lives in Ladâkh, mainly in the upper reaches.

Partridge, Chukar (*Alectoris Chukar*/ Rakhpa, Strakpa/34cm/ 14in). can be seen in dry areas like Chilling, Gya, Horzey, Igoo, Kanji, Miru, Nang, Ney, Nimo, Stakmo, Phyang, Rumtse, Sumdo and parts of Kargil where grass and bushes are likely to be found. The greyish-brown bird has a white abdomen, one black strip around its white neck and another across its forehead. Male and female chukars look similar.

Partridge, Snow (*Lerwa lerwa*)

Partridge, Tibetan (*Perdix hodgsoniae*/ Shagpa-giao, De-shrak/ 30cm/ 12in). spends time in the arid and rocky areas near Chushul, Hanle, east Ladakh, Sumdo and Tso Kar. Though this bird lives in Ladakh throughout the year its population is not very widespread. One of its breeding grounds is near Hanle. It is most likely to be sighted between Hanle and Chumur where, in the fading weeks of summer, groups of two or three adult couples and their chicks moving together have frequently been spotted, often near rocks.

Pelican: A small kind of pelican is found in the marshes.

Phalarope, Red Necked (*Phalaropus lobatus*/ Jingmar/19cm/ 7.5in). is a water-loving bird seen in east Ladakh, the upper Indus Basin and the marshes of Shey. The female is bigger than the male and has a white mark above the eye.

Pigeon, Blue Rock (*Columba livia*/ Phurgon/ 33cm/ 13in). This greyish bird has wide black stripes along its inner wing and seen near the inhabited parts of Leh, Nubra and Zanskar. However, sometimes it spends time in gorges. It nests in small colonies on cliffs and crags.

Pigeon, East Stock (*Columba eversmanni*)

Pigeon, Hill *(Columba rupestris)*

Pigeon, Hill (*Columba rupestris*) is commonly found in areas like Sumdo.

Pigeon, Snow (*Columba leuconota*/ Bujul, Phurgon/ 34cm/ 13in). is frequently seen near the gorges of Changthang, Nubra, Sumdo and Zanskar. Pfister reports having spotted in September 'a strange pigeon' near Sumdo 'which looked intermediate between Hill Pigeon and Snow Pigeon.' He concluded that it was be a hybrid.

Pigeon: The *purgon* is a small field pigeon, common in Ladâkh

Pipit, Oriental Tree- (*Anthus hodgsoni*)

Pipit, Red-throated (*Anthus cervinus*)

Pipit, Rosy (*Anthus roseatus*)

Pipit, Water (*Anthus spinoletta*): Solitary birds have been spotted near Tso Kar in late September. Their plumage indicated that they were all set for winter.

Plover, Common Ringed (*Charadrius hiaticula*)

Plover, Grey (*Pluvialis squatarola*)

Plover, Kentish (*Charadrius alexandrinus*)

Plover, Lesser Sand (*Charadrius mongolus*/ Mignagtsellay/ 21cm/ 8.25in). can be seen near Chushul, Hanle, Lungparma, Tso Kar and Tsomo Riri. It breeds on dry land near lakes.

Plover, Little Ringed (*Charadrius dubius*)

Plover, Mongolian: This is a very rare bird, and one with a spellbinding act. Ladâkh is one of its few homes. Naturalists call its routine the 'distraction display.' As soon as a male plover sights a predator he acts as if he has been wounded. He lets his wings droop towards the ground, on which he straggles as if with great effort. He goes through this act in order to catch the predator's eye—and invite the predator to come and attack him. While he is doing so, his female swiftly shepherds their child away from the predator. As soon as she has done so, the male, too, flies away, leaving the predator puzzled. The Mongolian plover nests and brings up its young in July.

Plover, Pacific Golden (*Pluvialis fulva*)

Pochard, Common *(Aythya retina)* is a water bird.

Pochard, Ferruginous (*Aythya nyroca*/ Ghustat/ 42cm/ 16in). seeks the water of Tso Kar and Tsomo Riri. Its down (feather)- and grass-lined nests are found on islands at junctures where land meets water. In the breeding season the throat and breast of the male turn white.

Pochard, Red-Crested (*Netta rufina* [old name] and *Rhodonessa rufina* [new]/ Marzangmo/ 50cm/ 20in). is a duck with a broad white stripe on its wings, sometimes seen in summer in groups of two or three near little ponds in east Ladakh, Hanle, the plains below Leh town, the Leh-Kargil highway, Shey and Tsigul Tso.

Pochard, Tufted (*Aythya fuligula*)

Pratincole, Collared (*Glareola pratincola*) has been sighted on some rare occasions near the river in Shey in August and September, one or two birds at a time.

Quail, Common (*Coturnix coturnix*): Pfister spotted a solitary quail amidst buckthorn bushes in Shey in late May.

Quail, Rain (*Coturnix coromandelica*)

Rail, Water (*Rallus aquaticus*)

Raptor: Found in the upper reaches of Ladâkh,.

Raven, Common *(Corvus corax)*

Raven: The large raven (*porok*) is very frequently found in the villages. Ravens are birds of prey. They go wherever humans and other animals go. They have been sighted at altitudes of as much as 6,150 metres.

Redshank, Common (*Tringa totanus*/ Kyalechit/ 28cm/ 11in). visits marshes, lakes and rivers in east Ladakh, Nubra, Shey and Suru valley in the summer. During the breeding season the bird develops streaks on the upper body and dark patches lower down.

Redstart, Black (*Phoenicurus ochruros*/ Tsilder, Santig-nagpo/ 15cm/ 6in). has a tail that vibrates, as is common among redstarts. It breeds in the grassy portions of lower Ladakh.

Redstart, Blue-capped *(Phoenicurus coeruleocephalus)*

Redstart, Blue-fronted (*Phoenicurus frontalis*)

Redstart, Common (*Phoenicurus phoenicurus*/ Kyakchit/ 15cm/ 6in). can be seen in the wooded areas of Leh, Nubra and Suru.

Redstart, Eversmann's (*Phoenicurus erythronotus*)

Redstart, Guldenstadt's: (Phoenicurus erythrogaster) Found in the Ladâkh region.

Redstart, Hodgson's (*Phoenicurus hodgsoni*)

Redstart, White Winged (*Phoenicurus erythrogaster*/ Sintic, Santic, Tsentic/ 18cm/ 7in).: Big as redstarts go, it is found in glacial moraines and rocky meadows near Hanle, the Upper Indus Basin, Nubra, Tso Kar and Zanskar.

Redstart, White-capped Water-*(Chaimarrornis leucocephalus)*

Robin, Orange-flanked Bush- (*Tarsiger cyanurus*)

Robin, Rufous-tailed Scrub- (*Cercotrichas galactotes*)

Roller, European (*Coracias garrulus*)

Roller, Indian (*Coracias benghalensis*)

Rosefinch, Common great (*Carpodacus rubicilla*/ Lama-chipa, Ichu-gomar/ 21cm/ 9in). can be seen in the rocky, arid parts of east Ladakh, Nubra and Zanskar. It builds nests on or under stones.

Rosefinch, Red-fronted *(Carpodacus puniceus*) has been seen in June near Chushul, Lalpari, Tsigul Tso and Tsomo Riri, on grass and sand, and breeds amidst bushes.

Rosefinch, Red-mantled (*Carpodacus rhodochlamys*)

Rosefinch, see 'Finch.'

Rosefinch, White-browed (*Carpodacus thura*)

Ruby throat, White-tailed or Himalayan *(Luscinia pectoralis)*

Rubythroat, Siberian: (*Ogla mamber*) The other name of this bird means 'throat in flames.' It visits Ladâkh in large flocks.

Ruff (*Philomachus pugnax*/ Tingrilmo/ 28cm/ 11in). visits the fields and marshes of Hanle, Nubra, Shey and Tso Kar.

Sandgrouse, Tibetan (*Syrrhaptes tibetanus*/ Caling, Kagaling/ 48cm/ 19in). is a handsome, fawn and cream coloured bird. It is pale orange neck upwards. The sole pin-tailed sandgrouse in Tibet-Ladakh, it visits the region in large flocks, stays between June and September and breeds in the arid and rocky areas near Chushul, Lam Tso/ Chumur, Leh, Shey and Thikse. Flocks of between six and fifteen have been seen near Tso Kar and slightly bigger flocks—sometimes as big as forty strong—near Hanle.

Sandpiper, Common *(Actitis hypoleucos)*

Sandpiper, Curlew (*Calidris ferruginea*): Pfister spotted a solitary bird at Lalpari in August.

Sandpiper, Green (*Tringa ochropus*/ Ldokbi/ 24cm/ 10in). is known for its loud, three-note whistle when it flies. It can be seen near the shallow water bodies of Chumur, Nubra, Shey, Startsapuk Tso, Tso Kar and Tsomo Riri.

Sandpiper, Marsh (*Tringa stagnatilis*/ Tselay Ling/ 25cm/ 10in). frequents the wet areas of Shey and east Ladakh. Its belly and under wings are white. In the breeding season dark patches appear on its back.

Sandpiper, Terek (*Xenus cinereus*) .

Sandpiper, Wood (*Tringa glareola*)

Serin, Fire-fronted *(Serinus pusillus)*

Shelduck/ Sheldrake, Ruddy *(Tadorna ferruginea):* Better known as the Brahminy Duck.

Shoveller, Northern (*Anas clypeata*/ Khamchu Kham/ 50cm/ 20in). can be seen near shallow water bodies in east Ladakh, Nubra, Shey, Suru and Tsigul Tso. Its breast and tail are white and the rest mainly black.

Shrike, Grey-backed *(Lanius tephronotus)*

Shrike, Lesser Grey (*Lanius minor*)

Shrike, Long-tailed/ Rufous-backed *(Lanius schach)*

Shrike, Red-backed (*Lanius collurio*)

Shrike, Rufous-backed (*Lanius schach*)

Shrike, Rufous-tailed (*Lanius isabellinus*)

Shrike, Southern Grey (*Lanius meridionalis*)

Skylark, Oriental/ East *(Alauda gulgula)*

Snipe, Common (*Gallinago gallinago*/ Tingtilling/ 25cm/ 10in). likes the marshes of Shey and Nubra. Its bill is long and its wings white from below.

Snipe, Pintail (*Gallinago stenura*)

Snipe, Solitary (*Gallinago solitaria*)

Snowcock, Himalayan (*Tetraogallus Himalayensis*/ Ribja/ 72cm/ 28in). is a grey, black and white bird that can be seen in groups of four to eight, scraping hillsides in Dras, Ganda-La, the Hemis National Park, Rumbak valley, Suru, Zanskar and parts of Kargil. It can be heard around daybreak

Snowcock, Tibetan (*Tetraogallus tibetanus*/ Ticok, Te-ok, Congmo/ 50cm/ 20in). can be seen in summer as well as autumn near important passes like Chang La and Taklang La as well as Hanle. In winter it comes down to 3,000 m./ 10,000ft. The adult bird has black stripes on a white base. As will be seen, the two snowcocks occupy different habitats.

Snowcocks, Himalayan and Tibetan, *(Tetraogallus* sp).: These are large and majestic birds that spend the entire year—indeed, their whole lives—in Ladâkh. Therefore, humans as well as predatory animals hunt them for their meat.

Snowfinch, Mandelli's (*Pyrgilauda taczanowskii*)

Snowfinch, Plain-backed (*Pyrgilauda blanfordi*) breeds in the slim tunnels dug in the ground by little animals like marmots and normally lines the nest with feathers and hair. It is frequently seen in the Tso Kar area between June and early September.

Snowfinch, Tibetan (*Montifringilla adamsi*)

Sparrow, House *(Passer domesticus)*

Sparrow, Spanish (*Passer hispaniolensis*)

Sparrowhawk, Eurasian (*Accipiter Nisus*): Solitary birds have been seen among trees and rocks near Hanle and Rizong between early June and October.

Starling, Brahminy *(Sturnus pagodarum)*

Starling, Rosy (*Sturnus roseus*)

Starts, red: Visits Ladâkh in large flocks.

Stilt, Black-Winged (*Himantopus himantopus*/ Tabia/ 32cm/ 13in). has long pink legs and white plumage and frequents the water bodies—include dirty ponds—of east Ladakh, Nubra, Shey and Suru.

Stint, Little (*Calidris minuta*)

Stint, Temminck's (*Calidris temminckii*)

Stonechat, Common (*Saxicola torquata*)

Stork, Black (*Ciconia nigra*) has been seen on the grass near Tso Kar in June.

Swallow, Barn *(Hirundo rustica)*

Swallow, Red-rumped (*Hirundo daurica*)

Swallow, sea: See 'Tern.'

Swallow, Wire-tailed *(Hirundo smithii)*

Swift, Alpine (*Tachymarptis melba*/ Kalakukti/ 22cm/ 9in). is mostly brown and seen near the cliffs of Dras, east Ladakh and Suru.

Swift, Common *(Apus apus)*

Swift, Fork-tailed *(Apus pacificus)*

Swift, House (*Apus affinis*)

Teal, Common (*Anas crecca*)

Teal: This is a water bird found in Ladâkh near the Rupshu lake. Even more likely to be found near the bigger rivers.

Tern, Arctic (*Sterna paradisaea*)

Tern, Common (*Sterna hirundo*/ Niaza/ 36cm/ 14in). is seen around water in Chushul, Hanle, Pangong Tso, Tso Kar and Tsomo Riri. In the breeding season its bill and legs turn orange-red.

Tern, Gull-billed (*Gelochelidon nilotica*)

Tern, Little (*Sterna albifrons*)

Tern, Whiskered *(Chlidonias hybridus)*

Tern, White-winged Black- (*Chlidonias leucopterus*): Seen in June between Startsapuk Tso and its neighbour, Tso Kar.

Thrush, black-throated: (*Turdus ruficollis*) It visits the Ladâkh region. Interestingly, it 'winters' in this region.

Thrush, Blue Rock *(Monticola solitarius)*

Thrush, Blue Whistling *(Myophonus caeruleus)*

Thrush, Dusky (*Turdus naumanni*)

Thrush, Rufous-tailed Rock- (*Monticola saxatilis*)

Thrush, Song (*Turdus philomelos*)

Thrush, Tickell's (*Turdus unicolor*)

Tit, Eurasian Penduline (*Remiz pendulinus*)

Tit, Fire-capped (*Cephalopyrus flammiceps*)

Tit, Great *(Parus major)*

Tit, Green-backed (*Parus monticolus*)

Tit, Simla Crested (*Parus rufonuchalis*)

Tit, Yellow-browed (*Sylviparus modestus*)

Treecreeper, Bar-tailed (*Certhia himalayana*)

Turnstone, Ruddy (*Arenaria interpres*/ Tangnak Ldogbi/ 23cm/ 9in). has distinct white lines on its wings and back, and a broad black stripe on its tail. It likes the rocks around Tso Kar, Tsomo Riri and Tsigul Tso (in Chushul) and dry areas within these lakes.

Twite *(Carduelis flavirostris)*

Vulture, Bearded *or* Lammergeier (*Gypaetus Barbatus*/ Skiaklag, Tangcar/115 cm/ 45in). prefers the inhabited areas and garbage heaps of Chushul, Hanle, Loma, Lungparma, Nyoma, Puga, Suru and Tso Kar. It has a black mask and beard on a white head.

Vulture, Cinereous (*Aegypius monachus*)

Vulture, Egyptian (*Neophron percnopterus*)

Wagtail, Citrine (*Motacilla citreola*/ Sterzi, Star-zee/ 19cm/ 7in). is seen in the wet grasslands of Drass, east Ladakh and Nubra. Its 'nest is a compact cup, made of dry grass, rootlets and moss; placed on the ground under a bush, stone or grass' (Chandan, Abbas and Gautam).

Wagtail, Forest (*Dendronanthus indicus*): Pfister notes having watched a solitary bird 'feeding near the spring on the southern edge of Startsapuk Tso' in the course of four days in early June.

Wagtail, Grey *(Motacilla cinerea)*

Wagtail, Large Pied (*Motacilla maderaspatensis*)

Wagtail, White *(Motacilla alba)*

Wagtail, Yellow *(Motacilla flava)*

Wallcreeper (*Tichodroma muraria*) has been sighted in small numbers near Hundar, Panamik, Rizong, Rumbak and Sumdo between June and mid- September.

Warbler, Black-browed Reed- (*Acrocephalus bistrigiceps*)

Warbler, Blyth's Reed- (*Acrocephalus dumetorum*)

Warbler, Dusky (*Phylloscopus fuscatus*)

Warbler, Garden (*Sylvia borin*)

Warbler, Greenish Leaf- (*Phylloscopus trochiloides*)

Warbler, Hume's *(Phylloscopus humel)*

Warbler, Large-billed Leaf- (*Phylloscopus magnirostris*)

Warbler, Long-billed Bush- (*Bradypterus major*)

Warbler, Paddyfield (*Acrocephalus agricola*)

Warbler, Plain Leaf- (*Phylloscopus neglectus*)

Warbler, Sedge (*Acrocephalus schoenobaenus*)

Warbler, Stoliczka's Tit- (*Leptopoecile sophiae*)

Warbler, Sulphur-bellied or Olivaceous Leaf- (*Phylloscopus griseolus*)

Warbler, Tickell's leaf *(Phylloscopus affinis)*

Warbler, Tytler's Leaf- (*Phylloscopus tytleri*)

Water birds: Their biggest concentration in Ladâkhis near the Rupshu lakes, at altitudes of 14,000' and more. Please also see individual entries in this chapter. (See also 'Hunting' in the chapter on 'Adventure Sports').

Waterfowl: Every species of waterfowl is to be found in Kashmîr, and in plenty, in winter when they come down from the colder Yârqañd and Mughalistan. They leave when spring begins. In Ladâkh some species are found in the wetlands.

Wheatear, Desert (*Oenanthe deserti*/ Chiu-logzi/ 15cm/ 6in). has a tail that is mostly black. It breeds on rocks in the arid parts of east Ladakh, Suru and Zanskar.

Wheatear, Hume's (*Oenanthe alboniger*)

Wheatear, Isabelline (*Oenanthe isabellina*)

Wheatear, Pied *(Oenanthe pleschanka)*

Wheatear, Variable *(Oenanthe picata)*

Wheeler: Visits Ladâkh in large flocks.

Whimbrel (*Numenius phaeopus*)

Whitethroat, Greater (*Sylvia communis*)

Whitethroat, lesser *(Sylvia curruca)*

Wigeon, Eurasian (*Anas Penelope*/ Gobrak pa/ 48 cm/ 19in). is a duck with an orange head that has sometimes been seen in shallow water bodies like the marshes of Shey, and Tso Kar.

Woodpecker, Large Scaly-bellied Green (*Picus squamatus*)

Wren, Winter *(Troglodytes troglodytes)*

Wryneck, Eurasian *(Jynx torquilla)*

Wryneck, Eurasian (*Jynx torquilla*) was spotted by Pfister in late September near Tso Kar.

Yellowhammer (*Emberiza citronella*)

References

1 Chandan, Pankaj, Abbas, Mohd. ' and Gautam, Parikshit, *Field Guide: Birds of Ladakh*, WWF India, is the main source of the Ladakhi names of birds and their length (in centimetres).

2 Pfister, Otto, Birds recorded during visits to Ladakh, India, from 1994 to 1997, *Forktail* 17 (2001): 81-90, http://www.orientalbirdclub.org/publications/forktail/17pdfs/Pfister-Ladakh.pdf

3 The names of the other birds have been collected over a period of time from a variety of sources, dating from British explorers' sightings in the 1800s to observations in the 1990s.

Chapter- 10

The Flora of Ladâkh-'Gilgit-Baltistan'

There are around 880 species of flora (angiosperms, gymnosperms and pteridophytes) in the parts of Ladâkh that are under actual Indian administration.[i] (Kashmir has 3,054 species and Jammu district 506). I have tried to list such plants, trees and flowers as grow in undivided Ladâkh and Gilgit, including Baltistân, Hunzâ and Astore. If those species grow in other parts of Jammu and Kashmîr (and adjacent areas), I have mentioned that as well.[1]

Ladâkh proper is an alpine (and, at places, arctic) desert. There is hardly any rainfall, snowfall or moisture in most parts of Leh district and only a little more in Kargil-Zanskar. This affects the vegetation of the region. Ladâkh proper is mostly a treeless desert. However, some plants grow along the banks of rivers and in the moist crevices of rocks. But within deserts there are oases. So, the flora of Ladâkh can be put in three broad categories: alpine, desertic and oasitic.

The alpine vegetation of Ladâkh includes several species that are also found in Kashmîr. Desert (or desertic) flora is mostly found at altitudes, especially barren mountain slopes, that are much higher than the plains of

1. The Râvi, the Chénâb and the Jehlum are the three big rivers of the state. (None of the three flows through Ladâkh.)

Ladâkh. This kind of vegetation has Tibetan and Siberian elements, is normally stunted and forms tufts. The vegetation of the oases grows along streams, rivulets and village ponds.

Many of the plants that grow in Ladâkh do so only when planted by men. Which means that they do not grow wild, on their own. These crops include barley, gram, lentils, onion, pea, potato and wheat.

Tree species introduced by humans in Ladâkh include apricot, mulberry, walnut and willow.[2] The government has brought in some species of salix and populus because they yield fodder and fuel. Small patches of the native Juniperus macropoda Boiss are also found in some places.

In Ladâkh alpine vegetation grows mainly in small, confined strips of territory to which some of the melting snow water flows down. The upper beds of mountain streams, too, have alpine vegetation.

Temperatures fluctuate wildly over the months, and often even during the course of a single day. Thus, most of the inhabited parts of Ladâkh could be as hot as 38°C in summer and minus 30°C in winter. Similarly, in summer it could be 38°C at noon and around 10°C at night. As a result, rocks start cracking up and mountains crumble. Therefore, 'rock ruin' is common in Ladâkh.

Most of the areas of Ladâkh-Gilgit under Pâkistâni occupation are similar to the ones administered by India. So is the Lahaul-Spiti region of neighbouring Himachal Pradesh. However, some parts of Pâkistân Occupied Ladâkh-Gilgit are greener and are in the temperate zone.

There are several high altitude (4,000 metres plus) lakes in Ladâkh (and in the Pir Panjal Range). Unlike lakes which are at lower altitudes, these lakes have no macro-phytic vegetation. There are twenty-six hotpots in India where rapid deforestation and 'endemicity' are taking place. Ladâkh (like Kashmîr and, indeed, the entire Himâlayas) is among this unfortunate twenty-six. Several species are endangered and will vanish unless all of us—residents as well as tourists—mend our ways.

Medicinal plants: Medicinal flowers are gathered only at mid-day, by hand, by the stem and carried in baskets. They should never be collected in the morning or cut mechanically (which includes the use of scissors and shears). The petals should never be touched and the plants should never be put in polythene or other synthetic bags.

2. This sentence is on the authority of a leading botanist. However, apricot and willow, to the best of my knowledge as a historian, are native to several parts of Ladakh, especially Kargil and Hunzâ.

A representative list is given below. The local name (in Ladâkhi and/ or Urdu-Persian) has often been given in italics, within brackets. The Ladâkhi name might be understood in Baltistân but the Urdu-Persian name will not be understood in Ladâkh. Urdu-Persian names are mainly used in the areas occupied by Pâkistân.

Acantholimon Iycopodioides (*Girard*) Boiss (*Longze*): This is a rare and endangered medicinal plant species found on hill slopes in Ladâkh.

Achillea millefolium L (*Gul-é-Biranjasif/ Chuang*) Flowers in August-March. Grows in Ladâkh, Gilgit, Swât, Poonch, Medicinal property: hypotensive and haemostatic. Arrests bleeding.

Achyranthes aspera L (*Gul-é-Charchitâ*) Flowers in September-April found in Gilgit. Used for bleeding piles.

Aconitum balfourii Stapf (*Bonga nakpo*): This is a rare and endangered medicinal plant species found in Ladâkh.

Aconitum heterophyllum (*Buma*): This is a rare and endangered medicinal plant species found in Ladâkh.

Achillea millefolium L

Achyranthes aspera L

Aconitum balfourii Stapf

Aconitum heterophyllum

Aconitum rotundifolium (*Bonkar*): This is a rare and endangered medicinal plant species found in Ladâkh.

Aconitum violaceum (*Yangtso; zinba; dusi-lama*): This is a rare and endangered medicinal plant species found in Ladâkh.

Actinocarya tibetica This is a medicinal plant species found in Ladâkh.

Adonis chrysocyathus (*Semshi*): This is a medicinal plant species found in Ladâkh.

Allium carolinianum (*Gogcheegma*): This is a medicinal plant species found in Ladâkh.

Allium humile Kunth (*Pocha*): This is a medicinal plant species found in Ladâkh.

Althaea officinalis L (*Gul-é-Khairo*) Flowers in July-October. Grows in the Muzaffarâbâd region, Medicinal property: demulcent, diuretic, emmolient. Used in the treatment of bronchial catarrh and rheumatism.

Anaphalis contorta (*Telgang*): This is a rare and endangered medicinal plant species found in Ladâkh.

Anaphalis cuneifolia (*Simula*): This is a medicinal plant species found in Ladâkh.

Anaphalis nepalensis (*Tawa*): This is a medicinal plant species found in Ladâkh.

Anaphalis nubigena DC. Grows in the alpine parts of Ladâkh (and in Kashmîr).

Anaphalis triplinervis (*Phulu mentock*): This is a medicinal plant species found in Ladâkh.

Androsace aizoon (*Sgatik mugpo*): This is a medicinal plant species found in Ladâkh.

Androsace mucronifolia (*Zigsolo*): This is a medicinal plant species found in Ladâkh.

Androsace rotundifolia (*Zigsolo*): This is a medicinal plant species found in Ladâkh.

Anemone rivularis (*Zupka*): This is a medicinal plant species found in Ladâkh.

Anemone rupicola (*Simaso*): This is a medicinal plant species found in Ladâkh.

Aquilegia fragrans (*Zadul-dorje*): This is a medicinal plant species found in Ladâkh.

Arabidopsis multiforum (*Imatso*): This is a medicinal plant species found in Ladâkh.

Arabis glandulosa (*Umnako*): This is a medicinal plant species found in Ladâkh.

Arctium lappa (*Miah*): This is a medicinal plant species found in Ladâkh.

Arenaria bryophylla (*Lekhum*): This is a medicinal plant species found in Ladâkh.

Arenaria griffithii (*Sokhtam*): This is a medicinal plant species found in Ladâkh.

Arenaria serpyllifolia L Grows in the cold deserts of Ladâkh.

Arnebia banthamii Johnston (*Gul-é-Afsantin*) Flowers in October-November. Grows in Kâghân, Poonch. Medicinal property: stomachic, tonic and vermifuge.

Arnebia euchroma (*Demok*): This is a rare and endangered medicinal plant species found in Ladâkh. The root, when soaked in (say, mustard) oil, colours the oil red. If applied to the hair, it is said to improve the health of the hair.

Artemisia biennis (*Khampa*): This is a medicinal plant species found in Ladâkh.

Artemisia brevifolia (*Khamchu*): This is a medicinal plant species found in Ladâkh.

Artemisia desertorum (*Khamlol*): This is a medicinal plant species found in Ladâkh.

Artemisia dracunculus (*Burtse*): This is a medicinal plant species found in Ladâkh.

Artemisia gmelinii (*Khampa or shridhi*): This is a medicinal plant species found in Ladâkh.

Artemisia laciniata (*Bintso*): This is a medicinal plant species found in Ladâkh.

Artemisia maritima: Found in Ladâkh.

Artemisia maritima L (*Gul-é-Kashmîrî/ Khamchu*) Flowers in August-September. Grows in Ladâkh, Astore, Chitrâl, Swât. Used in the treatment of cardiac problems, fever, and ailments of the throat and tongue. This is a rare and endangered species.

Artemisia maritime (*Phurnag*): This is a medicinal plant species found in Ladâkh.

Artemisia minor (*Phurnag*): This is a medicinal plant species found in Ladâkh.

Artemisia moarcroftiana (*Phurnag*): This is a medicinal plant species found in Ladâkh.

Artemisia parviflora (*Khamang*): This is a medicinal plant species found in Ladâkh.

Artemisia salsalaides (*Amango*): This is a medicinal plant species found in Ladâkh.

Artemisia scoparia (*Khamtso*): This is a medicinal plant species found in Ladâkh.

Artemisia sieversiana (*Khamchu*): This is a medicinal plant species found in Ladâkh.

Artemisia stracheyi (*Rumonlo*): This is a medicinal plant species found in Ladâkh.

Artemisia stricta Edgew Grows in the cold deserts of Ladâkh.

Aster diplostephiodes (*Ba-sha-ka* or *Luqchunq*)

Aster flaccidus (*Lugmig, Chunwa:* small): This is a medicinal plant species found in Ladâkh.

Aster strachey (*Lugmig metura*): This is a medicinal plant species found in Ladâkh.

Astragalus rhizanthus (*Sarma*): This is a medicinal plant species found in Ladâkh.

Astragalus spp. Grows in the cold deserts of Ladâkh.

Astragalus strictus (*Serpang*): This is a medicinal plant species found in Ladâkh.

Astragalus thizanthus Royle ex Senth: Grows in the alpine parts of Ladâkh (and in Kashmîr).

Astragalus tribulifolia (*Vanglo*): This is a medicinal plant species found in Ladâkh.

Atelanthera perpusilla: This is a medicinal plant species found in Ladâkh.

Berberis pachyacantha: Grows on alpine slopes and in sheltered ravines in Ladâkh.

Berberis zabe (*Sherpa*): This is a medicinal plant species found in Ladâkh.

Bergenia stracheyi (*Dak-kya-hawo, gatikpa*): This is a rare and endangered medicinal plant species found in Ladâkh.

Betula utilis (*Takpa*): This is a rare and endangered medicinal plant species found in Ladâkh.

Biebersteinia odora (*Khardung*): This is a medicinal plant species found in Ladâkh.

Bistorta affinis (*Langna*): This is a medicinal plant species found in Ladâkh.

Bistorta vivipara (*Naram, Langangpa*): This is a medicinal plant species found in Ladâkh.

Blumea bifoliata (*Leuman*): This is a medicinal plant species found in Ladâkh.

Bupleurum himalayense (*Sah-kuchak*): This is a medicinal plant species found in Ladâkh.

Bupleurum marginatum (*Zira-sherpo*): This is a medicinal plant species found in Ladâkh.

C. wallichii DO: Grows on hill slopes in Ladâkh.

Capparis spinosa: Found in shrublands and patchy forests at the bottom of valleys.

Capsella bursa-pastoris (*Zokka*): This is a medicinal plant species found in Ladâkh.

Caragana gerardiana (*Zomosing*): This is a medicinal plant species found in Ladâkh.

Caragana versicolor (*Loosing*): This is a medicinal plant species found in Ladâkh.

Caragana versicolor Benth Grows on hill slopes in Ladâkh.

Carum bulbocastanum (*Gosnyod*): This is a medicinal plant species found in Ladâkh.

Carum carvi (*Gonyot*): This is a medicinal plant species found in Ladâkh.

Centauria picris (*Konpa, Iqabskves*): This is a medicinal plant species found in Ladâkh.

Cerastium cerastoides (*Spangian, kamo, panqien*): This is a medicinal plant species found in Ladâkh.

Chenopodium botrys (*Sanyek*): This is a medicinal plant species found in the cold deserts of Ladâkh.

Chenopodium foliolosum (*Sanyek*): This is a medicinal plant species found in Ladâkh.

Chenopodium hybridum (*Sanyek*): This is a medicinal plant species found in Ladâkh.

Christolea crassifolia This is a medicinal plant species found in Ladâkh.

Chrysanthemum cinerarifolium (*Gul-é-Dâwoodi*): Flowers in March-July. Grows in Abbotâbâd Medicinal property: aperient. Used in the treatment of sore eyes, upset stomach.

Chrysanthemum griffithi (*Serpan*): This is a medicinal plant species found in Ladâkh.

Chrysanthemum pyrethroides (*Serpan; bhurse-khampa*): This is a medicinal plant species found in Ladâkh.

Chrysanthemum tibeticum (Hk f and Th. ex Cl). (*Jerium, Phemantso*): This is a medicinal plant species found on hill slopes in Ladâkh.

Circium arvense (L) Scop *(Soh-chlia):* This is a medicinal plant species found on hill slopes in Ladâkh.

Circium wallichii (*Kakar*): This is a medicinal plant species found in Ladâkh.

Clematis orientalis (*Emong nakpo*): This is a medicinal plant species found in Ladâkh.

Clematis tibetina (*Zakzic*): This is a medicinal plant species found in Ladâkh.

Codonopsis clematidea (*Ludut dorje*): This is a medicinal plant species found in Ladâkh.

Codonopsis ovata This is a medicinal plant species found in Ladâkh.

Codonopsis rotundifolia (*Klupdud dorje*): This is a medicinal plant species found in Ladâkh.

Conringia planisiliqua (*Khaskar*): This is a medicinal plant species found in Ladâkh.

Convolvulus arvensis (*Grachi*): This is a medicinal plant species found in Ladâkh.

Corispermum hyssopifolium (*Seimso*): This is a medicinal plant species found in Ladâkh.

Corydalis diphylla L Grows in the alpine parts of Ladâkh (and in Kashmîr).

Corydalis govaniana (*Tongru-silva*): This is a medicinal plant species found in Ladâkh.

Corydalis meifolia (*Tonzil*): This is a medicinal plant species found in Ladâkh.

Corydalis rutifolia (*Chimlo*): This is a medicinal plant species found in Ladâkh.

Corydalis tibetica (*Stong zil*): This is a medicinal plant species found in Ladâkh.

Cousinia thomsonii (*Chansar; nag po; batsatsuak*): This is a medicinal plant species found in Ladâkh.

Cremanthodium arnicoides (*Rekonpa*): This is a medicinal plant species found in Ladâkh.

Cremanthodium ellisii (*Dariya kan*): This is a rare and endangered medicinal plant species found in Ladâkh.

Crepis flexuosa (*Remang*): This is a medicinal plant species found in Ladâkh.

Crepis stoliczkai Cl.: Grows on hill slopes in Ladâkh.

Crocus sativus: This is a medicinal plant species found in Ladâkh.

Cuscuta approximata (*Amarlata*): This is a medicinal plant species found in Ladâkh.

Cuscuta capitata (*Amarlata*): This is a medicinal plant species found in Ladâkh.

Cuscuta europaea (*Amarlata*): This is a medicinal plant species found in Ladâkh.

Cuscuta reflexa (*Amarlata*): This is a medicinal plant species found in Ladâkh.

Cymbopogon jwarancusa Schult. (*Gul-é-Khawi*): Flowers in July-October. Grows in Chitrâl, Gilgit. Medicinal property: blood purifier, styptic and tonic.

Dactylorhiza hatagirea (*Sanchu; angbolakpa, wanoluk*): This is a rare and endangered medicinal plant species found in Ladâkh.

Daphne mucronate: This is a medicinal plant species found in Ladâkh.

Delphinium brunonianum (*Lunde-kaown*): This is a medicinal plant species found in Ladâkh.

Delphinium brunonianum (*Lunde-kaown*): This is a rare and endangered medicinal plant species found in Ladâkh.

Delphinium cashmerianum (*Lunde-kaown; cha-gotpa*): This is a rare and endangered medicinal plant species found above 4,500 metres in Ladâkh.

Delphinium cashmerianum Royle: Grows in the alpine parts of Ladâkh (and in Kashmîr).

Delphinium viscosum (*Bilamonokh*): This is a medicinal plant species found in Ladâkh.

Descurainia sophia (*Teri-latchij*): This is a medicinal plant species found in Ladâkh.

Dianthus anatolicus: Grows in Ladâkh.

Dianthus anatolicus Boiss: This is a medicinal plant species found in the cold deserts of Ladâkh.

Dioscorea deltoidea: Grows mainly in Kashmîr and Jammu. Its tubers are rich in diosgenin and yield cortisone, a steroid hormone.

Dracocephalum heterophyllum (*Zinkzer, driangu, priyanku*): This is a medicinal plant species found in Ladâkh.

Dracocephalum moldavicum (*Kirmir*): This is a medicinal plant species found in Ladâkh.

Dracocephalum staminium (*Ghiromanko*): This is a medicinal plant species found in Ladâkh.

Drumm. (*Gyamobdebyin*): This is a medicinal plant species found in Ladâkh.

Echinops cornigerus (*Ekzema*): This is a medicinal plant species found in Ladâkh.

Echinops niveus (*Ekzema*): This is a medicinal plant species found in Ladâkh.

Ephedra gerardiana (*Chhapat; tse*): This is a rare and endangered medicinal plant species found in Ladâkh.

Ephedra gerardiana Wall. ex Royle: Grows on hill slopes in Ladâkh.

Epilobium angustifolium. (*Utpal-wanbo*): This is a medicinal plant species found in Ladâkh.

Epipactis helleborine (*Penginlo*): This is a medicinal plant species found in Ladâkh.

Equisetum spp.: Grows near water bodies/ oases in Ladâkh.

Eragrostis poaeoides (*Gieng*): This is a medicinal plant species found in Ladâkh.

Erigeron alpinus (*Repan*): This is a medicinal plant species found in Ladâkh.

Eriobotrya japonica Lindley (*Gul-é-Lokât*) Flowers in July-August. Grows in the sub-Himâlayan Zone Medicinal property: Its flowers are expectorants.

Eritricum canam (*Changser, tukse*): This is a medicinal plant species found in Ladâkh.

Ermania lanuginosa (*Measlo*): This is a medicinal plant species found in Ladâkh.

Erodium tibetanum: This is a medicinal plant species found in Ladâkh.

Euphorbia stracheyi (*Tingling*): This is a medicinal plant species found in Ladâkh.

Euphorbia tibetica (*Tingling*): This is a medicinal plant species found in Ladâkh.

Euphrasia laxa (*Kianglo*): This is a medicinal plant species found in Ladâkh.

Ferula jaeschkeana (*Thunak, risho*):This is a rare and endangered medicinal plant species found in Ladâkh.

Fritillaria roylei: (*Chikmo*): This is a rare and endangered medicinal plant species found in Ladâkh.

Galium boreale L.: Grows in the alpine parts of Ladâkh (and in Kashmîr).

Galium pauciflorum (*Phomongo*): This is a medicinal plant species found in Ladâkh.

Galium serpilloides (*Pemantso*): This is a medicinal plant species found in Ladâkh.

Gentiana algida (*Pungen carpov*): This is a medicinal plant species found in Ladâkh.

Gentiana carinata (*Ziang*): This is a medicinal plant species found in Ladâkh.

Gentiana decumbense L.: Grows near water bodies/ oases in Ladâkh.

Gentiana kurrooa (*Pangyin*): This is a rare and endangered medicinal plant species found in Ladâkh.

Gentiana nubigena (*Pangyin*): This is a medicinal plant species found in Ladâkh.

Gentiana olivieri (*Khilche nagpo*): This is a medicinal plant species found in Ladâkh.

Gentiana squarrosa (*Ziang*): This is a medicinal plant species found in Ladâkh.

Gentiana stracheyi (*Ziang*): This is a medicinal plant species found in Ladâkh.

Gentianella moorcroftiana (*Teekta*): This is a medicinal plant species found in Ladâkh.

Gentianella paludosa (*Pallutso*): This is a medicinal plant species found in Ladâkh.

Gentianopsis detonsa (*Shiti*): This is a medicinal plant species found in Ladâkh.

Geranium pratens Linn (*Gagchuk; ngon-boo*): Grows in the alpine parts of Ladâkh (and in Kashmîr) and near water bodies/ oases in Ladâkh.

Geranium sibiricum (*Eyamlomentok*): This is a rare and endangered medicinal plant species found in Ladâkh.

Geranium tuberaria (*Yusiang*): This is a medicinal plant species found in Ladâkh.

GiGer microphyllum. (*Seri-jriboo*): This is a medicinal plant species found in Ladâkh.

Glechoma tibetica: Grows above 4,500 metres in Ladâkh.

Gnaphalium affine (*Gandha pattra*): This is a medicinal plant species found in Ladâkh.

Gnaphalium stewartii (*Peo*): This is a medicinal plant species found in Ladâkh.

Halepestes tricuspis: This is a medicinal plant species found in Ladâkh.

Heracieum pinnatum Cl: Grows in the cold deserts of Ladâkh.

Heracleum lanatum (*Tunak, tukar*): This is a rare and endangered medicinal plant species found in Ladâkh.

Herminium monorchis: This is a rare and endangered medicinal plant species found in Ladâkh.

Hibiscus cannabinus L (*Gul-é-Ambari*): Flowers in autumn-winter. Grows in Swât, Chitrâl. Used in the treatment of Gastritis and constipation.

Hippophae rhamnoides (*Tar-ngoo, starbu, zino*): This is a rare and endangered medicinal plant species found in Ladâkh. It is found in shrublands and patchy forests at the bottom of valleys. See 'Seabuckthorn' below.

Hippuris vulgaris L: Grows in the cold deserts of Ladâkh.

Humulus lupulus L (*Gul-é-Junjul*): Flowers in July-August. Grows in Ladâkh, Pangi on the upper Chenab. Medicinal property: antiseptic, stomach tonic diuretic. Used in the treatment of hardness of uterus, female inflorescence (hop) and swellings.

Hyoscyamus niger (*Thangdum, langtang-tse*): This is a rare and endangered medicinal plant species found in Ladâkh.

Hypericum leptocarpus (*Meerang*): This is a medicinal plant species found in Ladâkh.

Hyssopus officinalis L (*Gul-é-Zoffâ/ Jip-chi, chibu*): Flowers in June-September. This is a medicinal plant species found in Ladâkh, Kashmir, Pangi, Upper Chenab. Used in the treatment of chest congestions. A 'tea' made of its flowers is an expectorant.

Impatiens balsamina L (*Gul-é-Mehñdiâ*): Flowers in July-October. Grows in Chitrâl, Medicinal property: antibiotic. Used in the treatment of intercostal neuralgia and lumbago.

Impatiens glandulifera Royle: Grows in the alpine parts of Ladâkh (and in Kashmîr).

Iniula rhizocephala (*Riamko*): This is a medicinal plant species found in Ladâkh.

Inula racemosa (*Manu*): This is a rare and endangered medicinal plant species found in Ladâkh.

Inula royleana (*Ukchha*): This is a medicinal plant species found in Ladâkh.

Iris ensata (*Banpiaj*): This is a medicinal plant species found in Ladâkh.

Juglans regiaL. (*Akhrot*): This is a medicinal plant species found in Ladâkh.

Juniperus communis (*Shukpa*): This is a rare and endangered medicinal plant species found in Ladâkh.

Juniperus macropoda and J. indica: Found in steppe juniper forests in small patches on cliffs and sloping land.

Juniperus macropoda Boiss: Grows in very small quantities in some parts of the Ladâkhi desert.

Juniperus polycarpus: Grows on alpine slopes and in sheltered ravines in Ladâkh.

Juniperus recurva (*Shukpa*): This is a rare and endangered medicinal plant species found in Ladâkh.

Jurinea ceratocarpa (*Chholmong*): This is a medicinal plant species found in Ladâkh.

Koelpinia linearis (*Nodar*): This is a medicinal plant species found in Ladâkh.

Lactuca serriola (*Dudej*): This is a medicinal plant species found in Ladâkh.

Lagotis kunawurensis (*Tsermo*): This is a medicinal plant species found in Ladâkh.

Lancea tibetica (*Payak-tsa*): This is a rare and endangered medicinal plant species found in Ladâkh.

Lavatera kashmiriana Camb: Grows in the alpine parts of Ladâkh and Kashmîr.

Leontopodium nanum (Hk.f. and Th). Hand.-Mazz. (*Palu*): This is a medicinal plant species found on hill slopes in Ladâkh.

Leontopodium nanum: Grows in Ladâkh.

Lepidium latifolium (*Shangshu*): This is a medicinal plant species found in Ladâkh.

Leucas aspera Spreng. (*Gul-é-Tumbâ*): Flowers in August-February. Grows in Jammu, Ravi, Chenab, Used in the treatment of children's coughs and colds.

Leucopoa albida (*Fukche*): This is a medicinal plant species found in Ladâkh.

LIoydia serafina: (*Kangkar; tsa-awa, anwa*): This is a rare and endangered medicinal plant species found in Ladâkh.

lnula falconeri (Hk.f).**:** Grows on hill slopes in Ladâkh.

Lomatogonium rotatum (*Tsemrang*): This is a medicinal plant species found in Ladâkh.

Lonicera spinosa (*Lamora*): This is a medicinal plant species found in Ladâkh.

Loontopodium spp: Grows in the alpine parts of Ladâkh (and in Kashmîr).

Lotus corniculatus L: Grows in the alpine parts of Ladâkh (and in Kashmîr).

Luppula barbata: This is a medicinal plant species found in Ladâkh.

Lychnis nutans (*Lappu*): This is a medicinal plant species found in Ladâkh.

Lycium ruthenicum (*Umila*): This is a medicinal plant species found in Ladâkh, in shrublands and patchy forests at the bottom of valleys.

Malva sylvestris. (*Sotsal*): This is a medicinal plant species found in Ladâkh.

Malva verticillala (*Chirati*): This is a medicinal plant species found in Ladâkh.

Marrubium vulgare (*Trapper*): This is a medicinal plant species found in Ladâkh.

Mattiastrum thomsonii: This is a medicinal plant species found in Ladâkh.

Meconopsis aculeata (*Serhun, tsenmon*): This is a medicinal plant species found in Ladâkh.

Meconopsis aculeata (*Serhun, tsergnon*): This is a rare and endangered medicinal plant species found in Ladâkh.

Meconopsis horridula (*Udpalsnogpo*): This is a medicinal plant species found in Ladâkh.

Meconopsis simplicifolia (*Udpalsnogpo*): This is a medicinal plant species found in Ladâkh.

Meconopsls sinuate (*Udpalsnogpo*): This is a medicinal plant species found in Ladâkh.

Medicago lupulina (*Gunyok*): This is a medicinal plant species found in Ladâkh.

Melica persica (*Tandi*): This is a medicinal plant species found in Ladâkh.

Mentha longifolia (*Phololing*): This is a medicinal plant species found in Ladâkh.

Mertensia tibetica: Grows on alpine slopes and in sheltered ravines in Ladâkh.

Mirabilis jalapa L (*Gul-é-Abbâs*): Flowers in November-January. Grows in Hunzâ, Gilgit. Used in the treatment of haemarrhoids.

Morina coulteriana (*Khundaj, kare*): This is a medicinal plant species found in Ladâkh.

Morina longifolia (*Biskandara*): This is a medicinal plant species found in Ladâkh.

Myricaria elegans: Found in shrublands and patchy forests at the bottom of valleys.

Myricaria elegans Royle: Grows on hill slopes and near water bodies/ oases in Ladâkh.

Myricaria rose (*Hombuk*): This is a medicinal plant species found in Ladâkh.

Myricaria squamosa (*Ombu*): This is a medicinal plant species found in Ladâkh.

Nepeta cataria (*Gandhsoi*): This is a medicinal plant species found in Ladâkh.

Nepeta coerulenscens (*Neimlo*): This is a medicinal plant species found in Ladâkh.

Nepeta discolor (*Nyomalo*): This is a medicinal plant species found in Ladâkh.

Nepeta erecta (*Eripantso*): This is a medicinal plant species found in Ladâkh.

Nepeta eriostachia (*Zimthik Ie*): This is a medicinal plant species found in Ladâkh.

Nepeta floccosa (*Shamalolo*): This is a medicinal plant species found in Ladâkh.

Nepeta glutinosa. (*Gimanko*): This is a medicinal plant species found in Ladâkh.

Nepeta leucolaena (*Beimtso*): This is a medicinal plant species found in Ladâkh.

Nepeta longibracteata (*Teyanku*): This is a medicinal plant species found in Ladâkh.

Nepeta podostachys (*Shangukaram*): This is a medicinal plant species found in Ladâkh.

Nepeta spp.: Grows above 4,500 metres in Ladâkh.

Onosma hispidum Wall (*Gul-é-Laljari*): Flowers in March-July. Grows in Landikotal, Swât, Chitrâl, Kâghân. Medicinal property: cardiac tonic, stimulant.

Origanum vulgare L. (*Lachung*): This is a medicinal plant species found near water bodies/ oases in Ladâkh.

Oxyfropis microphylla (*Stagsha nagpo*): This is a medicinal plant species found in Ladâkh.

Oxyria digyna (*Chur-tse, chum tse*): This is a medicinal plant species found in Ladâkh.

Oxytropis cachameriana Camb.: Grows in the alpine parts of Ladâkh (and in Kashmîr).

Oxytropis microphylla (*Taksha, rechakpa*): This is a medicinal plant species found in Ladâkh.

Oxytropis tatarica (*Sarkash*): This is a medicinal plant species found in Ladâkh.

Paeonia emodi Wall. (*Gul-é-Ud-Salap*): Flowers in May-June. Grows on moist ground in Kâghân, Chitrâl, Bahrin, Poonch. Used in the treatment of diarrhoea

Paraguilegia microphylla: This is a medicinal plant species found in Ladâkh.

Parnassia palustris L.: Grows in the alpine parts of Ladâkh (and in Kashmîr) and near water bodies/ oases in Ladâkh. .

Pedicularis longifolia (*Phakchang, lunori zarpo*): This is a medicinal plant species found in Ladâkh.

Pedicularis megalantha (*Lungruk makpo*): This is a medicinal plant species found in Ladâkh.

Pedicularis pectinata (*Lungri muppo*): This is a medicinal plant species found in Ladâkh.

Pedicularis cheilanthifolia (*Kikimo*): This is a medicinal plant species found in Ladâkh.

Pedicularis tongiflora Rudolph: Grows in the alpine parts of Ladâkh (and in Kashmîr).

Peganum harmala (*Sepan*): This is a medicinal plant species found in shrublands and patchy forests at the bottom of valleys in Ladâkh.

Pervoskia abrotanoides Karel (*Gul-é-Shanshohai*): Flowers in September-October. Grows in Chitrâl, Gilgit, Hunzâ, Ladâkh and Ziarat Used in the treatment of fevers.

Phragmites karka (*Retz*). **Trin. ex-Steud:** Grows near water bodies/ oases in Ladâkh.

Physochlaina praealta (*Langthang*): This is a rare and endangered medicinal plant species found in Ladâkh.

Picrorhiza kurrooa Royle (*Honglen*): This is a rare and endangered medicinal plant species found in Ladâkh.

Plantago depressa (*Tharam*): This is a medicinal plant species found in Ladâkh.

Plantago erosa (*Tharam*): This is a medicinal plant species found in Ladâkh.

Plantago himalaica (*Karache, nikto*): This is a medicinal plant species found in Ladâkh.

Plantago major (*Riew kai*): This is a medicinal plant species found in Ladâkh.

Pleurospermum angelicoides (*Chhipi*): This is a medicinal plant species found in Ladâkh.

Poa annua L: Grows in the alpine parts of Ladâkh (and in Kashmîr).

Podophyllum hexandrum (*Demobkusu, tandik*): This is a rare and endangered medicinal plant species found in Ladâkh.

Podophyllum hexandrum Royle ex Camb: Grows in the alpine parts of Ladâkh and Kashmîr.

Polygonum affine D Don: Grows in the alpine parts of Ladâkh (and in Kashmîr).

Polygonum paronychioides (*Nhachu*): This is a medicinal plant species found in Ladâkh.

Polygonum polystachium (*Chutzi nagpo*): This is a medicinal plant species found in Ladâkh.

Polygonum viviparum: Grows on alpine slopes and in sheltered ravines in Ladâkh.

Potentilla anserine: This is a medicinal plant species found in Ladâkh.

Potentilla atrosanguinea (*Chisheng*): This is a medicinal plant species found in Ladâkh.

Potentilla bifurca L: Grows in the alpine parts as well as deserts of Ladâkh (and in Kashmîr).

Potentilla desertorum: Grows on alpine slopes and in sheltered ravines in Ladâkh.

Potentilla fruticosa (*Khiamġar*): This is a medicinal plant species found in Ladâkh.

Potentilla fruticosa: Grows above 4,500 metres in Ladâkh.

Potentilla salesoviana (*E-mong karvo*): This is a medicinal plant species found in Ladâkh.

Primula denticulata: This is a medicinal plant species found in Ladâkh.

Primula macrophylla (*Sulumentok, kilche*): This is a medicinal plant species found in Ladâkh.

Primula rosea (*Sulumentok*): This is a rare and endangered medicinal plant species found in Ladâkh.

Prunella vulgaris (*Syangave*): This is a medicinal plant species found in Ladâkh.

Psychrogeton andryaloides (*Lukchung ba*): This is a medicinal plant species found in Ladâkh.

Pterocephalus hookerii (*Spang-tsi-dowo*): This is a medicinal plant species found in Ladâkh.

Ranunculus brotherusii (*Maokiang*): This is a medicinal plant species found in Ladâkh.

Ranunculus laetus (*Sharchang*): This is a medicinal plant species found in Ladâkh.

Ranunculus lobatus (*Zamtso*): This is a medicinal plant species found in Ladâkh.

Rheum emodi (*Tukshu*): This is a rare and endangered medicinal plant species found in Ladâkh.

Rheum moorcroftianum (*Tukshu*): This is a rare and endangered medicinal plant species found in Ladâkh.

Rheum webbianum (*Tukshu*): This is a rare and endangered medicinal plant species found in Ladâkh.

Rhododendron anthopogon (*Balu*): This is a medicinal plant species found in Ladâkh.

Rhodiola heterodonta (*Sholo-marvo*): This is a medicinal plant species found in Ladâkh.

Rhodiola imbricate (*Shrolu*): This is a medicinal plant species found in Ladâkh.

Rhododendron anthopogon (*Balu*): This is a rare and endangered medicinal plant species found in Ladâkh.

Rosa foetida Herrm (*Gul-é-Briar*): Flowers in January-July. Grows in Kurrum, Ziarat Used in the treatment of diarrhoea.

Rosa webbiana: Grows on alpine slopes and in sheltered ravines in Ladâkh.

Rosa, sericea (*Rongsal, syan, sib*): This is a medicinal plant species found in Ladâkh.

Salix denticulata: Grows on alpine slopes and in sheltered ravines in Ladâkh.

Salix viminalis: Found in shrublands and patchy forests at the bottom of valleys.

Salsola collina Pall: Grows in the cold deserts of Ladâkh.

Sambucas nigra L (*Gul-é-Uti-Khaman*): Flowers in March-April. Grows in Parachinar, Nathiagali, Medicinal property: laxative; stimulates blood circulation. Used in the treatment of skin irritation.

Saussurea bracteata. (*Pang-tsi dowo*): This is a rare and endangered medicinal plant species found in Ladâkh.

Saussurea gnaphaloides (*Yuliang, pang-tsi*): This is a rare and endangered medicinal plant species found in Ladâkh.

Saussurea lappa (*Kut*): This is a rare and endangered medicinal plant species found in Ladâkh.

Saussurea obvallata (*Spangsetobo*): This is a rare and endangered medicinal plant species found in Ladâkh.

Saussurea subulata Cl: Grows in the cold deserts of Ladâkh.

Sedum ewersii. (*Churuppa*): This is a medicinal plant species found in Ladâkh.

Seabuckthorn (*Hippophae rhamnoides; chharma* in Ladâkhi) is the reigning superstar of Ladâkhi flora. The extracts of its berry are being credited with all kinds of miraculous medicinal properties, not least of which is this thorny shrub's ability to earn billions of dollars in foreign exchange for India, and neighbouring China. The shrub grows wild in various parts of the Indian Himâlayas, notably Ladâkh, Lahaul-Spiti (HP), Sikkim and Uttarâkhand.[ii]

Miraculous properties: Seabuckthorn is a deciduous shrub. It is said to have the ability to absorb nitrogen from the air and 'fix' it in the soil. This enhances the fertility of the soil. It is being claimed that the Seabuckthorn fruit has more than a hundred nutrients essential for the functioning of the human body. Besides, it is full of a gas that all of us need very badly in Ladâkh—oxygen.

The shrub yields small golden berries, products of which are being marketed commercially as 'Leh berries' (because that name is less of a mouthful than either seabuckthorn or Hippophae rhamnoides). Extracts from these berries are said to be rich in eight vitamins, including the vitamins A, B1, B2, E and K, as well as twenty-four minerals, eighteen amino acids and several anti-oxidants. The seabuckthorn berry is supposed to have the highest concentration of vitamin C among all fruits. Its extracts are now being sold in the form of juice, jam and sauce.

As mentioned, the shrub is good not only for men but also for the soil. It has an elaborate root system and a 'compact canopy system,' which protect the soil from wind and water erosion. The shrub upgrades fragile and marginal mountain slopes by binding the soil softly.

And after we humans have sucked all the goodies out of the berry and the soil has been pumped with nitrogen, what do we do with its seeds, leaves, branches and bark? Obviously, they can't simply be thrown away. So, the local people use them as fuel and animal fodder.

Why does this wonder shrub grow only in the Indian and Chinese Himâlayas? Apparently that's because of the clean air, pure snow, extreme cold and awesome altitudes of the Himâlayas.

Phytochemical studies: Two of the scientists[3] who had been posted in Ladâkh and had applied for a patent for a herbal beverage, teamed up with three scientists[4] based in Kerala, which is at the other end of the country. They conducted 'phytochemical investigations' on seabuckthorn samples collected from Ladâkh. They analysed the fruit, the seed and the leaves separately. They found:

i) carotenoids (mainly beta-carotene), tocopherols, fatty acids and steroids (mainly sitosterol) in the 'non-polar fractions;'

ii) terpenoids in the seed oil;

iii) phenolics and carbohydrates in the 'polar fractions;'

iv) plenty of beta-carotene (and some xanthophylls) in the fruit and the seeds;

v) decent quantities of ursolic acid in the seeds and leaves;

vi) beta-amyrin and uvaol as minor terpenoids; and

vii) palmitic acid, palmitoleic acid, stearic acid, oleic acid, linoleic acid and linolenic acid in the fatty acid;

viii) complex glycosides of flavonoids in the polar fractions.

ix) glycosides (mainly glucosides) of isorhamnetin and kaempferol;

x) the amounts of ascorbic acid and flavonoids were lower than the data contained in literature; and

---

3. S. Dwivedi and O.P.Chaurasia, both of the Field Research Laboratory (DRDO), Ladakh. The other pioneering scientists who had, together with these two, applied for the patent are Col DP Attrey, Basant Ballabh and Dr. Brahma Singh.

4. R. Kala, P.S. Hema and A. Banerji, all three of the Phytochemical Research Unit, Regional Research Laboratory, Trivandrum-695 019.

xi) the levels of the phytochemicals varied enormously, depending on which part of Ladâkh the sample had been taken from, as well as on 'the physiological stage.'

Note of caution: In the companion volumes 'Ladakh' and 'The Other Kashmir' I have written about the fabled longevity of the Hunzâkuts people and have sounded a note of caution. I have mentioned that a very large number of websites about the supposed elixir-like qualities of the water of Hunzâ had links to a commercial organisation. Now that seabuckthorn is being sought to be identified with the life-restoring Sañjîvani herb of the Hiñdu epics, I must say the same about the websites that tout the supposed wonders of seabuckthorn. Most of them uncritically quote the five scientists who discovered the berry's properties, and many of these websites have been sponsored by a Delhi-based corporation.

I do not have the qualifications to question the findings listed on the internet. Nor am I casting aspersions on them. However, in both cases it is my duty to point out the nature of the sponsorship of websites about the elixir-like water of Hunzâ and the wondrous berry of Leh. I should also mention that some Ladâkhi botanists, who do not have a direct commercial interest in the berry, are convinced that the berry's properties are every bit as good as they are cracked to be.

Mass appeal: Seabuckthorn's appeal transcends religious, and national, borders. Genghis Khan and his cavalrymen, it is said, ate seabuckthorn berries, seed and oil to improve the memory as well as physical strength. Obviously they overdosed on the noble berry. They could never forget a slight or an insult, and had the stamina and prowess to get even with everyone who had rubbed them the wrong way.

Russian cosmonauts, we are told, ate seabuckthorn products on board the Mir because it gave them some extra oxygen. No wonder they did better than their American counterparts.

Personally, I love the taste of all seabuckthorn products. However, their labels point out that they have all been sweetened artificially.

It is possible that I might live an extra eleven minutes because I have consumed a lot of delicious seabuckthorn juice, jam and sauce.

Selinum vaginatum: This is a rare and endangered medicinal plant species found in Ladâkh.

Senecio graciliflorus (*Zerjum*): This is a medicinal plant species found in Ladâkh.

Senecio leatus (*Hechiang*): This is a medicinal plant species found in Ladâkh.

Senecio tibeticus (*Niyamgar*): This is a medicinal plant species found in Ladâkh.

Silene indica (*Shukoa, luqsuk*): This is a medicinal plant species found in Ladâkh.

Silene longicarpophora: Grows above 4,500 metres in Ladâkh.

Silene moorcroftiana (*Timuksa*): This is a medicinal plant species found in Ladâkh.

Silybum marianum Gaertn. (*Holy thistle*): Flowers in March-April. Grows in Abbotâbâd, Mirpur, Its flower heads are used in the treatment of diabetes.

Sophora alopecuroides: Found in shrublands and patchy forests at the bottom of valleys.

Spiraea lycoides: Grows on alpine slopes and in sheltered ravines in Ladâkh.

Stachys sericea Wall: Grows in the alpine parts of Ladâkh (and in Kashmîr).

Stachys tibetica Vatck: Grows in the cold deserts of Ladâkh.

Swerlia petiolata (*Heising*): This is a medicinal plant species found in Ladâkh.

Swerlia thomsonii (*Tikta*): This is a medicinal plant species found in Ladâkh.

T. tibeticum (Hk. f and Th. ex Cl).**:** Grows in the cold deserts of Ladâkh.

Tamaricaria elegans (*Hombuk*): This is a medicinal plant species found in Ladâkh.

Tanacetum dolichophyllum (*Seigmanlo*): This is a medicinal plant species found in Ladâkh.

Tanacetum gracile Hook.f. (*Gul-é-Tansy/ Khamchu*): This is a medicinal plant species found in Ladâkh and Hunzâ. Flowers in June-August. Used in the treatment of children's worms.

Tanacetum longifolium (*Bhurse-khampa*): This is a medicinal plant species found in Ladâkh.

Tanacetum nanam (*Phulumentok*): This is a rare and endangered medicinal plant species found in Ladâkh.

Tanacetum tenuifolium (*Autang*): This is a medicinal plant species found in Ladâkh.

Tanacetum tibeticum (*Khurmang*): This is a medicinal plant species found in Ladâkh.

Taraxacum officinale (*Han, khurmang*): This is a medicinal plant species found in Ladâkh.

Tenacetum fruticulosum Ledeb.: Grows in the cold deserts of Ladâkh.

Thalaspi alpestre L.: Grows in the alpine parts of Ladâkh (and in Kashmîr).

Thalictrum alpinum: This is a medicinal plant species found in Ladâkh.

Thalictrum foetidum (*Haichinsah*): This is a medicinal plant species found in Ladâkh.

Thalictrum minus (*Chak-choo*): This is a medicinal plant species found in Ladâkh.

Thermopsis inflate (*Khymang; chudup*): This is a medicinal plant species found in Ladâkh.

Thlaspi arvense (*Bumak*): This is a medicinal plant species found in Ladâkh.

Thlaspt montanum L. (*Bumuk*): This is a medicinal plant species found in Ladâkh.

Thylacospermum caespitosum (Camb). Schischk.: Grows on hill slopes in Ladâkh. This plant has the habit to form a cushion. One variety has a diminutive or miniature 'habit.' The 'bushy habit' is the common adaptation found in plants of the cold desert.

Thymus linearis (*Taksha nakpo*): This is a rare and endangered medicinal plant species found in Ladâkh.

Tragopogon gracilis (*Thar-noo, akhron*): This is a medicinal plant species found in Ladâkh.

Tribulus terrestris (*Zema rave*): This is a medicinal plant species found in in shrublands and patchy forests at the bottom of valleys Ladâkh.

Trifolium pratense L. (*Gul-é-Trepatrâ*): Flowers in February-April. Grows in Chitrâl, 'Astore, Swât. Used in the treatment of asthma and spasmodic bronchitis. Medicinal property: expectorant.

Triglochin palustris (*Puga, gaike*): This is a medicinal plant species found in Ladâkh.

Trigonella emodi (*Bhusu hung*): This is a medicinal plant species found in Ladâkh.

Urena lobata L. (*Gul-é-Bachitâ*): Flowers in September-December. Grows in Changa Manga, Medicinal property: aphthosis, expectorant. Used in the treatment of sore throats.

Urtica hyperborean (*Pachoo, zasot*): This is a medicinal plant species found in Ladâkh.

Urtica urens (*Zabo, zatsut*): This is a medicinal plant species found in Ladâkh.

Verbascum thapsus L. (*Gul-é-Gidhar*) Flowers in June-August. Grows in Chitrâl, Mansehra. Used in the treatment of coughs, diarrhoea, and throat irritation. Medicinal property: febrifuge, stimulant.

Veronica macrostemon (*Shimiogar*): This is a medicinal plant species found in Ladâkh.

Vinca major L. (*Gul-é-Periwinkle*): Flowers in December-March. Grows in Parachinar, Abbotâbâd, hills. Medicinal property: its fresh flowers are laxative.

Viola biflora: This is a medicinal plant species found in Ladâkh.

Viola odorata L. (*Gul-é-Banafshâñ*): Flowers in March-May. Grows in Ladâkh, Nathia gali, Kâghân, Swât, Chitrâl. Medicinal property: protects livers, soothes lung congestion. Used in the treatment of sinusitis, sore throats.

Vitex negundo L. (*Gul-é-Nirgundi*): Flowers in March-June. Grows in Thal, Swât, Mirpur Medicinal property: cardio tonic, Used in the treatment of cholera, diarrhoea, liver problems.

Waldheimia tomentosa (*Makungla, lugmik serpo*): This is a rare and endangered medicinal plant species found in Ladâkh.

Waldhemia glabra (*Sa-palu*): This is a rare and endangered medicinal plant species found in Ladâkh.

Waldhemia stoliczkai (*Cl*). Ostenf. Grows in the cold deserts of Ladâkh.

Xanthium strumarium L. (*Gul-é-Cheero*): Flowers in July-August. Grows in Gilgit, Chitrâl, Swât. Its flowers are used in the treatment of toothaches.

Youngia tenufolia (*Stathis, jampa*): This is a medicinal plant species found in Ladâkh.

References

i. Sources of information for this chapter include

"Bio-diversity of Jammu and Kashmir" by A.H.M. Ali Reza with Hasan Z. Chowdhury.

"Medicinal flowers of Pâkistân," an incredibly detailed paper by Mohammad Afzal Rizvi of the Bait al-Hikmah Research Institute.

"Floristic Diversity of Indian region" compiled by R.R. Rao.

"Country report -4. India: Lessons from Ladakh" Down to Earth (Volume 9, No. 23, April 30, 2001), published by the Centre for Science and Environment in Delhi.

All four papers have been posted on the Internet.

I have also consulted the book

"151 Healing Plants of Jammu and Kashmîr" by O.P. Sharma Vidyarthi (a government publication).

I am grateful to Jigmet Takpa, IFS, for the notes that he has very kindly given me.

ii. Sources for this entry include:

"Phytochemical studies on Indian Seabuckthorn (Hippophae rhamnoides)" by R. Kala, P.S. Hema, S. Dwivedi, O.P. Chaurasia and A. Banerji.

"DRDO develops herbal beverage for troops posted at high altitude" a government press release of December 24, 2001;

"Wonder berry from Ladakh" by A.S. Prashar; *Tribune* News Service, Chandigarh, April 19, 200?.

Chapter- 11

The Rivers of Ladakh and River-Rafting

Leh/ the Indus Valley

The Indus

It is from this great river that India got its name. Several places—in Ladakh, near Sonamarg [Kashmir] and in Tibet—claim to be its source. Tibet wins. The place in Tibet where the Indus originates is around 17,000' above the sea and is at 32°N and 81°E. Thereafter, the river flows north-west for 160 miles.

It is called the Singh-ka Bab during that stretch. According to a local belief, the river springs out of the mouth of a lion. Therefore, the Tibetans also call it the Sengge(y) Chhu, or the water body (chhu) that flows out of the mouth of a lion (senggey/ singh). The Ladakhis call it the Sanspo.

The Indus enters India from the east in southern Ladakh. The place where it does is at roughly 13,800' and at 33°02'N/ 79°09'E. The river continues to flow in a north-western direction. It begins its journey in India along an extended, flat, alluvial bed in Lungbale. The Indus is calm and serene during this stretch.

Details of the course of the river are given later in this section.

The river flows through a narrow passage for the seven miles after Nakjubukle. The constriction ends at Harlaput. The Indus remains unconstricted till Mahe. The Indus and River Hanle merge at Loma, five miles upstream of Harlaput. It is estimated that River Hanle rushes down at almost 60 miles per hour before the confluence.

The Indus enters the mountainous Pûgâ valley at Mahe. It continues to flow through the rugged terrain of this region till Karo. It opens up somewhat at Tarchit. At Karo the river enters the Leh valley. The Valley is vast between here and Spituk (10,288'). From there the river is again pressed between narrow banks till it gets to Nimmu (10,150'). The blue waters of River Zâñskâr merge with the relatively dirty waters of the Indus above Nimmu. The Indus then widens somewhat between Nimmu and Khaltse (9,900').

The river remains under Indian administration till Garkun. After that it weaves through Pakistan Occupied Kashmir and finally leaves the state eleven kilometres downstream of Sazin. It enters Pakistan at 35°35'N and 73°23'E.

The more important towns that the Indus goes past in Pakistan include Attock (2,079'), Khushalgarh, Mianwali, Dera Ismail Khan, Dera Ghazi Khan, Mithankot, Rohri, Sukkur, Sehwan, Hyderabad, Kotri and Karachi. The river has a 160 km. delta that runs along the coast of the Arabian Sea.

The Course of the Indus Runs Thus:

(A word about pronunciation: the 'e' at the end of the names given below is meant to be sounded, as if it were an 'é'. Thus the last two syllables of Nakjubukle are 'book-lay' and not like the English 'buckle'. Hanle is pronounced aan-lay. For some reason the 'h' is silent in this word alone).

Lungbale 13,547'-Tagyarmale-Gangrale 13,547'	11 km.
Gangrale-Niuchele-Luzurma Yogma-Pemaririle-Nakjubukle 13,500'	23 km.
Nakjubukle-Khama Shishale/ Pema Laga-Tuble-Loma 13,500' (*confluence* with River Hanle)	8 km.
Loma-Harlaput 13,500'	8 km.
Harlaput-Nyoma Rap 13,500'	12 km.
Nyoma Rap-Yalapuk (L)-Rakaru (R)-Mahe 13,500'	19 km.
Mahe- Raldung-Yang-Chumâthâng 13,456'	18 km.

Chumâthâng-Jiro (hot spring)-Kidmang-Mudil/ Kesar-Nior Nis (or Nurnis) 13,161'	16 km.
Nior Nis (Nurnis)-Kangmar-Akeke-Kiari-Khatpâ Thâñgbo-Kumdok-Gaik 12,940'	16 km.
Gaik-Tirido-Thanka-Hémyâ 12,817'	19 km.
Hémyâ-Likché 12,707'	10 km.
Likché-Ikpadok-Khawâthâng-Tunah-Leh/ Manali road head 11,100'	17 km.
Roadhead-Igu-Karu 11,080'	15 km.
Karu-Changa-Stakna 11,060'	11 km.
Stakna-Ranbirpura-Thiksey-Shey	11 km.
Shey-Choglamsar Bridge (6.5 km. away from Leh town)	5 km.
Choglamsar-Spituk 10,286'	6 km.
Spituk (13 km. ahead is the *confluence* with River Zâñskâr)-Nimmu 10,150'	25 km.
Nimmu-Machakha-Umlung Gongma-Alchi Gompa-Saspol	19 km.
Saspol-Wuleh Tokbo	8 km.
Wuleh Tokbo-Nurla 10,130'	13 km.
Nurla-Chagri-Chokbu-Khaltse 9,900'	11 km.
Khaltse-Narmu	10 km.
Narmu-Skirbuchan	12 km.
Skirbuchan-Kanutse	23 km.
Kanutse-Sunnit	6 km.
Sunnit-Garkun (last Indian post)	5 km.
Garkun-Gurugurdu	12 km.
Gurugurdu-Marol (*confluence* with River Shingo)	15 km.
Marol-Kharmang (fort)	26 km.
Kharmang-Vaziri Gund	13 km.
Vaziri Gund-Mabrok	8 km.
Mabrok-Shokha	14 km.
Shokha-Sermi	7 km.
Sermi-Yagho (*confluence* with River Shyok)	6 km.
Yagho-Gol	3 km.
Gol-Goma Thurgon	18 km.

Goma Thurgon-Skardu 7,680' (*confluence* with River Shigar)	13 km.
Skardu-Ponedas	22 km.
Ponedas-Krabâthâng	13 km.
Krabâthâng-Kotmul	27 km.
Kotmul-Strongling	13 km.
Strongling-Juche	12 km.
Juche-Shingas	12 km.
Shingas-Burumdoir	14 km.
Burumdoir-Hanuchai	16 km.
Hanuchai-*confluence* with River Gilgit	16 km.
The confluence point-Bunji	12 km.
Bunji-Lichar	18 km.
Lichar-Drang	14 km.
Drang-Gunar	15 km.
Gunar-Chîlâs	27 km.
Chîlâs-Balugush	14 km.
Balugush-Sinai Much	17 km.
Sinai Much-Basha	17 km.
Basha-Harban	10 km.
Harban-Sazin	14 km.

The border between India and Pakistan is 11 km. downstream of Sazin at 35°35'N- 73°23'E. The first 4km. are under Indian administration and the next 7km. under Pakistani occupation.

Rafting: Gradient: (The grades are explained at the end of this chapter).

i) Karo to Choglamsar (including the stretch between Hemis and Choglamsar): Between Grade I and Grade II. The river is shallow and calm. It takes about three hours from Hemis to Choglamsar. En route are Stakna, Thiksey, Shey, Chushot and the Choglamsar bridge.

ii) Spituk to Nimmu: Between Grade II and Grade III, sometimes Grade IV. The stretch between Phay and Nimmu takes around four hours. The river is slightly faster here. Therefore, the rafting is far more exciting than in the previous stretch.

iii) Nimmu to Alchi: Grades III and IV. Not recommended for beginners. This stretch can take around 6-8 hours.

iv) At some places in Ladakh the gradient is of Grade V.

Considerable whitewater rafting has been done on several stretches of the Indus. Some stretches, like the one near Choglamsar, are easy enough for first-time rafters. Adventure tourism expert Asaf Mahmud writes, that "The first ever and pioneering whitewater rafting feat in India was performed [on the Indus] in the autumn of 1975." However, Asaf also offers a few words of caution. He says, "The river has a tendency to shift its bed at various sections... It has some gorges as well... To run the entire river requires [an] expedition approach as most of its upper section [passes through a] wilderness".

Foreigners can travel between Ḳaro and Khaltse without any special permission.

The Hanlé river

This river originates close to India's desolate, sparsely populated border with Tibet. A number of little streams emerge from the Lokphuk Gongru Tso (14,400') lake and the melting glaciers west of the Imis Lâ (pass) (16,760'). The lake is 5km. upstream of Samdole. Asaf Mahmud says, "The streams in this sub-region, clockwise, are, Pachatung, Tongongmalung, Tuang, Miksaḍiu, Nalung and Kuglung". The streams join each other at various points to create River Hanlé.

The Hunza River from the left joins the Indus coming from Baltistan, Ladakh and Tibet

A major source of the river is the Kongra Chu rivulet, which carries down the waters of the mountains east of the Tsomo Rîrî, extending to the Lanak pass in the south.

The river flows down northwards. Of its total length of 70 miles (112 km)., it spends around 30 miles (48 km). winding through the vast and level Mangkâng plain. It merges with the Indus at Loma.

19th century British accounts, quoting Major Alexander Cunningham, the explorer, say that he called "the above described swampy plain the Hanlé Tso (or lake), and [thought] it must be the largest sheet of fresh water in Ladák".

Between Samdole and Loma it follows the course given below:

(The 'e' at the end of *almost* all the names given below is pronounced like an 'é'. Thus 'Shade' really is 'shaa-they,' 'they' being as in English. All altitudes are in feet and distances in miles. Both are approximations).

From-to	Altitude	Distance
Samdole	14,900	0
Samdole-Ranksile	14,900	1
Ranksile-Zarser	14,900	1
Zarser-Hale	14,900	4
Hale-Ukdungle	14,412	8
Ukdungle-Zong	14,400	7
Zong-Shade	14,400	6
Shade-Hanle	14,270	7
Hanle-Târâkokpole	14,024	11
Târâkokpole-Nukzele	14,024	7
Nukzele-Tihrale	14,024	6
Tihrale-Loma	13,900	12
		Total:70 miles

How to get there: Every other day a bus or truck leaves Leh for Nyoma (almost 230 km. away). From Nyoma, which is the nearest town, you will either have to walk or, with luck, look for a lift if a vehicle happens to pass by.

Zâñskâr

The Zâñskâr river

River Zâñskâr is also called the Chiling Chu. Its headwaters include the Yunam, the Tsarap ('Serap') Lingti Chu and the Sarchu. The river then merges with the Sumgal, which comes down from near the Tsomo Rîrî lake. It takes 130 miles to reach Padam. In the process the river descends by almost 4,000'. It joins River Doda at Padam.

The river then turns north and travels 80 miles and falls another 1,500' (or 18.7' per mile) before it joins the Indus at Nimmu (Snimo). Thus, in all, the river is 210 miles long, and falls a little less than 6,000' (or 28.5' per mile).

River Zâñskâr winds its way through some gorges that are so deep that they are in the shade almost throughout the day. It goes past Thonde (Stongde) 11,460', Rinam 11,224', Pishu, Zâñglâ 11,050', Pidmu, Hanumil, Purfi Lâ, Niraq 11,000', Chiling and Nimmu 10,160'.

Cunningham, the British explorer, estimates its discharge at 1,000 cubic feet in winter, 3,000 cu. ft. in May and 9,000 cu. ft. in August.

Rafting: Much of the river freezes over for a few weeks in the winter. Travellers walk on this *chadar* (sheet) road at night—when it is least likely to melt and, thus, give way. It takes almost a week of walking on the chadar to travel from Padam to the roadhead in Leh district.

In summer, rafters take roughly the same amount of time, a little more than a week, to run the river. The going is not always easy. The river abounds in pools, drops and rapids. Some of the rocks that you will encounter have jagged edges.

Several teams have rafted down from Karshâ all the way to Nimmu, where River Zâñskâr merges with the Indus. M. Asaf Mahmud says, "The characteristics of River Zâñskâr call for an expedition approach. Detailed logistics based on complete self-sufficiency should be adhered to for running the river. Provisions for 7-10 days, including fuel for cooking, must be taken along, of course, in dry bags".

The river is of Grade III. Some adventure groups organise rafting in mid-August.

The Doda river

The source of River Doda is at the bottom of the Nûn-Kun Massif, where it is formed by the melting of the Drungdrung glaciers. As the 70 km. long river travels south, a number of streams join it. These include the Chinzum (left), Chumu (l), Hagshu (right), Bardur (r), Kyala (l), Shimiling (r) and Seni/ Sani (r). The Kargil-Zâñskâr (Padam) road runs along the river.

Rafting: It is possible to raft on the stretch between Abring (Abran) and Upti-Karshâ.

The Tsarap Lingti Chu

The Tsarap Lingti Chu originates at Purne. The Niri (Tsarap Chu) and Kargyâk streams emerge from the Tso Tak Phu Lake (33°21' N- 77°18' E), which is upstream of the Phugtâl monastery and the Shingo Lâ (pass).

As the Tsarap Lingti Chu goes down, it passes Char, Abnop, Dorzong, Ichar, Raru, the Bardan monastery, Trakkar, Chila, Kissara, Pipiting (a suburb of Padam), the Upti Fort and Karshâ. River Tema comes down from the Poat Lâ (18,752'), which is south of Padam. It joins the Tsarap Lingti Chu at Money.

Rafting: It is possible to raft on the stretch between Phugtâl and Padam. Some rafters start near the Purne monastery, run the course of the river till it joins River Zâñskâr and then continue rafting on River Zâñskâr till Nimmu, where the latter river merges with the Indus.

The Markha

River Markha flows towards the west briefly before joining River Zâñskâr. In spring and summer it is in spate. People trek along the river in autumn and winter.

Kargil

The Shigar

The Shigar originates in the Bara Deosai plateau and flows southeast.

River Drass

River Drass emerges from near the dZoji Lâ. The Mushkoo and Gamru streams join it before it merges with River Shingo.

The Shingo

The Shingo flows east from the Chhota Deosai plains (West Karakoram).

The Shigar and Drass rivers merge with it. It then joins the Suru north of Kargil and later merges with the Indus.

The Suru

The Karcha stream trickles down from Rangdum (34°03'N, 76°23'E), which is the place where the Suru valley meets Zâñskâr. The stream joins the substantial waters of the melting Shafat glaciers (which are at the bottom of the Nûn-Kun massif). River Suru forms when the two merge.

The river then travels west, draining the stunning valley of the same name, till it reaches Kargil town. En route it picks up three major tributaries. The Chalong stream, which comes from the Babong glacier, merges with it at Pânikhar. The Phulangma, the source of which is in Itchu, joins it at Sâñkoo. The Wâkhâ Chu combines with the Suru at Kargil town.

The Suru, in turn, merges with River Shingo at Yogmayul, near Kargil town. From there they travel together. They first go through an area where tourists are not allowed and then through POK. They finally reach Chathalung, where the Indus subsumes them.

There are further details about the Suru valley in the chapter on Kargil district. However, villages have been arranged in the reverse (upstream) order in that chapter.

Shafat Nalla joins the Suru from the left

The course of the Suru runs thus:

The altitudes given are of the place mentioned second and are in feet. Distances are in miles. 1 mile= 1.6 km. The distances and altitudes given are mostly approximate).

From-to	Altitude (feet)	Distance (miles)
Rangdum	12,150	0
Rangdum-Zuliduk	12,000	3
Zuliduk-Shama Kurpo	11,970	5
Shama Kurpo-Gulmatonga	11,810	7
Gulmatonga-Parkachik	11,500	10
Parkachik-Tangol	11,000	5
Tangol-Achambar	10,700	2
Achambar-Pânikhar (Suru)	10,500	5
Pânikhar-Damsna	10,300	5
Damsna-Thama/ Mangdom	10,200	3
Thama-Karpokhar	10,000	5
Karpokhar-Sâñkoo	9,800	2
Sâñkoo-Pharona	9,500	8
Pharona-Chaliskot	9,300	4
Chaliskot-Grantung	9,214	6
Grantung-Titichumig	9,000	5
Titichumig-Kargil	8,987	4
Kargil-Yogmayul	8,814	3
	Total	82 miles

Rafting: M. Asaf Mahmud has calculated that the drop works out to 40.68 feet per mile. The river is already a great favourite of international rafters. There's a 'jeepable' road (Kargil-Zâñskâr) running close to, if not along, the river, throughout. There are villages, and thus supplies, all along the route. There are no restrictions on tourists, Indian or international. The scenery is spectacular and the mountains are greener than in the rest of Ladakh. (The moist plains of Damsna, so reminiscent of Mongolia, are a personal favourite). And in the second half of the river, rafting is sometimes so safe that if you jump out of the raft in, say, early September, the water won't reach your hip.

Some stretches are rough, though.

(Kilometre references given below indicate the nearest corresponding point on the road that runs along or near the river).

The fall is very steep between Rangdum and Parkachik ('km. 101' to 'km. 90'). Rafting is not advisable on this stretch. In general, the section between 'km. 87' (Parkachik) and 'km. 42' (near Sâñkoo) is meant for experienced and skilled river rafters.

The 8 km. stretch between Parkachik and Tangole(e) is good for rafting. It is followed by a steep – and dangerous – gorge. The approximately 10 km. stretch from below Tangol(e) to Damsna is good.

Then there is a bad section that begins near the '52 km.' point (roughly Purtikchey) to the '46 km.' point (roughly Sangrâ). In other words, the stretch on either side of the bridge at 'km. 48' should be avoided.

The section between 'km. 46' (Sangra) to 'km. 43' is all right. But 'km. 43' to 'km. 42' is to be avoided. It is quite safe from 'km. 42' (two kilometres upstream of Sâñkoo) almost till 'km. 2' (the Iqbal Hydel Project).

The eastern Karakorams

The Shyok (or Shayaok) River

The Shyok is often called 'the river of death' because of what it did in 1929. It has behaved since then.

The Rimo glacier, which is east of Sîâchen, is the main source of the Shyok (aka River Khumdan). The stream from the Rimo flows south and joins River Chip Chap at Gapshang (Yapchan). The Chip Chap, in turn, flows along the northern limit of the Depsang plains to reach Gapshang (15,710'). Together they form River Shyok. The waters of other glaciers join it as it flows down. These glaciers include the Chong Kumdan, the Kichik Kumdan, the Aq Tash and the Kunchang.

Till 1929, the Chong Kumdan blocked the flow of the river and acted as a natural dam. That year the river cut through the glacier and destroyed several villages downstream.

The crystal clear Shyok river in the Khapalu valley near Skardu

Once the river leaves the Depsang plains, the Shyok goes through deep, and narrow, gorges. When it reaches the southern tip of the Saser Muztagh, which is the eastern extremity of the Great Kârâkorams, the river almost turns around to go back the way it came. Its course turns from N-S to N-W.

It widens near the Saser Brangsa. Between Chhong Jangal and Shoma and again between Asham and Tirit its bed is anything between 1.5 km and 2.5 km. And yet in its last leg, between Yaglung and the point in Baltistan where it merges with the Indus, it narrows once again.

The course: The Shyok mainly flows through the Nubra sub-division of Leh. It joins the Indus at Yagho (35°22'N, 75°22'E) in Baltistan.

(Altitudes in feet, distances in miles)

From- to	Altitude	Distance
Gapshan	15,710	0
Gapshan-Saser Brangsa	15,200	19
Saser Brangsa-Sultan Chhushka	15,000	15
Sultan Chhushka-Kataklik	13,860	9
Kataklik-Mandultang	13,430	16

Mandultang-Yarguluk	13,200	4
Yarguluk-Mundro	13,000	4
Mundro-Neya Yâkmik	12,500	15
Neya Yâkmik-Dong Yailak	12,300	3
Dong Yailak-Shukpâ Kunzâñg	12,200	6
Shukpâ Kunzâñg-Chhong Jangal	12,000	14
Chhong Jangal-Sirshak	11,860	7
Sirshak-Shyok	11,500	8
Shyok-Shama	11,000	17
Shama-Agham	10,500	13
Agham-Rongau	10,490	8
Rongau-Satti	10,480	7
Satti-Tirit	10,200	8
Tirit-Deskit	9,950	9
Deskit-Hunder	9,900	4
Hunder-Rakhura	9,900	7
Rakhura-Kharu	9,700	6
Kharu-Yaglung	9,600	12
Yaglung-Malakcha	9,400	7
Malakcha-Chalunka	9,200	10
Chalunka-Turtuk	9,000	6

After Turtuk the river enters POK.

History: Till the 1940s the river was the main link between north India and Central Asia, through Ladakh and Yarqand. The Shyok freezes over in winter. Traders and others would walk on it. In summer, caravans would ply on the old Central Asian Trade Route, part of which ran along the river from Shyok village to Sultan Chhushka. The river is known for sudden and terrible floods. As a result, there are hardly any villages near it.

How to get there: i) To Shyok village: Travel by vehicle from Leh, across the Chang Lâ (17,400') to Tangkse (Durbuk). From there you can reach the picturesque Shyok village in a day's trek along the Tangkse Nâllâh.

i-a) It is possible to travel by vehicle right up to Shyok village.

ii) To Gapshan: Trek across Skyangpoche, the Saser Pass and Saser Brangas, through Sasoma (Nubra) to get to Gapshan, where the river forms.

ii-a) Travel by vehicle, across the Kharduñg Lâ and over River Shyok, to get to Sasoma.

Non-Indians may please note that they require special permission to travel through much of the area.

Rafting: Not yet attempted by anyone.

The Nubra river

The Nubra emerges from the southern tip of the massive Sîâchen glacier. Various streams get together to constitute River Nubra at Tsamskangchan (12,170'). The river descends in a south-eastern direction through a Valley. On its left is the Great Kârâkoram Range and on its right the Saltoro Range. It is an enormous river, with islands within, throughout its 160 km. course. It merges with the Shyok at Lughzhum, opposite Deskit (9,950').

In September the river is less than a metre deep at its deepest, opposite Charasa. It freezes over by November and can be crossed at several places, including where it joins the Shyok. In summer, travellers use the route along the left bank till Changlung (10,760'). There are hares and considerable brushwood in much of the gravelly, 2-3 km. wide, Lower Nubra valley.

There are a number of villages downstream of Panamik. They are huddled together and live off agriculture. Apricots and the juicy little apples that Nubra is famous for grow in these villages.

The course: The river goes past the following villages and areas:

Tsamskangchan

Lhâyul

Warshi

Jardongsa

Nyungstet

Stongstet

Henache

Kimi

Changlung

Sasoma

Aranu

Ayi

Takshai

Panamik

Pulithâñg

Kuri

Yulskam

Chamshing

Pinchimik

Charbagh

Markala

Lughzhum

There is a monastery near Warshi, on the right bank of the river. On the bank opposite Panamik there is a hot water spring. From Sasoma you can trek along the right bank of River Shyok, through the Saser Lâ, across the Kârâkoram Range, to Saser Brangsa.

How to get there: You can drive from Leh, across the Kharduñg Lâ, over River Shyok, to Changlung. The road more or less follows the course of the river.

Restrictions: Tourists need special permits to travel to certain parts of Nubra.

River Chip Chap: The river emerges from near the Aksai Chin plateau. It then flows west and joins the Shyok.

River Galwan: The river emerges from near the Aksai Chin plateau. It then flows west and joins the Shyok.

River Chang Chenmo: The river emerges from near the Aksai Chin plateau. It then flows west and joins the Shyok.

The gradation of rivers

The rivers of Ladâkh have been graded according to gradient, the intensity of waves, obstacles (such as rocks), the width (or narrowness) of the passage, difficulties encountered and the ease of manoeuvring.

There are six grades.

The Grades: I: Easy. II: Slightly difficult. III: Difficult. Irregular waves. IV: Very difficult. Strong waves. V: For experts only. Violent waves. VI: Not possible to do any rafting on such stretches.

Jammu, Kashmir, Ladakh

The State as a whole

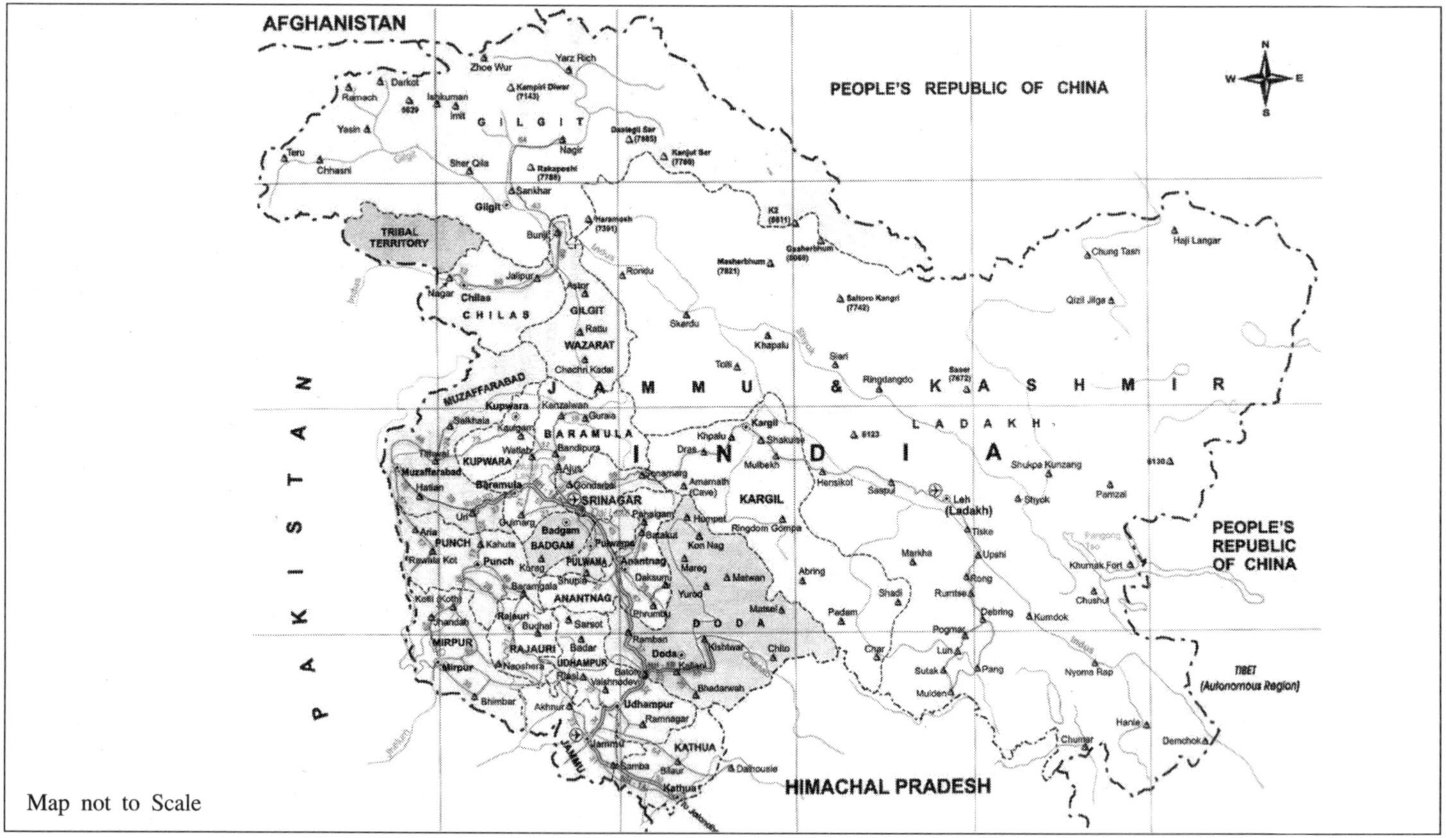

Jammu-Kashmir-Ladakh (whole State)

Chapter- 12

Lakes, Canals and Rivers in Jammu, Kashmir and Ladakh

Jammu province

Jammu rural and Samba

Surinsar: This is a small lake 42-45 km. from Jammu city (or roughly nine-km from the Mansar Lake of 'Udhampur'è). i) You can go all the way to Mansar and then approach Surinsar from there. This is the preferred route. ii)Or you can go to the Jammu city bypass. If you take the bypass from the Katrâ/ Nagrota side (i.e. north of Jammu), then you will drive southwards for a few kilometres, pass a long bridge, come to a junction and turn left on a wide road. If you take the bypass from the Bagh e Bahu/ Pathankot side (south) then you will turn right at the same tri- junction. There are signboards and a forest check post at the junction. Surinsar has a biggish tourist complex, rarely occupied.

There is a small island in the lake. Every inch of it is covered with vegetation, including palms not normally found in this part of India. There are taboos against boating on or swimming in this holy lake. The drowning of picnickers in the lake in the 1980s reinforced the taboos. (See also 'Mansar' in the section on the 'Udhampur, Resasi' districts for the legend).

Kathua

Rivers and canals

The Ravi (pron.: râvi) and the Ujh are the two principal rivers of the district. A major dam has been built on the Ravi at Thein and is known by that name. (One end of the dam is in J&K and the other in the Punjab. In Punjab the Thein Dam is known as the Ranjit Sagar Dam). On the Ujh there is a barrage which has led to the formation of a small artificial lake. Neither river is navigable.

Rajouri

Rivers

Many little rivers flow through the district. Among the important ones are the Sukh Tawi, the Jamola, the Darhal Tawi, the Ans and the Khandli.

Emperor Jehangir wrote in his memoirs that the water of a river that flowed through Rajouri 'became poisoned' during the rainy season. As a result, the people suffered from goitre and became yellow and weak. He did not name the river. It could have been the Munnawar Tawi, the quality of water of which has often been suspect.

Lakes

There are so many lakes in the Pir Panjal mountains of Rajouri that it could well be called the Lake District of India. There are twenty- seven lakes in the area between the Simar Sar and Nandan Sar alone. This is a stretch that measuress thirty kilometres by thirty kilometres. Seven of these lakes are fairly substantial in size. Most of them are located in the Peer Panjal range of mountains where Kashmir meets Jammu. Their waters flow into Kashmir. They are mostly perched at altitudes between 13,000' and 14,500'. Therefore, they freeze over in winter (Nov.-May). Some, like the Chandan and Nandan lakes, stay frozen longer than the others.

The Valley of the seven lakes is called Girgan.

Samot Sar: (3,550 m.; oval; length: 1 km). This is a blue- water lake immediately to the north of the Badjari Marg. *How to get there:* i) The easiest is a 4 hour trek from Budhal. Or ii) It could be part of a 4- 5 day trek that would include seven other lakes as well. Or iii) You could start from the Noori Chham waterfall, go to Behram Galla and then, past the Sarota Marg, to the Samot Sar. The other lakes in this circuit are:

Sukh Sar: (c.3,000m.; oval) This small lake is the northernmost of the group and the first if your trek begins from the north.

Akal Darshani: (c.3,300m.; triangular; width: 200m., length: 400m). This lake is a kilometre ahead of the Sukh Sar. It is sacred to the Bakerwal shepherds. Its waters seem black, as opposed to the blue of the other lakes.

Nandan Sar: (c.3,500m./ 13,200'; oval; length: 2 km., breadth: 1 km). This lake also happens to be a pass between Kashmir and the Girgan valley. The waters of the lake join the Jadi Marg Nallah, which leads to a valley. Later they flow towards Kashmir. To get to Nandan Sar, first climb up the slope near the Akal Darshani and then trek down in the direction of the valley. The whole valley, with tall mountains all around, seems to have become a lake. A thick fog covers the lake much of the time. There are strong winds throughout the year. Sometimes the winds blow the fog away. The mountains are so placed that there is an echo everywhere.

The (Muslim) Bakerwal shepherds consider the lake holy. They lose their sheep to the ice and the mountains of the area very often. They attribute the landslides and hailstorms that routinely plague them to Nandan Sar's wrath. So, they propitiate the lake by sacrificing a ram and offering prayers whenever they cross the Nandan Sar pass.

Chandan Sar: (c.3,800m.; circumference: 2 km.; kidney-shaped) This is a one-day trek from the Ravi Walli Marg. This is the source of the Chamar Nallah, which merges with the Bafliaz Nallah at the Behram Galla pass. Till the end of July you will find large chunks of ice floating on this lake.

Katoria Sar: (3,550m.; amorphous shape) Travel westward from the Chandan Sar and cross the Barhal Pass (3,650m). to reach the Katori(a) Sar. (Katori means 'cup'. By now you are in Poonch district). The waters of the lake are clear and cold. There are glaciers on three sides. Katoria Sar is the source of River Poonch.

Diya Sar: (c.3,600m.; length: 1 km). The lake got its name because it is shaped like a *diya* (clay lamp).

The Ravi Walli Marg Group of Lakes: This is a group of four lakes west of the Katoria Sar. Except for the Bhag Sar, they are at around 3,300m. above the sea level and thus at an altitude lower than Katoria's. The four lakes are:

Kokar Sar

Neel Sar

Ding Sar

Bhag Sar: (3,700m.; oval) It is very difficult for all other than accomplished mountaineers to reach this lake because it is surrounded by inaccessible mountains. Large chunks of ice float on it throughout the year. To get there you will have to go around the Chamar Sar from the left, then climb up to a c.4,000m. glacier, before descending to the Bhag Sar.

Other lakes:

The two Padyaran Sars: (c.3,400m.; both kidney shaped) First climb up the precipitous cliffs of the Diya Sar Gali pass (c.3,800m).. Continue through the Rupari Corridor in the direction of the Ans catchment. You will see the two lakes directly below the pass. The lakes are mostly covered by snow. The Rupari is a major pass. Bakerwal shepherds use it to travel between Rajouri and the Valley of Kashmir during their twice-a-year migration.

The Katori Sar of Bela Marg: (c.3,300m.; shaped like a *katori* or cup) This is a small seasonal lake at the western end of Bela Marg. It forms when the snow melts and dries up in late September when the water gets drained out.

Gum Sar: (c.3,600m./12,000') This is a small lake at the bottom of the pyramidal Dhakyar mountain, the peak (4,660m). of which is the highest in the range.

Panjtari (11,500'): This is a beautiful 'marg' (meadow), 3 km. long and 2 km. wide, close to the top of the Panjal range. Gulmarg is on the other side of the mountain. Panjtari is well above the tree-line, and, thus, above the forests. Views of sunrise and sunset are spectacular.

Girgan: the legend

It is said that in ancient times a king called Girgan Dev used to rule over this area. He had a daughter named Kali and six sons called Nandan,

Chandan, Neel, Sukh, Bhag and Gum. In those days it was the custom that when people grew old they would shift to the woods, where they would meditate and pray.

On reaching the specified age, Girgan, too, decided to do the same. He sent his children to the Panjal range to look for a suitable place for him in the woods there. So, his children fanned out into the mountains. They all came back, each recommending this place or that. All except Gum, who did not return.

Girgan, his sons and Kali set out in search of Gum. En route, Girgan was shown the places his children had selected for him. At last they came to a beautiful place at the feet of a tall mountain. They found Gum sitting there.

Gum had so fallen in love with the place that he wanted it for himself. He refused to give it to his father. This infuriated Girgan. Hindu mythology is full of saints who would do terrible things to people when they got angry. These saints just had to stare hard at and put a curse on whoever had been nasty to them and whatever they'd order would happen. Girgan decreed that Gum should sink into the earth and be buried there forever, never to come up again. He also said that Gum's name would be wiped off the face of the earth. Accordingly, Gum was swallowed up by the earth at the very spot where the Gum Sar lake now is.

Girgan then left for the places that had been selected for him by his other children. He rather liked those places. So, he blessed the other children and said that after they died they would be reborn as lakes and would thus live forever. And that is how the lakes named after the other five sons were created. The daughter became the Kali Dachani lake. As for Gum, his lake mainly flows inside, within the bowels of the earth. The Valley of these seven lakes has since been called Girgan.

Udhampur-Reasi

The mighty Chenâb, the Ans, the Tawi and the Ujh rivers flow through the undivided Udhampur-Reasi district. They often flow in deep troughs more than sixty or seventy feet below the nearest flat land, making their waters difficult to utilise. The Devika flows through Udhampur town and its waters are incredibly good for digestion.

The Mansar lake is at the south eastern extremity of the district, while the Sanasar was drained of its waters in the 1980s. An artificial lake has been created because of the Salal 'dam' (Hydro Electric Project). I inaugurated a tourist cafeteria next to it in 1992, but it has not been a commercial success.

Mansar Lake

This clear blue, spring- fed lake is the second most popular recreational destination in all of Jammu province, after Patni Top. In size it is much bigger than, say, the Naini Tal.

The lake: It is said that there is an underground link between this lake and Lake Surinsar, which is only eight kilometres away. That both lakes are, in turn, believed to be linked to the Kailash Kund which is in the high mountains. They say that if you throw a stone into the Kailash Kund lake it will turn up either in Lake Mansar or in Lake Surinsar.

The Mansar Lake

His Excellency the Governor, Mr. G.C. Saxena, and his wife, asked me to accompany them to Mansar in February 1993. Mr. Saxena observed that the lake was twice as big as the far more famous Naini Tal in his native U.P. So, if the Nainital could have yachts, why couldn't Mansar? Within two months I managed to borrow a yacht from the NCC to introduce this sport into Jammu province, in time for the first ever Mansar Mela (festival), which has since become an annual event (normally in early April). Mrs. Saxena found a tree with a fascinatingly child-friendly curve. At her suggestion I got a little 'club- house' constructed atop the curve.

There's plenty of fish in the lake but fishing is taboo because it offends religious sentiments. A small wildlife sanctuary has been created on the lakefront and houses the spotted deer, the nilgai, and peacocks. From November to mid-March migratory birds hover around by the thousand. Ducks can also be found. Lotuses grow on the lake.

*Religious significance:*The lake was created in the era of – youguessedit – the *Mahabharata*. Arjun, the great hero and marksman, was chasing the Shesh Nag (the Lord of the Cobra snakes). He shot an arrow to kill Shesh Nag. Water oozed from the spot, ultimately resulting in the present lake. (Snakes almost certainly live in it. Tortoises definitely do. The humps of a gigantic water- snake, but not the snake itself, are reported to have been seen above the surface of the lake in the early part of the 20th century. Shades of Nessie).

[A second arrow shot by the exiled warrior- prince is said to have created the nearby Surinsar lake – which is administratively in Jammu district. The two lakes are believed, quite reasonably, to be linked to each other by an underground fjord.]

A second legend treads the path beaten less often. It dares place the origin of the lake to a full generation later. So, apparently Arjun catches up with Shesh Nag and, instead of killing the snake- god, does the next best thing: he marries the Nag's daughter, Alupi. He goes away to resume making war. In his absence Alupi gives birth to a son whom she names Babruvâhan and who turns out to be as good with bows and arrows as his legendary father.

Arjun wins the war. To underline his victory he sends the Ashwamedh horse all over India, as was the custom. Only Babruvâhan has the courage to halt the horse in its tracks, and does so near the present Mansar. Unbeknownst to him that it is his father whom he is challenging to war, the younger warrior wounds Arjun mortally. Alupi arrives on the scene and begs her son to save his father by bringing a rare herb which is found only under the surface of the earth (i.e. in Pâtâl).

The son did so but, in order to puncture the surface of the earth (so that he could dive in), he had to shoot two arrows into it. This resulted in the twin lakes of Mansar and Surinsar. He entered the earth at Mansar and came out at Surinsar. Together, the two lakes are called Dwigart [lit.: two pits] in Sanskrit. It is believed that the words Duggar and Dogra are derived from Dwigart. Dogra and Duggar are the names of the clan which lives in the districts of Jammu, Kathua and Udhampur and in much of Himachal Pradesh. 'Duggar' is the word used locally. 'Dogra' is more Hindi-ised.

Since the lake is considered auspicious, there are two old temples near it. One of these is dedicated to Umapati- Mahâdev and the other to Lord Narasimha. There also is a shrine of Nag Devta, the snake gods. Several communities perform the *mundan* (ritual shaving of head) of their male children here.

Climate: Days are a few degrees less hot than in, say, Delhi. Nights are substantially cooler. Which means that the best seasons are autumn, winter and spring. Because of the hills and pine forests that surround the lake, it is extremely photogenic.

How to get there: i) The lake is 64 km. from Jammu town. There is a fairly regular bus service from Jammu city. Or drive straight south along the national highway from Jammu for about 40 km. till you come to the temple of Chi Chi Mâtâ (on the left). Drive on for a few hundred metres. There'll be a huge road on the left, which will take you, uphill, to Mansar. ii) If you are coming from the Punjab, drive straight north from Pathankot till you come to Sâmbâ town. Drive on for a kilometre and turn right on the above mentioned uphill road, which is around 25 km. long. iii) From Udhampur the lake is 40 km. south, mostly on the Dhar-Udhampur road.

Where to stay: The accommodation is entirely in the public sector, and is mid- market. There are rooms as well as two self-catering 'huts'.

The valley of Kashmir

Baramulla, Bandipora

High-altitude lakes: The two-mile long **Kausar Nâg** lake (c.13,000'), the largest mountain lake of Kashmîr, is also in the Pîr Pañjâl range. Also at altitudes between 12,000' and 14,000' are the **Kontar Nâg** and the **Gagri Nâg**.

The Mânasbal Lake

Mânasbal Lake: This deep lake is 32 km. from Srinagar, on the road to Bâñdîpore and in the same direction as the Wular lake. It is about 4 km. long and 1.2 km. wide. Mânasbal is famous for its clean waters, water-nuts and lotus roots (nadroo), as well as white and red lotus flowers, which start blossoming in early July. Migratory and other birds abound. The historic Jharokhbal park (aka Jaregba) is located nearby.

The ruins of Badshah Bâgh include the remains of a palace that was never completed, and a garden, which had been built at the behest of Emperor Jehangir and Noor Jehân. N.L. Bakaya calls the ruins northern banks 'Darogabagh'.

Mânas means 'mountain' and 'bal' means 'lake' (or even 'place'). Thus, the lake's name means 'the mountain lake'. Bakaya says that the word has been derived from the Sanskrit Mânassasarovaras or Mansarover.

Andrew Wilson wrote in 1875 that Mânasbal's 'shores are singularly suggestive of peacefulness and solitude.' Another 19th century British writer described the lake as 'secluded, profound, silent.' It still is.

The Mânasbal is connected to the Jehlum by a mile- long canal half a kilometre below Sumbal Being up to 12.8 metres deep, it is the deepest lake in all Kashmîr. According to Hindu mythology the lake is bottomless. A saint is said to have spent many years fashioning a line long enough to touch the bottom. Each time he tried, the line was found wanting and short. In desperation he jumped into the lake, never to be seen again.

The waters of the Mânasbal remain a clear deep- green because they come from springs inside the lake. Some of these springs can be seen, 'like miniature fountains', at the edges of the lake when its waters are low. In the south is a range of hills, including the 6,200', conical Aha Tung/ Ahateng peak, which can be seen from several other parts of the Valley as well. In the east is the Baladar range of mountains. From there, the Amrawati stream forms a 'fine cataract' which falls over a steep, white cliff made of limestone, into the lake below. Near this waterfall is a small Hindu ruin.

There is supposed to be a Tourist Bungalow. It is not likely to be functional till mass tourism returns.

Wular Lake

The 'lily- embroidered' Wular is the largest fresh water lake in Asia. It is 5,180 feet above the msl and 54 km. from Srinagar. Normally the lake is 20.13 km. long and 8.05 km. wide. The circumference of this elliptical lake normally is 48 km. and its average depth around 4 metres. Its normal

The Wular Lake

area is 125 sq. km. Other estimates variously put it as 16 km. long and 8 km. wide or 24 km. long and 10 km. wide. In any case its area increases by nine times – that's right, by 900 per cent - during the floods. The Wular thus functions as a flood reservoir. That is why you will find considerable silt everywhere.

It is at its deepest (5 metres) on its western side, i.e. opposite the Shakur ur din hill. Located between Bâñdîpore and Sopore, it is 33 km. by road from Srinagar City. The other way of getting there is by a 10-hour boat ride on the river Jehlum. (Motor-powered boats reach considerably faster). The Wular is supposed to be one of the 'last relics' of the pre-historic Satisar Lake mentioned above.

History: Wular's ancient name was Mahapadma-saras, after its presiding deity. The word 'Wular' is perhaps a corruption of the Sanskrit *ullola* ('turbulent' or 'with high waves'). Turbulence is occasional in this otherwise calm lake. Mahârâjâ Ranjit Singh lost 300 boats carrying his troops and supplies on one such occasion. Navigation on the lake can be dangerous when torrents of water suddenly come down from the mountains around it.

At the centre of the lake is an artificial island, **Zaina Lank** (rhymes with 'monk'). It was built in AD 1443 by Kashmîr's celebrated King Zain ul Abedin (a.k.a. Budshah), after whom it takes its name. It is "used by boatmen who dread the waves of the lake in storm though in the dry season it is no more than an island" (GMD Sufi).

It is said that Sundarsen, a tyrannical king, used to live on this island till it was submerged following the curse of a saint called Kalâl.

An alternate version goes like this: Sadangula, the Naga (serpent) king of Wular, was exiled from the island. A town called Chandrapura was built where his capital had stood. Later, Neel, the chief of the Naga serpents of Kashmîr, asked a Naga called Maha Padam to take the island over. Maha Padam disguised himself as a Brahmin and went to the court of Viswagasu, the then king of Wular. He asked to be allowed to live in Chandrapura. The king agreed. Maha Padam then told the king who he really was. He also asked to be allowed to submerge the island. The people of the island were evacuated and Maha Padam literally took the place over. The island was drowned inside the lake, which came to be named after him for several centuries after that.

The Rajatarangini records a third legend as well. Apparently a Dravidian sorcerer threatened to dry up the lake. Maha Padam appeared in King Jayapida's dream and asked for protection. In return he promised to lead the king to a goldmine. Jayapida agreed to help. However, he was also curious to see the sorcerer's magic. So, he first allowed the sorcerer to desiccate the lake. The water-serpent's family began to writhe on the bed of the now waterless lake. This hurt the Naga. Jayapida quickly got the lake restored. However, Maha Padam no longer felt bound to implement his original promise. He merely showed the king a copper mine instead.

Legends apart, it is almost certain that an ancient city – called Sindmatnagar by some historians – was submerged in the lake. The floods that often plague Wular probably sank it. However, some believe that it was sunk by volcanic upheavals. Zain ul Abedin sent divers down to lay the foundations of the present island at the spot where Sundarsen's palace- complex had once stood. They found not only the ruins of a temple (which they filled up with stones to build the island on), but also two idols of solid gold, which paid for the construction of the Lank. Zain ul Abedin got a palace and a mosque built on the Lank, ruins of which can still be seen. The pious king would often go to the island for forty-day meditation spells.

Fish and water plants: This gigantic lake produces water- nuts (*singharas*) and large quantities of fish. The people of the numerous villages on its shores eat and sell both. The fish include the sattar gad and chhari gad, both of which are caught by net and hook; the pikut gad, which can only be netted; and the chash gad and the harj, for which hooks are used. The larger fish are caught with spears. The nets are shaped like very large cones and managed by men sitting in at least two boats brought fairly close together. Lotuses are found in plenty.

Birds: Water-fowls come in large numbers in the autumn. In early spring they fly northwards across the Himalayas to the plains of Yarqand, Kashghar and Mogulistan. Like First World travellers going to less developed countries, these birds stock up for their journey to the relatively barren Tibet. They take *singharas* along in their bills. As a result, the shells of these water-nuts mark the places where they camp en route. The Kashmîris would traditionally hunt water-fowls with very long matchlocks. Swans, geese and a variety of seagulls are commonly found. These seagulls breed in the Wular area and lay their eggs on the thickly matted leaves of the water plants.

Sources and hydrology: The Bohnar, Madhumati and Erin nallahs (streams) enter the lake from the east, while the Jehlum passes through it in the south. The Wular "like every other lake surrounded by mountains, is liable to the action of sudden and furious hurricanes that sweep over it with such extraordinary violence that no boatman can be induced to face it. This fact led to the construction, in very early times, of the Noru canal, whereby, when the waters are high, the passage of the lake may be avoided." (*The Gazetteer,* 1890).

The banks of the lake are very marshy. The rains, snow and streams bring soil down from the mountains and deposit it on these shores every year. This silts up the lake, especially on the Bâñdîpore side. However, the water is generally clear and, towards the centre, of a deep green colour. Some land springs can be seen bubbling nearby.

How to get there/ excursions: There's no place to stay in near the lake, unless you bring your own tent. So you might want to plan a day return. The traditional tourist excursion has been thus:

Leave Srinagar by chartered bus or taxi or your own vehicle. Pass the Anchar Lake. Cross River Sind at Dodarhom. Then go to Tulmula (Kheer Bhawânî: see 'Srinagar, Ganderbal' districts). Soon you'll enter Bârâmullâ district. Safapur (see 'Mânasbal' in this chapter) will the next major stop. Bâñdîpore follows. The road now goes up a mountain and then through the Rajdiangan (also Rajadanangan) pass. The Gurêz valley lies beyond. However, take the road to Watlab instead. It will be time for lunch by now. Sopore and then Pattan are the next major towns. The lake will be the next, and last, stop.

You can return to Srinagar by late evening as long as you don't linger too long at the places en route. (There are separate entries on each of these places – except the pass – in the sections on 'Srinagar, Ganderbal' and 'Bârâmullâ, Bandipora' districts).

Budgam

Rivers, Streams and Springs

Budgâm is dotted with springs. There are thirty perennial, round- the-year fresh water springs in the Khag region alone, with another twenty coming to life in the summers. Because of this a nameless employee of the Jammu & Kashmîr government's information department once wrote that Khag should be called the 'land of springs'.

The better known *nags* (springs) are:

Gandhak Nâg: The sulphurous waters of this spring are believed to have medicinal and curative properties, especially for those with skin diseases. (Gandhak means 'sulphur'). The spring is located in Darang Khaiporâ, a village in the Khag administrative 'block'.

Nârâ Nâg: Also known as Narain Nâg, this spring is located near Khag village. It is said to get its waters from the TosaMaidân Sar Lake. These waters seep into the ground to re-emerge downhill as the Nârâ Nâg. In support of this plausible theory is the legend of a mendicant who accidentally dropped some sheep-dung into the ToshâMaidân Sar Lake, floating on the Nârâ Nâg when he reached the Nâg a few days later. To be sure that there was indeed an underground link between the Sar and the Nâg, he went back to the Sar and threw turmeric powder into it. After a few days the turmeric- coloured waters reached the Nâg and proved the mendicant's theory right.

Pushkar Nâg: The ancient Kashmîri Hindu scripture, the Neelmata Purana, contains the oldest extant mention of this spring, which originates in Pushkar village, which is between Khag and Ferozpura. The Purana says that bathing in the spring carries as much spiritual merit as reading the Vedas, the oldest of all Hindu scriptures, all night long. The Nâg flows eastward. The Kashmîrî Pandits would perform the Divai Path in the month of Savan (July-Aug) every year and then bathe in the spring.

Sukh Nâg: This perennial spring flows from the several small lakes between the Toshâ Maidân and Nurpur passes, on the east of the Panjal range. It cascades down the mountains and pours off a 20' cliff at Kanj Zubji, near the Toshâ Maidân, as a waterfall. It is then joined by other springs, in particular the Magam stream at village Bailheran and the Khor stream at Trekolabal. They merge together to become the Ahij brook.

The Ahij then branches into several streams such as the Mala Kol, the Lâr Kol and the Sona Maen Kol, which irrigate the Beerwah area.

Vigne observed that the Suk(h) Nâg, like many other rivers of the Valley is considered pre-eminently good on account of its freshness and power of creating an appetite. However, he adds that the hono(u)r of having filled the drinking- pipe of the old kings of Kashmîr is claimed for this stream.

Sut Haran: The name is probably a corruption of the Hindi/ Sanskrit expression 'Sita Haran' (lit.:the abduction of Sita). However, the local legend does not refer to the abduction of Goddess Sita. Instead, it is about her having bathed in this spring at some stage during the 14-year exile (*banvâs*) of Lord Ram. It is said that Shri Ram camped in these woods, accompanied by his wife, Sita, and brother, Lakshman. Near the spring there is a rock which the goddess is supposed to have sat on.

This spring, known for the sweetness of its water, is located in a dense forest. It is close to the Toshâ Maidân meadow on one side and the 'Line of Control' on the other. The Tos(h)a Maidân Sar lake found in the middle of the Toshâ Maidân meadow originates at this spring.

Streams: Sometimes several springs combine to form a stream. And at others a single spring, the Sukh Nâg for example, gives birth to as many three streams – in this case the Ahij, the Laen and the Sona Maen. The Ahij and the Mala Kol are examples of the former type, for the two merge with the Jehlum.

The streams of Budgâm have full-fledged identities of their own, in legend as well as in observable reality. The silent Mala Kol was nicknamed the 'deaf- mute stream' because it noiselessly followed the sage Syed Taj ud Din from the Sukh Nâg to Sikandarporâ when he visited the Khag area. The reticence of its character is most noticeable when it is in spate. Conversely, the Laen Kol is the noisy one, kicking up a ruckus even when its waters are low. The Laen, Maen and Zaen are seen by the locals as being three sisters.

Other major streams of the district are the ShaliGañgâ Nallah and the Ferozporâ Nallah

Kupwara

Springs and Streams: The Qazinâg spring is said to be the source of the various springs and streams of Bungus. The *Doudh Kol* is seven kilometres long and its waters are sweet and cold. It emerges from the Dudi hill and merges with the Tilwan Kol at the Buddi Behek meadow. The *Roshan Kol* is a picturesque seasonal stream that cuts through Budda Bungus, which is one of the more important meadows in the plains. It joins the Tilwan Kol at Gud Bari. The *Satkol Nâg* comes out of the Satkol hill. It gives birth to another seven streams before flowing into the

Leepa valley. The *Tilwan Kol* is the longest (15km)., widest, deepest and best- known stream in all Bungus. It unites with the Kahmill stream near the Baddi Behek pasture.

Glaciers: There are major glaciers at Shamshabari and Daejlungun.

Pulwama, Shopian

Aharbal: (61 km from Srinagar or 13 km. from Shopiâñ). Surrounded by fir forests, Aharbal is famous for its 24.4 metre waterfall created by river Vishav (Veshau). There is supposed to be a tourist bungalow (but please check its state of repair before deciding to spend the night there) and a PWD Rest House. The best views of the fall are from its right bank. The best times to see it are the morning and noon, because the rays of the sun that hit the spray create rainbows. See also the entry on 'Veshau' in the chapter on 'Rivers.')

Kounsar Nâg lake, the: (Roughly 12,000) Bakaya says that the name of the lake derives from the Sanskrit *Krama Saras, 'krama'* meaning 'footstep' and '*saras*' being 'lake'. It is also called the *Vishnû Paudh* ('Lord Vishnû's foot'). Either way, the lake seems to be associated with Lord Vishnû, unusual for a valley where the Hindus are supposed to belong entirely to Lord Shiv's sect. Its old name – and that of the three tall surrounding mountains, one of which is 15,253' high – was Kysur.

This blue lake is three kilometres long. It is around 2.25 km. at its widest. Vigne, c. 1870, wrote, 'Judging from the angle at which the slopes enter the lake, the bottom must originally have been about 200 feet in depth below the present level of the water... The formation is a beautiful amygdaloid, containing spots of quartz in a dull, dark, purple-coloured matrix. This formation, which is very common in Kashmîr, the natives cal the *chitur deyu*, or the *devil's small-pox*, supposing it to be a disease in the rock caused by the evil eye.'

The Nâg freezes over till mid-June. Even after that large chunks of ice remain on the surface. To the south of the lake is a glacial Valley. A stream flows out of the lake. It goes on to become the Veshau/ Vishav river.

Legends: There are two alternative legends about the three basaltic peaks and the lake. i) According to the older one the peaks were the thrones of the Hindu trinity, the Lords Brahma, Vishnû and Mahesh (Shiv) when they fought the demon Jalodbhav and dried up the Satisar (or Satisaras).

(For details see 'Bârâmullâ, Bandipora.') ii) Others say that the highest – western – peak was the throne of a king. The next, the middle peak, was where his vizier would sit, and the nobles on the eastern one.

Those who believe in the former version go on to link the highest peak with the Manu (Noah) legend. Apparently, Goddess Durgâ transformed herself into a huge ark (all right, boat). Lord Vishnû became a fish, in what is known as his *Matsya Avatar* ('fish incarnation'). After the 'ark' had been filled with all those who had been chosen to be saved from the flood, the Lord brought it to the western peak and moored it there. Ever since, Hindus have been going to the lake and the western peak on the '*Naubandhan Teerth*' or 'the pilgrimage of the mooring of the boat'. (Nau= boat; bandhan= mooring of; teerth= pilgrimage).

All the same, Vigne observed that the Kounsar Nâg was "not held in the same estimation as the Gañgâ Bal on the opposite side of the Valley".

Târsar and Mârsar: "When you were away," King Yusuf Shâh Chak (late 16th century) wrote of his beloved, "your plaits reminded me of the Târsar and Mârsar lakes". These twin lakes are located in the mountains and are 3 and 5 km. respectively from Nagberan. Both lie between the valleys of the Sind and Kashmîr. You can get to the Târsar either from the northern end of Trâl valley or from Lidderwatt. The Mârsar is almost a mile long and more than half a mile broad and shaped like an arc. It is covered with snow till late summer and is also the source of the Arrah river. It can be reached either from Trâl or from Lidderwatt. There are two trails from Trâl: from Narastan, which is the best path, or from Zostan.

In South Asia, any food or drink that has been touched by the human (or animal) mouth is considered unclean (*jhoothâ*). Ditto for food or water touched by unclean hands. The shepherds who live near these two lakes believe that 'fairies live inside these lakes.' Therefore, one should not gargle or spit into these lakes or otherwise dirty their waters.[1] Even the Muslims consider it a sin to catch fish in these lakes.

---

1 Such tales have obviously been made up to keep people from dirtying up the pure waters of these lakes.

In Safâpur near Lake Mânasbal there's a taboo against catching fish. The real reason is that the fish of the area are so defenceless and easy to catch that one can grab them with bare hands. This has been dressed up as an elaborate superstition, according to which fish caught in the Safapur area will turn into blood in the vessel when you cook them.

Srinagar city

The Lakes of Srinagar

Most people have heard of just the 11.25 sq. km. Dal Lake. Some have heard of the Nageen as well. In fact, Srinagar has five lakes. This is how they are linked: The Dal merges with the Nageen. It is also connected, through a small estuary, to the 6.5 sq. km. Anchar Lake. The Khushhâl Sar and Gil Sar are two small, interlinked lakes that flow into the Anchar. The Brari Nimbal could be considered Srinagar's sixth lake. However, the Khushhâl and Gil Sars, as well as the Brari Nimbal, are not at present meant for casual, recreational tourists.

The Sind river flows into the Anchar. The waters of the Anchar, in turn, flow into the Jehlum. The Dal Lake and the Jehlum would have flowed into each other had the Dal Gate not been built to separate the two. This gate ensures that the Dal Lake does not empty itself into the Jehlum when the waters of the river are low. It also prevents the Dal from getting flooded by the Jehlum when the river is in spate. As things stand, between the Dal and the Jehlum is a canal called the Tsont (or Chunt) e Kol. The Tsont e Kol begins near the Dal Gate, were it meets the Dal Lake. It ends near the Badshah Bridge/ Shergarhi (Divisional Commissioner's office) complex, where it merges with River Jehlum. Actually, the Tsont e Kol begins well before the Dal Gate, but that end is closed at present.

The **Dal Lake**: The word Dal could have either come from "bal," the Kashmîri word for "lake," or from the Tibetan word "dal," which means

The Dal Lake

'still'. It is believed that there used to be a vast plain called Vitâlamarg, which was converted into the Dal lake by an ancient Hindu king. This must have been before the Christian era, because the Drogjun sluice gate – where the Dal joins the Tsont-i-Kol canal on the Jhelum – was originally built by King Pravarsena in AD 59. So was the old embankment leading to the city.

Historian Hassan estimated the circumference of the lake at 10 miles (16km). "According to historians," he wrote, "in ancient times it was a waste land called Talni Marg. Rajá Pravarasená dammed the Behet [the Jehlum] at Nawapurá and made it flow into the town up to the foot of the Maran mountain [the Hari Parbat]. After a period of time, the Behet had a flood in the time of Rajá Duralab Darun and caused the field to be flooded, thus it turned into a lake. The governors of the time did not dam it and hence after a long time it became very deep. Sultan Sikandar... constructed a strong dam from Naidyar to Nishat garden... and then built six stone bridges over it.

"After that Saif Khân built a dam from Khwajá Yarbal to Aishabad as a thoroughfare to the gardens".

That explains the thoroughfare. Or does it? *The Gazetteer* says, 'The lake is crossed by a narrow path running along a raised causeway called the Súttu or Sut-i-Chodri, said to have been constructed by a wealthy Hindú pandit. [It starts at] Naid Yár...'

For the histories of the two main islands in the lake, please see 'Char Chinar/ Rop Lank' and 'Son Lank' in this chapter.

The lake used to have an area of 22.5 square km. in the 19th century. However, it has now shrunk to almost exactly half of its former self, to 11.25 sq km. Much of what has gone consisted of marsh. Going by 19th century accounts, however, the lake's depth has not changed much – or at all. *The Gazetteer* (1890) says that the average depth of the lake is around 7 to 10 feet, going up to 26 feet at one place. This is still true of the lake.

The lake is shrinking only partly due to the silt that comes down from the mountains with the rains. The main reason is human greed and shortsightedness. At the close of the twentieth century there were as many as 60,000 people living inside the lake, on islands and in houseboats. For centuries, some of them have been growing vegetables and flowers on the surface of the lake, legally. However, many of them have also been creating artificial islands, to live and build hotels on, and also to grow trees and vegetables on.

Among the plants to be found on the Dal are the white lily, the annesleya horrida (called juwur by the local people), the delicious singhârhâ (horned water nut), the lotus (the roots of which are called the nadroo and constitute one of the few vegetarian dishes of Kashmîr), the kamal doda, reeds and rushes (used for thatching the roofs of boats and for making sieves), and grass and floating leaves used as fodder for animals.

Son(a) Lank: (Pron. 'sown lunk', rhymes with 'lone hunk'). The Son(a) Lank (the Golden Island) is an artificial island in the Dal Lake. It was built by the Mughals, apparently to be one up on the Kashmîri King Zain ul Abedin, who had originally built the island. It is roughly 35m. square and, in the mid- 19th century, used to host a jail, the ruins of which might still be seen.

"In the middle of the Large [section of the] Dal, opposite to Hazratbal, Sultan Zain-ul-Abidin had built an island, Sona Lank, and a palace with three stories on it, but it cracked in an earthquake. Then, the Mughal kings turned it into a pleasant scenery. [Afghân governor] Ameer Khân made changes in it and caused the water to be drawn up the chinar with the help of a water- wheel and built a fountain in the courtyard of the building. He spent his time enjoying it. Today the building is desolate." (Hassan, mid-19th century)

Next to nothing of Ameer Khân's building survives.

The Shikârâs

History: These are flat-bottomed boats with a cloth canopy. The canopy is higher at the rear and lower in the front. While researching Kashmîri art I came upon a 15th century miniature painting which showed full-fledged shikârâs. So, this type of boat is at least that old.

Seating capacity: A shikârâ is allowed to carry five adults, or three adults and four children. Please don't overload the shikârâ. Your own life could be in danger. You have to pay extra 'halting charges' if you extend your trip beyond the specified period.

Routes: Shikârâs ply on the Dal and Nageen lakes, mainly to provide joyrides to tourists. Their less comfortable (and infinitely less expensive) cousins carry local commuters across the Jehlum, from one bank to the one immediately opposite. 16 joyride- routes and 3 river- crossings are popular with tourists.

The Jehlum- crossings you will find most convenient are all from the Bund (parallel to and just off the Residency/ Sherwani Road). 'Aab'-

means 'water' and 'guzar' is 'to cross'. Aab e guzar, thus, indicates the point at which to cross the Jehlum.

Go to Lâl Chowk. Stand in front of the clock tower. Tyndale Biscoe School will now be in front of you, on the left. Amira Kadal will be on your right. In front will be a major lane. This is the Forest Lane. Go through it to the Bund. You'll find boats to take you to the SPS Museum/ Lâl Mandi area.

Listed below are the most popular routes and crossings. Unless specified otherwise, all timings are for return trips. (A *ghat* is a riverbank, normally a bank on which a stone platform and/ or steps have been constructed).

a) *From the Boulevard:* The best known shikârâ rides from here are to i-ii) the Nishat and Shalimar (Mughal) gardens. The two gardens are quite far apart from each other; iii-v) the Kuttar ('Kabootar') Khânâ and Char Chinar islands. (There are two Char Chinars: Rop Lank and Son Lank. The Rop Lank is the closer of the two and is the one most shikârâs go to).; vi) the Cheshmashahi Ghat. (This is next to the Nehru Memorial Botanical Gardens. The Cheshmashahi garden is an uphill walk of almost 2 km. from here).; and vii-ix) Hazratbal, Nageen lake and Naseem Bâgh(5 hour return trips to any one of these three places; or a 6 hour loop- return trip for all three).; x) the Chhattabal Wier (3 or 4 hours one way; return by vehicle, because the water will be upstream. This shikârâ ride is on River Jehlum and not on any of the lakes).

Normally tourists combine e or ii with iii or iv (4½ to 6 hours return, including halts). You can also combine iv and vi (3 hours).

b) *From the Dal Gate:* There are short rides from the 'First Ghat' to i) Nehru Park (2-2½ hours return); and ii) the bathing boats in the middle of the Dal Lake (2½ to 3 hours return). (Incidentally, there are bathing boats in the Nageen, too).

c) *From the Nehru Park ghat (bank)* to i) the bathing boats of the Dal (1 to 1½ hours return); ii) the Nehru Island (This ride takes a few minutes. You can pay per passenger or for the entire shikârâ).

d) *From the Jehlum:* You can take a shikârâ from one of the registered ghats to i) the Nishat and Shalimar gardens, via Kuttar Khânâ and the closer Char Chinar island (Rop Lank) (6½ hours return; skip one of the two gardens and save half an hour); ii) Char Chinar and Cheshmashahi (5 hours); iii) the Chhattabal Wier (3½ to 4 hours).

e) *From the Nageen Club* to the bathing boats of the Nageen (1 to 1½ hours).

f) Visit a houseboat on the Dal (thirty minutes return) to see what one looks like from the inside. Most shikârâ- operators can arrange such a visit for you.

g) *Nageen Lake:* Cross it from east to west (in less than thirty minutes).

h) *From the Char Chinar ghat* to the Char Chinar island: (1½ to 2 hours). Here, too, you can pay per head or for the whole shikârâ.

I strongly recommend any trip that takes you down the Jehlum to the Chhattabal Wier (aka 'Vier' and 'Veer'). Forget joyrides. This will be a trip through history, culture and architecture, with Hindu temples and bathing ghats as well as stunning Muslim shrines along the banks of the Jehlum.

Anchar Sar: "Formerly, the said lake was much smaller. In 1300 AH [AD 1882], the Sindlar being flooded turned its course and entered Anchar Sar [sar= lake]; it destroyed the agricultural land on every side, and widened the space of the lake three-fold. In its middle Raja Jayapid had built a dam which is called Ramu Sathu." (Hassan, the 19th century historian).

In 1999, this author got a sixth of this 6.5sq.km. lake cleared of weeds to prove that the Anchar can be made as pretty as the Dal merely by 'deweeding' it. I also got a low wall constructed at one end. This prevents the waters of the lake from flowing into the Jehlum when the level of the river is lower than that of the lake. In 2000 I got constructed gates to regulate the flow of water.

The Jenab Sâheb shrine is on the banks of the lake. One of the many springs that feed the lake can be seen at the ghat nearest to the shrine.

Hârwan lake: This is an artificial reservoir, upto 30' deep. It was constructed by Mahârâjâ Pratap Singh as part of the waterworks of Srinagar City. The waters of Lake Tarsar flow down to the reservoir and are collected there, before being supplied to the city.

The catchment area of the reservoir is almost 150 square miles. The Dogrâ Mahârâjâs had banned the grazing of cattle and sheep in the entire catchment area, so that the water of the reservoir did not get contaminated. Srinagar was then prone to epidemics like cholera. Therefore, the Mahârâjâs' caution was well-advised.

A covered masonry canal runs from this lake to the Nishat reservoir, winding its way through the hills.

Khushhâl Sar: "It is a lake situated in the northern parts of the city; on its eastern bank is situated Muhalla Jadibal, and on its western is the Idgah. Its circumference is about four miles. Around it grows the reed grass in abundance, half of which is used for manufacture of matting for the Jami [Jâmâ] Masjid and the other half for [religious] mooring places and the Khânqâh of Jadibal. In it there are plenty of birds of prey…" (Hassan)

Things have changed considerably since Hassan's time (mid 19th century). The Khushhâl Sar is still quite pretty. However, since the last decades of the 20th century, garbage has often been dumped in it. In the evenings it emits a foul smell. Aided by some NRI scientists I tried to introduce enzymes into the lake, which would neutralise the organisms that were caused the stench. The experiment was a non- starter. Such enzymes work only in still, stagnant waters, and not in lakes that flow into a river.

The birds of prey are still there.

Srinagar-Ganderbal rural

Gañgabal Lake: (3,570m./ c.12,000 feet). About 60 km. north of Srinagar, this lake is on the north- eastern slopes of the Haramukh mountain. It is a little more than 2 km long and around one kilometre wide. Its waters are not very clear or deep. Its beauty owes to its being at the foot of the Haramukh glacier and to what tourist literature calls 'its varied scenery'.

The Gañgabal Lake

The lake is also called the Uttar Gañgâ, the Harmukhat and the Har Mukt Gañgâ. Sacred to the Hindus, it has a status among them that no other place in the higher mountains of Kashmîr does. The ashes of the dead are immersed in the lake in September. It is believed that Goddess Parvati (Uma) had, at this spot, squeezed the Gañgâ out of her husband, Lord Shiv's top- knotted hair. The annual Hindu pilgrimage to the lake is on the 8th of Bhadra (roughly 20th August).

There are pretty wild flowers in the nearby meadow. There are several lakes, notably the Nund Kol (see below), around the Gañgabal, which is in the centre. Parshu Ram, the great pre-historic saint, is believed to have meditated near these lakes.

These lakes include the Lool Gul and the Andan Sar. Both are to the north of Gañgabal and both are at around 13,500'.

To get to Gañgabal you can drive up to the Nârâ Nâg ruins of Wâñgat after which you will have to trek uphill to the lake.

Nund Kol is also called the Nandi Sar and the Kaladaka. It is 500 feet below, and to the east of, the Gañgabal. 'Kala' is another name for Lord Shiv. Nandi is the Lord's faithful bull. This lake is supposed to be the place where the Lord and his bull lived together. Because the Harmukh mountain (16,872') towers over it, N.L. Bakaya calls the Nund Kol a 'blue carpet at the feet of the mighty Lord Hara'.

Nearby lakes include i) the Kola Sar, which is almost five kilometres away, and at a lower level. Because of the surrounding mountains little light reaches this lake; and ii) the shallow, little Brahm Sar, between which and the Kola Sar is the rocky Hamsdar.

The Ladakh region

Leh

Rivers

The Indus is the principal river of Ladakh and travels south to POK and Pakistan. However, before it leaves India it is joined by rivers Suru, Shayok and Zâñskâr

Lakes

'Tso' means 'male lake', and 'tsomo' means 'female lake'.

Chang Chenmo: This is a large lake in northwest Ladâkh. Streams from the surrounding mountains, especially the northern slopes of the Karakoram Range, feed it. It has no outlet. Therefore, its water is brackish.

Lingzi Tang: This large lake is near Ladâkh's northwestern border with Tibet. It is near the southern mountains of the Karakoram Range. When snow melts in the mountains around the lake the water thus formed turns into streams. These streams flow into the Lingzi Tang. Its water is brackish.

Pangong Tso/ Lake: (13,936 feet). Also called Tso Monanglari ('the lake of the great hollow'). This L-shaped lake is around 148 km./ six hours from Leh by taxi. You travel in the direction of Hemis, and turn left near Hemis. The last major village before the lake is Tangtse. Chushul is 47 km. ahead of the lake.

It is a salt- water (brackish) lake, the highest of its kind in the world. The waters of the lake (or, correctly, this series of inter-connected lakes) are mostly sapphire blue, with different shades of blue or green at different places. People have counted as many as seven shades. The general formula that the colour is green where shallow, blue where deep and other shades in between.

The lower lake is called Pangong Tso, is around 65 km. long, is the longest lake in Ladakh and is in Ladakh itself. (The upper lakes, on the other hand, are in Rudok. The Chinese have annexed parts of Pangong proper, too). The total length of the lakes is 144 km. and almost three-quarters are under Chinese ownership or occupation. The lakes are 3 to 6 km. wide.

The Pangong is 142' (around 45m). at its deepest, in the north- west. British officers reported around 1860, "We looked in vain for fish, and, with the exception of a species of bug... we failed to see any animal of signs of life..." In September they noted that the temperature of the water was 55°F.

Local people told me that the lake freezes over punctually on the 14th November every year. This is one report I would like to check out personally for I, too, have visited the lake only in September. It remains frozen for three months when it can be walked upon.

Till 1993 tourists, not just foreigners but even Indians, could visit the lake only if they obtained special permits. That year, as the Tourism Secretary of Jammu and Kashmir, I was able to get the rules changed and this was one of seven thitherto prohibited areas thrown open to tourists. A major Indian film, *Dil Se*, was shot at the Pangong.

There are barren, rocky mountains in the east and north-east, with peaks at between 18,000' and 19,500'. The mountains in the south-west are taller and go up to 21,500'. One of the peaks is always covered with snow. The glaciers on some of these mountains melt into little streams, some of which merge with the lake.

The Gazetteer notes, "The Lukung stream enters the lake at its north-west end... The lake has no effluence, and shows signs of gradual subsidence. The waters of the western end are much more salt [sic] than those of the eastern end near Ot. In the stream connecting the Pangong Tso with the Tso Nyâk the water becomes drinkable... Wild geese are plentiful here, and in the Tso Nyâk there are fish, a species of tench".

Lukung is at the northern edge of Pangong. You first get to see the lake from here. Two roads emerge at Lukung. One, obviously, leads to the lake. The other goes to Phobrang, which is next to the areas occupied by China.

Tangtse: There are old engravings on some boulders near Tangtse.

Durbuk: It is learnt that there is a large statue of the Chambâ at Buddha.

Thukung: This is a place at the southern end of the lake. It is here that the lake turns at a right angle, towards the east, into Chinese occupation. In 1962 there were bloody battles here.

Accommodation: There are two rooms for certain categories of travellers near the lake. You would do well to take your own tent, though. The Tourism department has a two bedroom hut at Tangtse, a distance away. Or you can camp at Spangmik, the last village you will be allowed to visit. You cannot camp close to the lake.

How to get there: There are no buses to the lake. Jeep-taxis are the only option. Unless you trek much of the way.

Spanggur: Now under Chinese occupation, this little lake can be seen from the Indian side. It is in the same area as the Pangong, and is to the southeast of Shyok. When snow melts in the surrounding mountains, the water flows into this lake. Its water is mainly brackish.

Tso Kar: (150km. from Leh; 75km. from Tsomo Riri). 'Kar' means 'salt'. For that reason, many guidebooks refer to it as the Salt Lake. Over the centuries table salt would be extracted from this lake. This was stopped in 1959.

The lake is located in the Aksai Chin region, and is near the Indo-Tibetan border. The Tso Kar is close to the Tsomo Riri. It is believed that in the distant past the Tso Kar and the Lingzi Tang were inter-connected.

Indeed, there is a theory that thousands of years ago there was a small sea where the Tibetan plateau now is. Several salt lakes dot the Aksai Chin area now. They might be remnants of that sea.

It is more likely that they are not. That's because most of them, the Tso Kar included, receive fresh water from the streams that flow down from the surrounding mountains. In addition, a river flows into the Tso Kar from the Karakoram range, which is in the north.

The *Changpa* nomads live in the pastures between and near these two lakes. So does a wealth of wildlife: the bharal, the kiyang, the lynx, the marmot, the nyan and the wolf.

Thukje monastery: This is a small monastery in a village close to the lake. It comes under the Kurzok monastery.

Tsomo Riri: (4,595m). 215 km. south- east of Leh town. This large, brackish water lake is 19km. long and 7 km. wide. Its colours change as the sun moves during the day. In June it starts getting bright as early as 4.30am. There continues to be light till around 8.30pm. Tso means 'male lake' and a Tsomo is a female lake.

There are many glaciers uphill from the lake. When they melt their waters form little streams that flow to the flat land below. All these streams merge to make up the Tsomo Riri. However, there are no drains to take water out of the lake. So, because of the dryness all around, and the summer sun, the waters of this lake evaporate considerably, especially in summer. As a result the water left behind is brackish and there are no living organisms inside the lake.

Outside the lake is a different matter altogether. There is an 80m. by 60m. island near its north eastern shore. (In the road directions to the Tsomo, this point is at 'Km.209.') This island is where the Bar-headed Goose and Brown-headed Gull set up their nests. In season as many as 3000 birds congregate at the lake. Groups of as many as 500 Bar- headed Goose at a time are common. The reason is obvious. When birds migrate southwards in April and May they have to fly over hundreds of miles of desert. Suddenly they see this huge expanse of water. They are naturally tempted to stay there for a while.

The rare and endangered Black-necked Crane is the lake's star attraction. Other visitors include the Craig Martin, the Horned Lark, the Red-billed Chough, the Tibetan Snow-finch and several kinds of Wagtail.

Like the Pangong, the Tsomo is partly under Chinese occupation. For that reason, tourists were not allowed to visit the lake till 1993 when… well, you've read the story already. Except that I regret my enthusiasm to get the ban on tourists lifted. The World Wildlife Fund considers this one of the ten wetlands of global importance. But 'development' is scaring the birds away: mostly to Tso Kar. A couple of ugly buildings and camps have since come up near the lake, more ominously, so has a firing range where policemen learn how to use rifles. True, they fire on paper targets, not birds. But there's too much noise pollution. I am attempting to curb this. If I can't then I'm afraid I'll have to lobby for a ban on tourists visiting the lake, this time for reasons of ecology. The firing range, too, has to be shifted.

I last visited the lake in 2001, in the middle of June. Around 8 in the morning there were around three dozen birds on the island itself. There were twenty or thirty Brahmini ducks on the marshy eastern banks of the lake, well away from the island.

'Km. 209' is where the tip of the lake closest to the road is. It is also the part of the lake where the road from Leh first meets the lake.. The island as well as the eastern banks, where the Brahmini ducks were, are both close to the 'Km.209' point. To reach either you will have to trudge through half a kilometre of alluvium and occasionally jump over narrow streams. In the case of the island, a good long-jumper can jump over from the marsh to the island. With practice it is possible to walk noiselessly towards the birds without scaring them off. Tough sandals or floaters, neither of which I ever wear, are the recommended footwear. My shoes and socks were soggy for several hours thereafter.

The lake is too far for a day return from Leh town. I have travelled from Leh to the Tsomo in a 'Traveller' in as little as 5 hours and 45 minutes and, with several photography stops, in as much as 8 hours. Accommodation during the tourist season: You can stay in tents that are, on order, set up by Snow Leopard Adventures, Zâñgsty, Leh.

Kurzok is a tiny village on a hillock close to the banks of the Tsomo. There are a couple of privately owned guesthouses in the village. It has a medium-sized monastery that is said to have been built around AD 1650. *Reach Ladâkh* disagrees with this oral account that I picked up at the monastery. It says, instead, that Lama Kunga Lodos Snyingpo founded the Thupstan Sningpo Druprgout Chosling (monastery) between 1851 and 1861. It adds that Tsering Tashi Namgyâl, the head of the Rupsho monastery, sponsored the construction.

The monastery has murals and a small library. Both are said to date to the seventeenth century. By the end of the twentieth century several sections of the monastery started falling apart because of poor maintenance. Therefore, in 2001 its management launched a major renovation and expansion of the lhakhang. It belongs to the same red hat Drug Pâ sect as Hemis, but is not subordinate to the latter. There are three major idols in the monastery.

There is a tall mountain behind Kurzok from which several little streams flow down towards the Tsomo. Southwest of the village, much too close to the banks of the lake, is the palatial, white, 20th century, summer residence of the head lama of a distant gompa. He comes over just once a year.

Hot-water springs

There are famous hot water springs at Chumâthâng, Panamik/ Panamic (Nubra), Pûgâ (Chang Thâñg) and near Zâñglâ (in Zâñskâr, Kargil district). An official publication describes all of them as sulphur-springs. The springs at Pûgâ have borax.

Ladakh has mineral water springs, too.

Hot-water springs: Panamik village has two famous hot-water springs at the exits of which the water is at 167°F. It is 155°F even in the baths. People from all over the district visit these springs for their supposed curative qualities. Before borders hardened, so did travellers from Yarqand. These scalding waters are said to cure rheumatism and syphilis. (The last bit is interesting. I first visited Ladakh in 1981. That's before AIDS became widespread. In those days venereal disease (VD or STD) meant syphilis, gonorrhoea etc. STD was rampant in some of the neighbouring hills. However, STD was totally unknown in Ladakh. I was told that the viruses of these diseases couldn't survive Ladakh's incredible cold. Just as snakes can't. So, who were these people who came to get their syphilis cured? Yarqandis? Or is Panamik the reason why there's no syphilis in Ladakh?)

Chapter- 13

Wildlife and Flora in Jammu, Kashmir and Ladakh

Poonch

Wildlife

Almost 30 per cent of Poonch district consists of forests – 83,914 acres, to be precise. Its wildlife is supposed to be unique because both oriental and 'palearctic' species are found. Urbanisation and 'development' have played havoc with the wildlife of Poonch by encroaching on the forests where this wildlife used to live.

Before independence (1947) there were nine markhor game reserves just in the Poonch-Haveli tehsil. In addition there were 41 shikargahs (hunting reserves). However, a lot still survives.

Mammals found: The ghoral, leopard, brown bear, musk deer and markhor live in the district, some of these species being rare.

Birds ('avifauna'): Again, some of the species are rare and include the moral, rock partridge, kohlas, snow cock, chakors, black partridge and pheasant.

Flora

As we have seen, the climate of Rajouri varies from place to place, depending on the altitude of the place. So does the vegetation. Chir (pine) trees are found in most parts of the district, except in the alpine zone. As a result, resin is an important product of the district. i) The vegetation of the semi-tropical zone includes the kamila, khair phulai, amaltas, amla, shisham, jamun, anardana, kau and bargad. Shrubs that grow by the rivers and rivulets include garund, rausont, snathe and nerium indicum. ii) The temperate zone: Here we find the rare chikri tree, fir, oak and quercus senioarpifolia (kharsu). The endangered chikri tree grows mainly around Thanna Mandi, where they sell you kitschy handicrafts (including toothpicks) made of its wood. What a fine use of the wood of a dwindling specie. iii) The 'alpine' zone: Fir, rhododendron, willow and juniper grow here.

Wildlife

Animals that live in the district include the black bear, the brown bear, the wild bear, the jungli (wild) cat, the cheetah, the log deer, the musk deer, the Indian fox, the goral, the hare, the jackal, the langur, the snow leopard, the monkey, the porcupine, the grey musk shrew and squirrels.

Birds: Birds found in the district include the bulbul, chakor, Ram chakor, house crow, jungle crow, dove, egret, falcon (shikar), common pea fowl, red jungle fowl, kingfisher, common pariah kite, koel, Indian myna, nutcracker, green partridge, monal pheasant, koklar pheasant, Himalayan tree pie, black rock pigeon, grey quail, the swallow, tailor bird, white backed vulture and wagtail.

Silk: Eight thousand families of Rajouri are involved in the making of silk: mainly rearing silkworms.

Fish: The government has established a trout hatchery at Phaini (Budhal). In addition there are fish farms at Muradpur, which is seven kilometres from Rajouri town. Fish to be found there include the common carp, gross carp, silver carp, rehu and rigal. There are fish- ponds at Behrote, Chhani- parat, Dharamsal, Panjah, Rajpora- Kampla and Saranoo as well.

Udhampur-Reasi

Flora

Pines grow almost everywhere in this district. Forests of deodar, kail and fir can be found in the higher mountains that receive snow. There is one chinar tree in Sudh Mahâdev and a few chinar trees at Chirhai Muttal Bamboos and khair grow in the plains.

Mangoes, apricots, apples, guavas and walnuts are among the fruits grown.

Fauna

Birds found in the district: peacocks, doves, parrots and sparrows.

Wild animals: panthers, leopards, boar, foxes, wild goats and the wild cow. Camels are found in some parts.

Budgam

Forests

More than half of Budgam district consists of forests (750 sq. km. out of a total of 1,371 sq. km).. These are divided into three forest ranges, Doodh Gañgâ, Raithan and Srî Pratap Pora.

Kupwara

Flora

62 per cent of the district consists of forests. Trees that grow in the district include deodar, kail, pine, fir, blue fir, elm, chinar, poplar, willow and walnut. Some of the important medicinal herbs found in these forests are rattan jog, kutth, memaikh, booja khaupittries and gugal dhoop. (See also the entry on 'Bungus' later in this chapter).

Fauna

With forests of the kind Kupwara has, animals, including birds, naturally abound. Among the four legged kind are wild bulls and wild goats, 'red' and black bears, markhores, jackals, the musk deer, monkeys, tigers and foxes. And then there are doves, fly- catchers, wild cocks, woodpeckers, falcons, swallows and wild ducks, in addition to the usual crows, sparrows, pigeons and vultures.

Bungus: *Meadows- cushioned and nutritious:* True to the 'gus' part of its name, Bungus has more than a hundred meadows. A little more than half of these are on top of plateaux, while the rest are in the plains. These meadows are known all over Kashmîr for their cushioned feel. (Damsna in Kargil [Ladâkh] has a similar exalted reputation). The texture and quantity of the grass determines the cushion. Cowherds and shepherds take their flocks to these meadows because of their unique nutritional and medicinal qualities. Indeed, as we shall see below, several medicinal plants grow in the meadows of Bungus.

Fauna: Bungus has around 50 species of mammals and plays host to some 200 species of birds.

The higher chordates found in Bungus include antelopes, black bears, brown bears, the red fox, monkeys, the musk deer, snow leopards, and, Mr. Majrooh adds, lions (felius padres).

The Rodents of Bungus: Hedgehogs, the mongoose, rats, shrews and squirrels.

Resident birds: Pheasants, the tragophan, the monal pheasant, the Indian black partridge, wild fowls and the jungle bush quail.

Migratory birds: Doves, hoopoes, parrots (spectacular) and swallow golden orates.

Non- chordates: Mr. Majrooh says that these include several species of protozoa (free living as well as parasitic), coelenterate, mollusc and anthropod. There are no echinodermates in Bungus. Earthworms are the dominant specie of annelid.

Anthropods: Bees, bugs, flies, mosquitoes, pediculus species and scorpions.

Reptiles: Mainly lizards (calottes) and snakes (mostly non- poisonous). On occasion poisonous snakes, too, have been found, mainly the pit viper and the rustles viper.

Fresh water fish: Mainly schizothrox.

Hunting: This is now prohibited. However, before the ban people used to hunt the markhor (capra falconeri), the musk deer, jackals, tigers and snow leopards.

Flora: The word Bungus itself ('forests and grass') hints at extremely rich vegetation. Mr. Majrooh has classified the flora of Bungus according to its use.

Aromatic plants and incenses: Jurinea macrocephala (gogal dhupa), saussurea lappa (kuth) and salix capra (bed i mushk).

Condiments: Artemesia vestila (buna zeur), daucus carota (bera mujhar), Joeniculum vulgare (jungli bediyan), mentha arvensis (pudina), alium cepa (wana pran) and jhymus serphyllum (javend).

Drugs (as in hallucinogenic): Artemesia brevifolia (tehthwan), aconitum heterophylleum (patrees) and cannabis sativa (bhang).

Fibres (for mats, roof thatching etc).: Betula utilis (burza), cannabis sativa (bhang), celtis australis (bremy), parrotia jacquimontiana (poh), salix sp. (willow), ulmus wallichiana (bren).

Firewood: Bergia ammannoides (pahand), crataogus oxyacentha (rung), cedrus deodara (deodar) and picea soimthiana (kachkul).

Fodder: Adinatum capillus veneris (gew theear) and several other varities.

Fruits: Strawberry, juglans regia (doon), podophyllum emodi (bun wangan), solanum nigrum (kamby) and vitisveniferal (duch).

Medicinal plants: Macrotima benthami (gaw zaban), saussurea sacra (jugi padshah) and aconitum heterophylleum (patrees).

Poisons: Aconitum nepllus (mohund gal), conium maculatum (faka badiyana), datura stramonium (datura), phytolacca acinosa (brand) and rhus succedence (arkhur).

Resins: Pinus excelsia (kayer), cedrus deodara (deodar) and abbeis webbiana (budul).

Timber: Betula utilis (burza), abbeis webbiana (budul), ulmus wallichiana (bren) and æsculus indica (haw).

Upmarket foods: Morchella esculenta (guchhi) and hydnum coralloides (kao khoor).

Pulwama, Shopian

While saffron and the ambrî apple are the districts' best known crops, they mainly grow paddy, maize, mustard and pulses.

Srinagar city

The Fauna of the Dal Lake: Grebes, moor hens, ducks, swans and bald coots are often found near the lake. Herons and kingfishers have their favourite spots, away from the houseboats and shops. Eagles often swoop down to devour ducks. In autumn and winter you can expect to sight wild fowl instead.

Index